Molly Miller

About the Author

Molly Broadbent Miller was graduated
with a B.A. degree in classics from the
University of Manchester and received a
Ph.D. degree from the University of
Glasgow in 1953, completing her disser-
tation on "Prologomena to the Study of
Greek Chronography." She has taught at
the University of Glasgow and, as Visiting
Professor of Classics, at the State University of New York at Buffalo. She has
authored *Studies in Greek Genealogy*
(Leiden: E. J. Brill, 1968) and several
learned articles on chronographic and
demographic aspects of Greek history.
Mrs Miller is now at work on a study of
Athenian legendary history in relation to
the archeological evidence and is
collaborating on a study of Aristotelian
economic theory.

The Sicilian Colony Dates

A thirteenth century Armenian translation from the *Chronicle* of Eusebius (MS. 1908), from the Mashtotz Institute of Ancient Manuscripts, Erevan

The Sicilian Colony Dates

Studies in Chronography I

Molly Miller

State University of New York Press
Albany

PUBLISHED BY STATE UNIVERSITY OF NEW YORK PRESS
THURLOW TERRACE, ALBANY, NEW YORK 12201

© 1970 BY THE RESEARCH FOUNDATION
OF STATE UNIVERSITY OF NEW YORK

ISBN 0 – 87395 – 049 – 6 / LC 69 – 14646

PRINTED IN THE UNITED STATES OF AMERICA

CONTENTS

FIGURES

TABLES

THE PROBLEM

IN GREEK HISTORY, contemporary evidence for the dates of persons and events—in so far as it survives—begins in the fifth century B.C., with the creation of Greek historiography. But the Greek historians claimed to be able to give dates for earlier events and persons, and to correct each others' dates, in increasing detail and scale. This continued until their work was summed up in the Chronicle of Eusebius; thence, through translations, it became part of the historical doctrines accepted in European and Near Eastern scholarship.

The rise of modern critical standards, and the discovery of a medieval Armenian version of Eusebius to set beside Jerome's Latin translation, first raised the question of how Eusebius was able to give these ante-historiographic dates. Successive enquiries increasingly restricted the supposed amount of the original written sources, from temple or dynastic records hypothetically providing the whole, to records going back only to the Dorian Invasion, or only to the First Olympiad, or only to the establishment of annual magistracies, until Jacoby's demonstration that written local history, as a genre within historiography, can only be substantially traced back to the generation after Herodotus, and that it took its rise mainly as a reply to the insufficiency of Herodotean information about each city-state severally taken.

The present position, therefore, is that from Herodotus we may learn the kind of historical information available from the elders and experts in the major city-states around 450 B.C. Examination of his statements shows that they are in agreement with other ancient accounts—for exactitude of dating—only for (at most) a century before his own time. The power and persuasiveness of the Eusebian tradition is most clearly seen in the general acceptance of his dates over those of Herodotus; and there is a similar, but more painful,

1

difficulty when Eusebius and Thucydides differ. The natural expectation is that one of the sources will be 'right', the other 'wrong'.

But the true question is not whether Eusebius, or his predecessors were right, but how they were able to give any ante-historiographic dates at all. In other words, what were the ultimate sources for dates earlier than 450 B.C.; what were the methods of dating used by these sources; what was the treatment of these sources by the historians from 450 B.C. to the time of Eusebius?

In this study, these questions are asked of the series of Sicilian colony dates which are treated both by Thucydides and by Eusebius. The series extends from the later eighth to the early sixth century B.C., so that all the dates are earlier than the horizon of accurate memory furnished to Herodotus by the elders and experts.

The enquiry is divided into eight parts:

the first is devoted to an examination of what the surviving fifth-century sources (Pindar and Thucydides) say and how they say it; and to the evidence (from extant translations and derivatives) for what Eusebius actually said, and how. This is primarily a textual investigation—narrow therefore and laborious, but by no means unnecessary or unilluminating;

the second is concerned with classes of possible ultimate sources for Sikeliote history (oracular and other poetry, genealogies, exact living memory), and makes some preliminary remarks on the use and treatment of these sources by various historians;

the third looks at the dates arithmetically, and puts forward a chronographic hypothesis: that the dates were calculated, according to certtain established conventions, from a rather restricted body of evidence not uncritically used;

the fourth is concerned with fragmentary evidence from the historians—primarily the specialist Sikeliote historians—on their treatment of the colony dates;

the fifth consists of a collaborative enquiry into the kinds of generations represented by the ancient chronographic conventions. For independence' sake this is based on skeletal evidence and demographic techniques; and from these independent results we are able to distinguish and identify the kinds of generations recognised by the chronographers;

2

the sixth attempts, from all the evidence available, to discover the original information accessible in Sicily to the pioneer historiographers;

the seventh discusses the relationship, in Universal History, between western and mainland historiography in two principal cases: the Corinthian connections, and the attempted Messenian correlations;

the eighth attempts a modern treatment of the historical context of the Sicilian colonies in the organization of the international market over the two centuries of our period.

PART ONE

EVIDENCE FROM COMPLETE TEXTS

A. PINDAR.   Pindar's second Olympian ode celebrates a victory in the games of 476/5 B.C. won by Theron the Emmenid, tyrant of Akragas.[1] The poet asserts that, aiming his observation at Akragas, he swears that no city these hundred years has bred a man like Theron. This was taken in ancient times to mean that Pindar believed Akragas was about a century old in 476/5.

It is probable that Pindar was in Sicily himself when this ode was first performed; and in any case his connections with Sicily were so close that we can certainly assume that he is here reproducing local tradition—at least, a local tradition approved by Theron. While we can be certain about his source however, we do not know how it counted the years, whether through archives, Emmenid family tradition, or some other means. But we can again be sure that Pindar's treatment of the tradition was poetic: the hundred years are probably a very rounded number.

We are therefore likely to be fair to Pindar's source if we say that its date for the foundation of Akragas was 575 B.C.$\pm$20 years.

B. THUCYDIDES:i. The date of Akragas.   Unlike Pindar, Thucydides undoubtedly based his excursus about the Sicilian colonies on previous written material from at least one author. His possible or probable sources include Hekataios, Hellanikos, and Antiochos, whom we shall examine among the fragmentary authors in Part Four. Here we should note that in the seventy or so years which separate Pindar from Thucydides we move from oral to written sources behind the extant statements, and, at the same time, from poetic to precise figures.

---

[1]The date of the victory is known from *Pap. Oxy.* 222 (Jac 415 F 1).

4

Thucydides, as usual, does not name his source; and, as is his exasperating habit when quoting from other authorities, he gives no absolute date. The fall of Megara Hyblaia to Gelon of Syracuse would, however, be assigned in the source to some definite year or campaigning season (it has not survived in any of our authorities) in the period 485–480 B.C. Since Thucydides says that Megara fell 245 years after its foundation, that event occurred, according to this source, within the years 730–725 B.C.

Thucydides also tells us that, before the Megarians founded their city, they had encamped at Thapsos, taking refuge there after their expulsion from Leontinoi which they had helped the Chalkidians of Naxos to found. Leontinoi is dated five years after Syracuse: so that Thucydides implies dates for these foundations within the decade 740–730 B.C. Gela is said to have been founded 45 years after Syracuse (so within the decade 695–685), and Akragas 108 years later still, or within the decade 587–577.

Thucydides' source therefore believed, for whatever reason, that Pindar's 'hundred years' was a rounding of a slightly higher figure: that is, historiography claimed to be able either to correct Pindar, or to express the same tradition more exactly.

ii. Relation of the poetic and the historiographic in ancient dating. The Pindaric scholiasts are quite explicit about the superior precision of historiography. One of them (to *Ol.* 2.166e) says: 'Akragas was founded in Ol.50 while Theron's victory was in Ol.76. Thus from the foundation to the victory was 104 years; Pindar uses a rounded (ἀπηρτισμένῳ) number.' The other (to *Ol*.2.168) reports: 'The foundation of Akragas is dated (λέγεται) to Ol.50, whence to Theron's victory a hundred years in twenty-five Olympiads, added to Ol.50, gives us Ol.75. But the victory was in Ol.76; so Pindar uses a rounded number when he says "a hundred years".'

These two scholia seem to be different summaries of a single original, which was primarily interested in the rounding of the number by Pindar. In the course of the summarizing, the name of the historiographic authority used by the original commentator, if it was mentioned, has been omitted.

The scholia are nevertheless firm evidence that the difference between poetic and historiographic datings was fully discussed, and that the historiographic date nearest to the Pindaric placed the founding of Akragas in 580/79 B.C. But we know neither which

5

historian gave this date, nor whether Thucydides' source agreed with it, though the disagreement (if any) cannot have been great.

iii. The characteristics of the Thucydidean account. The most obvious characteristic of Thucydides' account is that it is a list with comments, a Register or Ἀναγραφή of Sicilian colony foundations. Consequently its information is readily represented, in modern terms, by a table.

TABLE I

THE THUCYDIDEAN REGISTER OF SICILIAN COLONIES

at specific year(s) within the period	Foundations*
740–730	(a) Naxos; Syracuse in the following year; Leontinoi in the 5th year after Syracuse; and after that, Katane.
	(b) 'at the same time': Megarians settle at Trotilon; join the Chalkidians at Leontinoi; expelled, they camp on Thapsos; finally
730–725	they found Megara Hyblaia, 245 years before it is destroyed by Gelon. Meanwhile, they
630–625	found: Selinous, 100 years after their own establishment.
695–685	(c) Gela was reinforced (ἐποίκους) 45 years after Syracuse; and herself founded
587–577	Akragas, 'most nearly' 108 years after her own establishment.
	(d) Zankle was at first a pirate settlement; then was regularly constituted and planted Himera.
	(e) the Syracusan secondary colonies were:
670–660	Akrai, 70 years after Syracuse;
650–640	Kasmenai, 'nearly' 20 years later;
605–595	Kamarina, 'most nearly' 135 years after Syracuse.

*For the metropoleis and oecists mentioned by Thucydides, see Part Two.

6

The general plan of the list is to name a colony and her secondary colonies, then to proceed to the next colony in chronological order, and her secondary colonies, and so forth. The exceptions are (1) Syracuse intervenes between Naxos and her secondary colonies, Leontinoi and Katane, and (2) the Syracusan secondary colonies are placed together at the end of the list.

More important, so far as the dates are concerned, the foundations fall into three groups: those with exact figures, those with approximated figures, and those with no figures. The foundings which are not dated are those of the first settlers at Gela, the pirates and the regular polity at Zankle, and the Zanklaian secondary colony at Himera.

In our later sources Zankle and Himera are dated (though the first Geloan settlement has no surviving date); but there is also some evidence which may illuminate the absence of dates in Thucydides. Kallimachos (F 43 Pfeiffer) reports that the Delphic oracle forbade the citizens of Zankle-Messene to invoke their founders by name at the annual festival of these heroes. This is evidence for a quite exceptional situation in the conditions of local traditions and associated rituals at Zankle; and it may have affected their historiographic treatment in a way which made Thucydides unwilling to go into the question of the dates.[2]

The approximated dates are those of Kasmenai and Kamarina from Syracuse, and of Akragas from Gela—three out of the 'four latest foundations, that is, the nearest to historiographic times. Not only are these among the most recent foundations, and for that reason alone establishments which might be expected to have the most certain dates, but Akragas had already been dated by Pindar, and the other two are colonies of Syracuse, whose citizen Antiochos had written his History, almost certainly, before Thucydides. The fact that it is these dates which Thucydides designates as approximate must therefore be regarded as of outstanding historiographic importance, so that if we knew how to interpret this fact, it should be informative either about the historiography of Thucydides' source, or about his judgement of it.[3]

Thucydides' source or sources were then written; their methods and his treatment of them may be reflected in the ἀναγραφή form,

_____

[2] See further Part Two below.
[3] See further Part Three below.

7

in the lack of dates for one group and in the explicitly approximate dates for another. These questions are within more general problems: the relation of the written historiographic sources to previously written poetic accounts; and to the oral material of the local elders and experts.

C. THE EUSEBIAN DERIVATIVES: i. The entries. Our next complete text for the Sicilian colony dates is nearly a thousand years later than Pindar and Thucydides: it is Jerome's Latin translation of the lost Greek chronicle of Eusebius. We possess a number of Eusebian derivatives dating from the fifth to the thirteenth centuries A.D., of which the oldest is the O(xford) manuscript of Jerome. The others are translations, or rather editions, of Eusebius in Syriac and Armenian, and excerpts in Greek and Syriac.

The general source of all these documents is the Chronika of Eusebius. In the case of the colony dates, there are some cases which may be marginally doubtful, and these are discussed below. The methods used by the derivative authors in editing, translating, or excerpting are usually transparent and tedious; while their use of the information available to them from Eusebius cannot often be dignified by the name of deliberate treatment. The study of these documents for their own sake is part of the study of the medieval struggle against barbarization, which is not our concern here: consequently we shall not consider any of these matters except where, in particular details, they affect the question of what Eusebius said.

Our first purpose is to reconstitute as far as possible the information collected and restated by Eusebius. It is only to the degree to which this can be done that we can move on to consider the question of his sources, their methods, and his treatment of them. And just as, in passing from Pindar to Thucydides we cross the frontier from the poetic to the historiographic—from one system of creation and convention to another—so with Eusebius we pass from the historiographic to the chronicle form—that is to say, from the causal, consequential, or polemical narrative to a tabulation of chronological sequence. In the most general sense, this means that all Eusebius' statements in the Canons are excerpts: his Sacred History, for example, consists of excerpts from the Bible, as understood by himself and earlier scholars; and restated in sentences suitable to the chronicle form.

8

Since we still possess the chief Eusebian source for Sacred History, it would be possible and useful to make a detailed study of the nature of his excerpting, the general principles of which could then be a starting-point for studies where his sources are unknown. In the absence of such a study, what must strike the uninstructed observer is the purity of Eusebius' chronological interests: he counts many years in multiple series, unwearyingly, but pays little or no attention to cause and effect, or to any other historiographic matter than chronological sequence. It would be impossible to arrive at the principles of (let us say) *Kings* and *Chronicles* from the representation of their subject-matter in Eusebius, though we should of course know that they included chronological information.

The general principles governing our consideration of Eusebius' sources for Profane History (including the colony dates) have therefore yet to be formed. We have a certain amount of external information, the chief among which is that the chronicle form matured, but did not begin, with Eusebius. His great Christian predecessor was Africanus; but there were pagan predecessors too, like Phlegon and Cassius Longinus in their *Olympiades*. Papyrus fragments give us some idea of the range of possibilities in the principles governing such works, and we have fragments from Phlegon's own book. What we do not know in this field is how much already excerpted material was simply copied from such sources by Eusebius—in other words, how much 'Eusebius' should be called 'Africanus' or 'Phlegon' or whoever first *chroniclized* (if we may invent a word) Sikeliote history in the tradition which descended to Eusebius. In this particular case, moreover, the question is unwontedly complicated by the fact that the last of the great classical Sikeliote historians, Timaios, himself published chronological tables in which (no doubt) his own dates for the colonies were set forth: it is not impossible therefore that whoever first chroniclized in the Eusebian tradition did so on the basis of Timaios' own tables. But this is only a possibility to be borne in mind; it is at least equally possible that whoever first chroniclized did so in deliberate opposition to Timaios' historiographic principles and any chronology derived from them.

In this situation of almost total uncertainty, the primary task is clearly to determine as closely as possible what Eusebius actually said.

There is no *a priori* reason to believe that for Eusebius or any of his surviving derivatives the Sicilian colony dates formed a topic

9

separate or essentially distinguishable from the general history of Greek colonization in all parts of the Mediterranean and Euxine in the archaic period. Consequently, in order to infer from our derivative sources what Eusebius himself said about the Sicilian colonies, and on that basis consider what Eusebius' sources may have been, we have to take all the colonial entries for the eighth to sixth centuries and attempt, first of all, to reconstitute their Eusebian texts and dates. Our immediate authorities are:

(a) *Greek:* the colonial entries excerpted from the Eusebian Canons by George Synkellos in his *Chronographia.* Synkellos is erratic in his excerpting, but is our only source for the Greek wording of the colony entries according to the Greek text available in Constantinople in the ninth century A.D. His *Chronographia,* in whole or in part, is reported to exist in four manuscripts, of which one is dated to A.D. 1201. The only usable edition is that hastily and not too carefully put out by Dindorf in 1829.[4]

(b) *Latin:* the colonial entries translated from the Eusebian Canons by Jerome in his Latin edition of that work, made early in the fourth century. The earliest manuscript is of the fifth century, and the authoritative edition is that of Fotheringham, published in 1923. The main general difference between Jerome and his Greek original is naturally a much greater interest in Roman history, and this may have affected the colony entries negatively; at least, Jerome omits some early Italian colonies found in other representatives of the Eusebian text. Apart however from this rather small margin of doubt, Jerome is much the earliest and fullest witness to the Eusebian text and generally his testimony carries more weight than that of any other of our sources. Some scholars, for example Gelzer, have indeed gone so far as to hold that entries not witnessed by Jerome are additions to the original Eusebian text, but when we come to examine the formulae of the entries we shall see that this probably, in some cases at least, is an unjustifiably extreme opinion. References are to Fotheringham's edition, by page, or *annus Abrahae.* Helm's second edition of Jerome (1956) is concerned exclusively

---

[4] *Georgius Syncellus et Nicephorus Cp. ex recensione Guilielmi Dindorfii:* vol.I (*Corpus Scriptorum Historiae Byzantinae 10*), Bonn 1829. References are to page and line of this edition.

with the Latin tradition, and is therefore less useful for our purposes than Fotheringham.[5]

(c) *Syriac:* the three works known to me as representatives of Eusebius in this language seem to be the second most important witnesses to the Eusebian text—though, since my Syriac is non-existent, this opinion is hardly cogent. The earliest work is however about contemporary with Synkellos, and is more useful than his in that it gives dates.

(i) the colonial entries in the *Epitome* of the Eusebian Canons compiled by Dionysius of Tell Mahre, who was the monophysite Patriarch A.D. 825 to 845. This survives in a single manuscript: I have used the Latin translation by Siegfried and Gelzer published in 1884.

(ii) the references to colonial foundations in the *Chronicon* of Michael the Great, monophysite Patriarch A.D. 1166 to 1199. These are not explicitly dated, but the excerpts are often less distant from the original than are Synkellos' Σποραδήν lists. I have used the French translation by J. B. Chabot in Tome I Fascicule I of his *Chronique de Michel le Syrien* (Paris 1889). Michael has a marked tendency to run his colony entries together, and sometimes their positions relative to neighbouring entries are as erratic as in Synkellos' lists. Synkellos and Michael are consequently often witnesses only to the existence of the entry, and not to its wording, nor to its date.

(iii) a few references to colonies in the *Chronography* of Gregory Barhebraeus, monophysite Patriarch A.D. 1264 to 1286. I have used the English translation by E. A. W. Budge published in 1932, based on a manuscript of the fourteenth century, and on the edition by Paul Bedjan published in 1890. For the entries which interest us, Budge (p.24n.) copies Bedjan who 'corrected the vocalization' from Dionysius. It would be useful to possess an examination by a Syriac scholar of the Syriac texts of the colony entries: my remarks in the following pages are to be read with the knowledge that I speak blindly on such matters.

---

[5] *Eusebii Pamphili Chronici Canones latine vertit . . . Hieronymus,* ed. I. K. Fotheringham (Oxford 1923). *Eusebius Werke VII: Die Chronik des Hieronymus,* herausgg. von Rudolf Helm (*Die Griechischen Christlichen Schriftsteller* 47) 1956.

(*d*) *Armenian:* two thirteenth-century manuscripts of an Armenian translation of the lost Syriac edition of the Eusebian Canons: I have used the German translation by Karst published in 1911. This representative of Eusebius, like Jerome and Dionysius, gives dates.[6]

These medieval witnesses to the text of Eusebius are very various, but at least so far as the colonial entries are concerned their span from Jerome to Barhebraeus and the Armenian is scarcely more than the variations in languages and purposes in modern scholarship from Dindorf to Budge. In these conditions, the ambition to reconstitute Eusebius himself on the colony entries must at present be confined to his purport, and not (usually at least) extended in detail to his text.

For the sake of clarity and convenience. I give first a table (TABLE II) of the Eusebian colony entries, then the evidence in the form of a note on each entry. The table is arranged as follows: the extreme left-hand column gives the sources, designated by the abbreviations:

G:	the Greek of Synkellos;
L:	the Latin of Jerome's *Canons;*
S(i)	the Syriac of Dionysius;
S(ii)	the Syriac of Michael the Great;
S(iii)	the Syriac of Barhebraeus;
A:	the Armenian *Canons;*

the second column gives in English what appears to have been the purport of the original Eusebian entry; suggestions, if any, for the Greek text are given in the notes. The entries are numbered for ease of reference.

the column of dates is divided under four headings according to the verbal formulae, so far as they are recoverable:

F (Founders): entries which name the founders of colonies;

P (Pairs): entries which give pairs of eastern and western colonies (for example, Gela in Sicily and Phaselis in Pamphylia) at a single date;

S (Singletons): entries recording simply a foundation with no other information;

SR (Singletons with regions):
entries which state both the name

---

[6] *Eusebius Werke 5: Die Chronik*, hrsgg. von J. Karst, Leipzig 1911 (*Die Griechischen Christlichen Schriftsteller 20*).

of a city and of the region in which it was established.

TABLE II
THE EUSEBIAN COLONY ENTRIES

Sources	Entries	F	P	S	SR
G Si Sii A	1. In Italy the cities Pandosia and Metapontion founded				771/0?
G L A	2. Thebans settle Kyrene in accordance with an oracle. But the oecist of Kyrene was Aristoteles known as Battos	762/1?			
G (part) Si	3. In Sicily ⟨Megara the metropolis of⟩ Selinous, and Zankle, founded; and in Pontos ⟨Sinope the metropolis of⟩ Trapezous		758/7		
L (part) Sii Siii A (part)	4. In Italy (?) Kaulonia and (?) Makalla founded; and in Bithynia Kyzikos		757/6		
L Sii	5. Milesians . . . found the city of Naukratis in Egypt	749/8			
G L Si Sii A	6. In Sicily Naxos founded				741/0
L Si Sii Siii A	7. In Sicily Syracuse and Katane founded				736/5
Si Sii Siii	8. In Sicily Leontinoi and Megara founded; and Maroneia		732/1		
G L Si Sii Siii A	9. In Sicily Chersonesos founded				717/6
L Si Sii A	10. Nikomedeia founded under its original name of Astakos			711/0	
L Si Sii A	11. Kroton and Sybaris founded, and Parion		709/8?		

13

Source	Entries	F	P	S	SR
L Si Sii	12. The so-called Partheniai found Taras, and the Corinthians Corcyra	706/5			
L Si A	13. In Sicily Gela, and in Pamphylia Phaselis, founded		691/0		
L Si Siii	14. Kalchedon founded			685/4	
G (part) L	15. Kyzikos founded, and in Italy Lokroi		679/8		
L Si Sii Siii A	16. Byzantium founded			659/8	
G L Si Siii A	17. Istros in Pontos founded				657/6
G L Si Siii A	18. In Emathia Akanthos and Stageira founded; Kardia; in Asia, Lampsakos; Abdera		655/4		
G L A	19. Phalaris tyrant in Akragas			652/1	
G L Si Siii	20. In Sicily Selinous founded				650/49
G L Si	21. In Pontos Borysthenes founded				647/6
G L Si Sii A	22. Battos refounds Kyrene	632/1			
G L Si Sii A	23. In Pontos Sinope founded				631/0
G L Si Sii A	24. Lipara founded			630/29	
G L Si (part) Sii A	25. Prousia founded, and Epidamnos (now called Dyrrhachium)	627/6			
G L A	26. Phalaris' tyranny ended			625/4	
L A	27. Panaitios, the first tyrant in Sicily, takes power in Leontinoi				615/4
G L Si Sii A (part)	28. Kamarina founded, and Perinthos		601/0		
L Si Sii A	29. Massalia founded			598/7	
L A	30. Phalaris tyrant for 16 years			571/0	

STATISTICS OF TABLE II

1. Of the thirty entries, the following totals of notices (in whole or part) are found in:

Synkellos	17
Jerome	25
Dionysius	23
Michael	18
Barhebraeus	10
Armenian	24

2. Entries mentioned in only one language:
Leontinoi, Megara, Maroneia, entry 8, in Syriac

3. Entries omitted by Jerome:

Wholly omitted	*Partly omitted*
1. Pandosia, Metapontion	4. Kaulonia, Makalla
3. Megara, Zankle, Sinope	18. Kardia
8. Leontinoi, Megara, Maroneia	28. Perinthos in early manuscripts

4. Dates agreed by all three sources:
9. Chersonesos in Sicily: 717/6
17. Istros in Pontos: 657/6
23. Sinope in Pontos: 631/0

5. Dates agreed by both of two surviving sources:
20. Selinous (Jerome and Dionysius): 650/49
21. Borysthenes (Jerome and Dionysius): 647/6

6. Dates agreed by two out of three sources:
7. Syracuse and Katane (Dionysius and Armenian against Jerome)
11. Kroton, Parion, Sybaris (Jerome and Armenian against Dionysius)
13. Gela and Phaselis (Jerome and Dionysius against Armenian)
16. Byzantium (Jerome and Dionysius against Armenian)
18. Akanthos etc. (Jerome and Armenian against Dionysius)
22. Kyrene (Dionysius and Armenian against Jerome)
25. Prousia and Epidamnos (Dionysius and Armenian against Jerome)
28. Kamarina, Perinthos (Jerome and Dionysius against Armenian)
29. Massalia (Jerome and Dionysius against Armenian)

7. Dionysius is one year earlier than Jerome at entries:

> 6. Naxos
> 11. Kroton, Parion, Sybaris
> 12. Taras, Corcyra
> 22. Kyrene
> 25. Prousia, Epidamnos
> He is two years earlier at
> 10. Astakos-Nikomedeia
> 14. Kalchedon

These instances of earliness may be due to his tendency to state the date of Sacred History, and to add the Profane event by saying *eodemque anno*: this would directly account for the dates of entries 6, 12, 22, 25, and 10.

8. Wide discrepancies of dating are found at the entries:

> 1. Dionysius four years later than Armenian
> 2. Interchange of entries in Armenian
> 6. Disturbances in text of Armenian
> 10. Interchange of entries in Armenian
> 13. Disturbances in text of Armenian
> 15. Additions to Syriac and Armenian
> 27. Armenian depressed by preceding entry
> 29. Armenian depressed by Jeremiah entry

9. The entry formulae divide the notices as follows:

there are 4 with founders named:	nos.2, 5, 12, 22
and 9 east-west pairs:	nos.3, 4, 8, 11, 13, 15, 18, 25, 28
and 8 singletons:	nos.10, 14, 16, 19, 24, 26, 29, 30
and 9 singletons with regions:	nos.1, 6, 7, 9, 17, 20, 21, 23, 27

10. Geographical Distribution of the foundations named:

Sicily:	12	(including Megara twice)
Propontis:	9	(including Kyzikos twice)
Italy:	8	
North Aegean:	5	(including Maroneia and Kardia)
Pontos:	4	(including Sinope twice)
Africa:	3	(including Kyrene twice)
Adriatic:	2	
Gaul:	1	
Pamphylia:	1	
Total	45	

NOTES TO THE SEPARATE ENTRIES

1. PANDOSIA and METAPONTION in Italy: 771/70?

Texts of the entry

Synkellos 400.14: Ἐν Ἰταλίᾳ Πανδοσία καὶ Μεταπόντιον πόλεις ἐκτίσθησαν.

Dionysius 20: Anno MCCXLVI ⟨Pan⟩dosia et Metapontius duae urbes conditae sunt

Michael 79: Les villes de Pandosia et de Metapontus furent bâties en Italie

Armenian 181: In Italia ward Pandosia et Metapontios gegründet

These texts seem to differ no more than might be expected of translations. The absence of this entry in the Latin could be due to Jerome's neglect, or to his low valuation of the entry as history, or to the introduction of the entry into the Greek Eusebius after Jerome's time.

Date of the entry

Syriac (i) aA 1246   Armenian aA 1242

If aA 1241 is 776/5 B.C. as in Jerome, then the Syriac date is 771/0, and the Armenian 775/4. But the Armenian equation is of aA 1240 with 776/5 B.C. and this may have been in the mind of the editor here (though it is not usually): in that case the Armenian date is 774/3. In no other case in the colony entries is the Syriac so much later than the Armenian date, and perhaps the Armenian has been disturbed by the entry on Micah at 1246, which corresponds to an entry in Dionysius at 1249, and to two notes in Jerome which extend from 1247 to 1255.

Pandosia is held by Dunbabin (*Western Greeks 33*) to be the town near Siris. Siris had *nostos* founders (Trojans): and was also Rhodian; and Kolophonian (in the time of Gyges, so about 655). Metapontion had *nostos* founders (Nestor of Pylos); and was also Achaian; and Phokian (Daulios tyrant of Krisa).

2. Thebans at KYRENE: 762/1?

Texts of the entry

Synkellos 400.16: Θηβαῖοι Κυρήνην ὤκισαν κατὰ χρησμόν, οἰκιστὴς δὲ αὐτῆς Βάττος ὁ καὶ Ἀριστοτέλης.

Jerome 151: Theraei Cyrenen condiderunt oraculo sic iubente: conditor urbis Battus cuius proprium nomen Aristoteles.

Armenian 181: Die Thebäer besiedelten Krine nach einer Offenbarung; und es war Besiedler Battos, dessen eigentlicher Name war Aristoteles

In spite of Jerome, we should keep the Theban name in this entry, and in spite of both translations take οἰκιστὴς δέ as adversative: Jerome also mistranslates the second entry on Kyrene: see (22) below. For other non-Theraians at Kyrene see the Lindian Anagraphe (Jac 532) entry 17 (Pankios and his sons from Lindos), and Pausanias III 14.3: Chionis of Sparta – both accompanying Battos. The 'Thebans' of this otherwise unknown tradition are presumably derived from the Aigeid tradition of the kings of Thera.

Date of the entry

Latin aA 1255   Armenian aA 1258

Jerome has the foundation of Phoenician Aradus at 1258 and the Armenian places it at 1255—that is, one of our sources has interchanged the entries, and this is more probably the Armenian. Michael p.81 says: 'A cette époque fut fondée l'île d'Aradus qui est Rouad: elle subsista pendant 1460 ans, jusqu'à ce qu'elle fut détruite par les Arabes'. This destruction is dated by Theophanes (*Chronographia* ed. C. de Boor [Leipzig 1883] I 344) to A.D. 648/9 so Michael's figure is not Eusebian: cf. (16) Byzantium.

3. MEGARA and ZANKLE in Sicily, SINOPE in Pontos: 758/7

Texts of the entry

Synkellos 401.1: Ἐν Πόντῳ Τραπεζοῦς ἐκτίσθη.
Dionysius 20:   Anno MCCLX in Sicilia urbes Selinus et S . . . a conditae sunt.
Michael 81:   A cette époque fut fondée en Sicile la ville de Selinus, et Scale (?); dans le Pont: Trapezus.
Barhebraeus 24: And also in Sikilia the city of Salinos was built, and Sakali, and Trapizonta in Pontos . . .
Armenian 181:   In Sikilia ward Silinus und Zankle gegründet
         182:    In Pontos ward Treapezos gegründet

Date of the entry

S(i) aA 1260   Arm. aA 1259
                                                          1260

4. KAULONIA and MAKALLA in Italy, KYZIKOS in Bithynia:757/6

Texts of the entry

Jerome 153:   Cyzicus condita: (v.l. in Jerome L: bysantium)
Michael 81:   . . . en Bithynie, Cyzicus: en Italie: Callicum et Lyconia.
Barhebraeus 24: . . . Kuzikos in Bithynea and Kalonon and Lycania in Italy.
Armenian 182:   In Italia wurden Kalikon und Likonia gegründet.

Date of the entry

Latin aA 1261   Arm. aA 1260

The dating here is part of the textual evidence, for in the original pagination of Jerome (and probably also of Eusebius himself), the year aA 1260

18

is at the bottom of a page, and the year aA 1261 at the top of the next. Consequently, comparison in entry 4 of the Latin and Armenian texts with the Syriac suggests that the Latin and Armenian have each preserved one half of the original entry. Moreover the variant reading in Jerome, of 'Bysantium' for Kyzikos, may derive from an attempt to make sense of some spelling of Bithynia, part of the fuller entry. The dating of Jerome's entry at aA 1261, on the first line at the top of the page, could easily be due to the second half of the entry being crowded over the page from the beginning of the original entry at aA 1260, equivalent to 757/6 B.C.

The identification of the Italian towns through the corrupt text of their names presents difficulties. Kalonon-Callicum-Kalikon may be Kaulonia (as suggested to me by A. R. Burn). If Makalla, a dependency of Kroton, was the same place as Petelia (as held by Berard with some approval from Dunbabin, *The Western Greeks*, p.159, n.11) it was important in the fourth century and could have received a (Rhodian?) non-heroic history then, as well as the nostos-story of Philoktetes. Textually, ΚΑΥΛΩΝΙΑ ΚΑΙ ΜΑΚΑΛΛΑ does not seem too far from the Syriac and Armenian, with Kaulonia as more probable, perhaps, than Makalla.

The text of entry 3 presents different difficulties: all the witnesses agree on Selinous in Sicily and Trapezous in Pontos, although no previous entries have recorded the foundations of their metropoleis, Megara and Sinope, and although it is very difficult to believe that any Greek historian dated these secondary colonies so early. It is of course an old and often-repeated suggestion that the names of Selinous and Trapezous have somehow replaced those of their metropoleis. But this is not likely to be due to a historical error, that is, that Eusebius' mind somehow thought of Selinous and Trapezous when he saw the names of Megara and Sinope in his authority (but did not think of Himera when he saw the name of Zankle); and this is even less probable for any later writer. If the names of the secondary colonies have in fact replaced those of their metropoleis, there must have been a textual reason: that is, we assume the entries were originally of the form:

’Εν Σικελίᾳ ⟨Μέγαρα ἐξ ὧν ⟩ Σελινοῦς, καὶ Ζάγκλη ἐκτίσθησαν
καὶ ἐν Πόντῳ ⟨ Σινώπη ἐξ ἧς ⟩ Τραπεζοῦς ἐκτίσθη.

Now at aA 1259 in both the Latin and the Armenian *Canons* there is an entry on the Spartan ephorate: Jerome says: In Lacedaemone primus ΕΦΟΡΟΣ, quod magistratus nomen est, constituitur: fuit autem sub regibus Lacedaemoniorum an. CCCL. The Armenian *Canons* however have only the first part of the entry at this year: Zuerst ward in Lakedmonia ein Ephor aufgestellt: the second part has been transferred to the long historical notice at the first Olympiad: Bis hierher haben die Lakedamonier Gesetze geherrscht, 350 Jahre. Karst (p.270, n.280) suggests that these Spartan 'laws' arose from a Greek ⟨βασιλεῖς αὐτό⟩νομοι, that is, a lacuna of about the same length as those required for the colony entries at this same year. Consequently, we are brought to conceive of the en-

19

tries in aA 1259 and 1260 as originally having something of this shape in relation to the 21st and 22nd regnal years in the Lydian *filum*:

’Εν Λακεδαίμονι πρῶτος ἔφορος. ἦν δὲ ἐπὶ   **ΚΑ**   βασιλέων αυτο
νόμων τῶν Λακεδαιμονίων ἔτη τν. ’Εν Σικελία   Μέγαρα ἐξ ὧν
Σελινοῦς, καὶ Ζάγκλη, ἐκτίσθησαν. ἐν Πόντω   **ΚΒ**   Σινώπη ἐξ ἧς
Τραπεζοῦς ἐκτίσθη.
’Εν ’Ιταλία Καυλωνία καὶ Μακάλλα ἐκτίσθησαν. ἐν Βιθυνία Κύζικος ἐκτίσθη.

From this all the characteristics of our immediate sources could be derived: the three lacunae common to all[7] and the omission of Bithynia in all Jerome's manuscripts except L, while it survives in the Syriac; the dating of the ephors to 1259 in both Jerome and the Armenian, of Selinous and Zankle to 1259 and Trapezous to 1260 in the Armenian; the dating of the Italian cities to 1260 in the Armenian and of Kyzikos to 1261 (over the page) in the Latin; the corruption of the Italian names due probably to crowding and wear at the bottom of the page.

5. Milesian NAUKRATIS in Egypt: 749/8

Texts of the entry

Jerome 153:   Mare optinuerunt Milesii an. XVIII construxer
                   untque urbem in Aegypto Naucratin.

Michael 85:   Les Milésiens occupèrent la mer en neuvième lieu
                   pendant 18 ans; ils fondérent une ville en Egypte:
                   Naucratès.

This is not an independent colony entry, but one subjoined to the notice of a thalassocracy.

Date of the entry

Latin aA 1268

6. NAXOS in Sicily: 741/0

Texts of the entry

Synkellos 401.2:   ’Εν Σικελία Νάξος ἐκτίσθη.
Jerome 155:   Naxus condita in Sicilia.
Dionysius 21:   et eodem anno Anaxus urbs Siciliae condita est.
Michael 85:   La ville de Naxos fut fondée en Sicile.
Armenian 182:   In Sikilia ward Anaxos gegründet.
Karst suggests that the spelling Anaxos has annexed the last letter of the preceding word, Sikilia: he does not quote Dionysius here, but at p.xlvii refers to other cases: Adelphier, Area, Arier, for Delphians, Rhea, Rhaitoi.

Date of the entry

Latin aA 1276   Syriac (i) 1275   Armenian 1280

---

7. In the ephorate notice Jerome's lacuna is partial only: he has *regibus* but does not translate αὐτονόμων; his grammar however suggests that he was guessing.

The Armenian has divided and depressed entries at this period, and this, together with the combined Latin and Syriac evidence, puts its date out of court. As between the Latin and Syriac, the Latin is to be preferred and has a reasonably good text: manuscripts of four families agree on this year, including the fifth-century *O*.

7. SYRACUSE and KATANE in Sicily: 736/5

Texts of the entry

Jerome 155: Syracusae in Sicilia conditae. Catina in Sicilia condita.
Dionysius 21: et eodem anno Syracusae et Catana Siciliae urbes conditae sunt.
Michael 86: Syracuse fut bâtie en Sicile.
Barhebraeus 24: And at that time Syracuse and Katana . . . were built in Sikilia.
Armenian 182: Sirakuse und Katane in Sicilia wurden gegründet.

Jerome here has the form of two entries, and in a number of manuscripts they are assigned to different years: either Jerome's division, or the conjunction in the other texts, may be due to negligence. The Greek text clearly cannot be satisfactorily reconstituted.

Date of the entry

Latin aA 1281   Syriac (i) 1282   Armenian 1282

The balance of the manuscript evidence is in favour of 1281 as Jerome's year; both the other texts run this entry together with the fall of Messenia, which is two years later in Jerome. It is probable, therefore, that Jerome most nearly represents the Greek date.

8. LEONTINOI and Megara in Sicily; and MARONEIA: 732/1

Texts of the entry

Dionysius 22: Anno MCCLXXXV Leontinoi et Megara et Martonia Siciliae urbes conditae sunt.
Michael 86: Mégara et Marathonia furent bâties aussi en Sicile.
Barhebraeus 24: And at that time . . . Leontino and Maghlara and Martoniya . . . were built in Sikilia.

This entry survives only in the Syriac texts, but it is difficult to think of any reason why Eusebius should choose to speak of Katane and reject a mention of Leontinoi; therefore we should probably regard this entry as Eusebian, in spite of the paucity of evidence. The text is, however, damaged: Martonia is not a Sicilian city, nor does it resemble any name of a Sicilian foundation. The alternative is to suppose that this entry was originally one of the east-west pairs, and that Martonia is to be sought among the 'eastern' colonies; then Maroneia, founded from Chios on the coast of Thrace, leaps to the eye. Megara may be derived from some such phrase as σὺν Μεγαρεῦσιν.

Date of the entry

Syriac (i) aA 1285

21

9. CHERSONESOS in Sicily: 717/6

Texts of the entry

Synkellos 401.2:   Ἐν Σικελίᾳ Χερρόνησος ἐκτίσθη.
Jerome 157:   In Sicilia Chersonessos condita.
Dionysius 22:   Anno MCCC in Sicilia Chronsos urba condita est.
Michael 86:   Chersonesos fut aussi bâtie en Sicile.
Barhebraeus 24:   . . . and Chreronesus were built in Sikilia.
Armenian 183:   In Sikila wurde Cherrenos gegründet.

Apart from the gradual degeneration of the proper name, these texts naturally translate one another.

Date of the entry

Latin aA 1300   Syriac (i) 1300   Armenian 1300

This is one of the three colonial entries on whose dates all witnesses agree; see entries 17 and 23.

10. ASTAKOS-NIKOMEDEIA: 711/0

Texts of the entry

Jerome 159:   Nicomedia condita quae prius Astacus uocabatur.
Dionysius 22:   Et Nicomedia urbs condita est.
Michael 86:   La ville de Nicomédie, qui s'appelait auparavant Astacus, fut alors bâtie.
Armenian 183:   Nikomeda ward gegründet, das ursprünglich Astakos hiess.

Date of the entry

Latin aA 1306   Syriac (i) 1304   Armenian 1310

The Armenian reverses the sequence of entries (10) and (11) and omits (12), so its dates are not reliable here: probably (10) has by misplacement extruded (12). The Syriac may not accurately represents its original, for the event explicitly dated to 1304 is the death of Hezekiah: the first year of Manasseh would then be in 1305, and Nicomedia would thus be at earliest in that year. Jerome's text is reasonably good, and easily to be preferred to the other witnesses.

This is one of the few Eusebian colony dates known from earlier sources: Memmon (434 F 1 §12) τήν Ἀστακὸν δὲ Μεγαρέων ὤκισαν ἄποικοι, ὀλυμπιάδος ἱσταμένης ιζ᾽ (712/1-709/8).

11. KROTON and SYBARIS, and PARION 709/8

Texts of the entry

Jerome 159:   Croton et Parion et Sybaris conditae.
Dionysius 22:   Anno MCCCVII urbes Croton et Parion et Sybaris et Egbatana conditae sunt.

22

Michael 86:   Les villes de Croton, de ⟨Parion et de Syb⟩ aris furent alors bâties.
Armenian 183:   Kroton ward gegründet, und Pathron et Sybaris.
Jerome has Ecbatana at the same year, on the Sacred History page 158. The three other names are apparently in alphabetical, not geographical, order.

Date of the entry

Latin aA 1308   Syriac (i) 1307   Armenian 1308

The Syriac is as usual a little early; the agreement of the Latin and Armenian is fairly rare. Dionysius of Halikarnassos dated the foundation of Kroton to Ol.17.3 (710/09).

12. TARAS and CORCYRA: 706/5

Texts of the entry

Jerome 159:   Hi qui Partheniae uocabantur Tarentum condiderunt et Corinthii Corcyram.
Dionysius 22:   Anno MCCCX ... Pathenii Tar⟨   ⟩et Corinthii condiderunt Corcyram.
Michael 87:   Les Parthéniens ⟨fondèrent Tarente, et les Corinthiens, Corcyre⟩.
For the absence of this entry from the Armenian, see entry 10.

Date of the entry

Latin aA 1311   Syriac (i) 1310

13. GELA and PHASELIS: 691/0

Texts of the entry

Jerome 163:   In Sicilia Gela, in Pamfylia Faselis condita.
Dionysius 22:   Eodem anno Gela in Sicilia condita est et Phaselia in Pamphylia.
Armenian 184:   In Sikilia ward Agela gegründet.
Ebenso Phaselis in Pamphila.
The Armenian splits the entry into two, dated two years apart; but the original is no doubt represented more correctly by the Latin and Syriac. For the spelling Agela see 6 above.

Date of the entry

Latin aA 1326   Syriac (i) 13⟨2⟩6   Armenian 1328 and 1330
The Latin and Syriac date is of course to be preferred.

14. KALCHEDON: 685/4

Texts of the entry

Jerome 163:   Calchedon condita.
Dionysius 22:   Anno MCCCXXX Calchedon urbs condita est.

Barhebraeus 25 : And in the 21st year of Manasseh the city of Chalcedon was built . . .

Date of the entry

Latin aA 1332 Syriac (i) 1330

For the apparent meaning of Barhebraeus' date see 16 below. The Syriac date is as usual earlier than the Latin.

15. KYZIKOS (II) and LOKROI: 679/8

Texts of the entry

Synkellos 402.3 : Κύζικος ᾠκίσθη.
Jerome 163 : Cyzicus condita et Locri in Italia.
Dionysius 23 : et eodem anno Cyzicus urbs condita est et in Italia urbs Locri
Armenian 184 : Kizikon ward gegründet.
In Italia ward die Lokrer gegründet.

Synkellos has only the first half of the entry: the Armenian splits it into two. The sequence of the names is apparently alphabetical.

Date of the entry

Latin aA 1338 Syriac (i) 1342 Armenian 1341 and 1342

The Syriac dating (and hence the Armenian) has apparently been disturbed by additions to the biography of Manasseh; Jerome's text is good.

16. BYZANTIUM: 659/8

Texts of the entry

Jerome 165 : Byzantium conditum.
Dionysius 23 : Anno MCCCLVIII Byzantia urbs condita est.
Michael 88 : A cette époque Byzance fut premièrement fondée par Byzos. Après 970 ans, elle fut restaurée et agrandie par Constantin . . .
Barhebraeus 25 : And Bozantia, the first building, was built by Bozos, and after ⟨nine hundred⟩ and ninety-seven years Constantine restored it and enlarged it . . .
Armenian 185 : Byzantion ward gegründet.

Date of the entry

Latin aA 1358 Syriac (i) 1358 Armenian 1357

Michael and Barhebraeus draw on non-Eusebian information: compare Hesychius Illustris in the sixth century (Jac 390). Barhebraeus dates the foundation 997 years before A.D. 330, i.e. 667 or 668 B.C. This probably accounts for his dating of Kalchedon (26 years earlier as in Eusebius, not 19 years earlier as in Hesychius) to the 21st year of Manasseh, which in the Eusebian Canons is aA 1325 or 692/1 B.C. The Eusebian date for Byzantium is given by the Latin and Syriac (i).

24

17. ISTROS in Pontos: 657/6

Texts of the entry

Synkellos 402.8: Ἐν Πόντῳ πόλις ʺἸστορος ἐκτίσθη.
Jerome 167: Histrus civitas in Ponto condita.
Dionysius 23: Anno MCCCLX urbs Asturas in Ponto condita est.
Barhebraeus 25: and in Pontos were built the cities Mithia, Istris . . .
Armenian 185: In Pontos ward die Stadt Istoros gegründet.

Date of the entry

Latin aA 1360 Syriac (i) 1360 Armenian 1360

18. AKANTHOS and others: 655/4?

Texts of the entry

Synkellos 402.9: ʺΑκανθος καὶ Στάγειρα ἐν ʽΕλλάδι ἐκτίσθησαν.
      402.10: Λάμψακος καὶ ʺΑβδηρα ἐκτίσθησαν.
Jerome 167: Acanthus condita et Stagira [in Asia *add. T*]
    Lampsacus condita et Abdera.
Dionysius 23: Anno MCCCLXIII urbes Acanthus et Stagira, et
    Lampsacus et Abdera conditae sunt.
Barhebraeus 25: . . . Akanthos, Akardia, and Estaghira . . .
Armenian 185: Akanthos und Strandia wurden gegründet.
    Lampsakos und adera wurden gegründet.

Date of Entry

Latin aA 1362 Syriac (i) 1363 Armenian 1362
     1363   1365

There are some curious textural phenomena in these two entries:
Mithia in 17 Barhebraeus; ἐν ʽΕλλάδι in 18 Synkellos; *in Asia* in 18 Jerome *T*; Akardia in 18 Barhebraeus. Dionysius has a single entry in 18 where the Greek, Latin, and Armenian have two, but the *in Asia* of Jerome *T* must originally have referred to Lampsakos, and joined the two entries into one, either in the Greek or in the Latin. (*T* is a fine ninth-century manuscript, of which Fotheringham says 'uidetur aut librarius ipse aut archetypi librarius uir doctus fuisse et, ut credo, non modo propria eruditione, sed Chronicis Graecis collatis textum emendasse'.) Therefore we should take the cities under 18 as having probably in origin constituted a single entry.

Of these, Akanthos is mentioned by all our sources; Akardia appears only in Barhebraeus, but may mean Kardia in the Thracian Chersonese (compare Anaxos, 6 and Agela 13); Stageira appears in the Greek, Latin and Syriac; Strandia in the Armenian may represent Stageira, or a mixture of Stageira and Kardia; Lampsakos and Abdera appear in all except Barhebraeus.

The Greek text says that Akanthos and Stageira were founded ἐν ʽΕλλάδι, which is not true, but presumably masks the original name of the region, contrasted with Lampsakos 'in Asia'. Barhebraeus' Mithia suggests that the original was ἐν Ἐμαθίᾳ, eastern Macedonia (ΕΝΕΜΑΘΙΑΙ: ΕΝΕΛΛΑ . . . Δ Ι): and that the region-name has become misplaced and so mistaken for a city-name. The original text for 17 will then be represented reasonably accurately by Synkellos; the text for 18 will have included ἐν Ἐμαθίᾳ ῎Ακανθος καὶ Στάγειρα, Κάρδια in the Chersonese and ἐν Ἀσίᾳ Λάμψακος, and ῎Αβδηρα in Thrace, the last an unsuccessful foundation.

Jerome's first date is probably to be preferred.

I have taken this entry, with settlements in Europe and Asia, as an east-west paired entry: perhaps wrongly.

19. PHALARIS becomes tyrant in Akragas: 652/1

Texts of the entry

Synkellos 402.15: Φάλαρις Ἀκραγαντίνων ἐτυράννησε.
Jerome 167:   Falaris apud Acragentinos tyrannidem exercet.
Armenian 185:   Phalaris führte über die Akrakantiner die Gewaltherrschaft.

Date of the entry

Latin aA 1365   Armenian 1366

This entry is not preceded by any notice of the foundation of Akragas, though it necessarily assumes it; see also 26, 27, and 30.

20. SELINOUS in Sicily: 650/49

Texts of the entry

Synkellos 402.12: Ἐν Σικελίᾳ Σελινοῦς ἐκτίσθη.
Jerome 167:   In Sicilia Selinus condita.
Dionysius 23:   Anno MCCCLXVII Selinus urbs in Sicilia condita est.
Barhebraeus 25:   and Salinos was built in Sikilia.

Date of the entry

Latin aA 1367   Syriac (i) 1367

The sources show an unusual agreement, and the date is confirmed by Diodorus XIII 59.

21. BORYSTHENES in Pontos: 647/6

Texts of the entry

Synkellos 402.18: Ἐν Πόντῳ Βορυσθένης ἐκτίσθη.
Jerome 167:   In Ponto Borysthenes condita.
Dionysius 23:   Anno MCCCLXX Borysthenes urbs in Ponto condita est.

Date of the entry

Latin aA 1370   Syriac (i) 1370

Agreement is again marked.

26

22. Battos founds KYRENE (II): 632/1

Texts of the entry

Synkellos 403.5: Βάττος Κυρήνην ἐπέκτισε.
Jerome 169: Battus condidit Cyrenen.
Dionysius 23: eodemque anno Batus Cyrinam condidit.
Michael 91: Battus fonda la ville de Cyrène.
Armenian 185: Battos gründete Yrene.
The translations do not render the Greek accurately.

Date of the entry

Latin aA 1385   Syriac (i) 1384   Armenian 1385
The Syriac resumes its habit of being earlier than the Latin.

23. SINOPE (II) in Pontos: 631/0

Texts of the entry

Synkellos 403.1: Σινώπη ἐκτίσθη.
Jerome 169: Sinope condita [in Ponto *add. T*].
Dionysius 23: Anno MCCCLXXXVI urbs Sinope condita est.
Michael 91: A cette époque fut bâtie Sinope . . .
Armenian 185: Sidon war gegründet.
Karst says that the Armenian text arose from a misreading of the Syriac. On the strength of the learned Jerome *T*, I have put this with the colonies whose regions are noted in the entry formula.

Date of the entry

Latin aA 1386   Syriac (i) 1386   Armenian 1386

24. LIPARA founded: 630/29

Texts of the entry

Synkellos 403.7: Λιπάρα ἐκτίσθη.
Jerome 169: Lipara condita.
Dionysius 23: Anno MCCCLXXXVIII urbs Lipara condita est.
Michael 91: Lipara . . . furent bâties.
Armenian 186: Lipar ward gegründet.

Date of the entry

Latin aA 1387   Syriac (i) 1388   Armenian 1389
The balance of evidence in Jerome is in favor of aA 1387.

25. EPIDAMNOS and PROUSIA: 627/6

Texts of the entry

Synkellos 403.8: Ἐπίδαμνος, ἡ νῦν καλουμένη Δυρράχιον, ἐκτίσθη.
403.9: Προύσια ἐκτίσθη.

27

Jerome 171:	Prusias condita.
	Epidamnus condita quae postea est uocata
	Dyrrhachium.
Dionysius 23:	eodemque anno Dyrrhachium urbs condita est.
Michael 91:	... et Prusias furent bâties; Epidamne fut bâtie,
	elle fut appelée Dyrrachium.
Armenian 186:	Prussia ward gegründet.
	Epidoros, welches Dyrakilon geheissen ward,
	wurde gegründet.

Jerome has two entries, at the same year, and therefore I have placed this as an east-west pair; possibly Synkellos shows alphabetical order of the names.

Date of the entry

Latin aA 1390   Syriac (i) 1389   Armenian 1390
                                                                                    1391

26. PHALARIS' tyranny ends: 625/4

Texts of the entry

Synkellos 403.10:   Φάλαρις τυραννῶν κατελύθη.
Jerome 171:   Falaris tyrannis destructa.
Armenian 186:   Phalaris ward von den Gewaltherrschen gestürzt.
Karst points out that the Armenian's translation arises from reading τυραννῶν as ὑπὸ τυράννων.

Date of the entry

Latin aA 1392   Armenian 1393

27. PANAITIOS, the first Sicilian tyrant: 615/4

Texts of the entry

Jerome 171:   Panaetius primus in Sicilia arripuit tyrannidem.
Armenian 186:   Panetios übte zuerst in Sikilia die Gewaltherrschaft.

Date of the entry

Latin aA 1402   Armenian 1407

The Armenian's date is depressed by a long entry on Josiah.

28. KAMARINA and PERINTHOS: 601/0

Texts of the entry

Synkellos 453.8:   Καμαρίνα πόλις ἐκτίσθη.
          453.9:   Πέρινθος ἐκτίσθη.
Jerome 175:   Camerina urbs condita [et Berintus condita M].
Dionysius 25:   ⟨Anno mil⟩ lesimo CCCCXVI Abrahami urbs
                   Camarina condita est atque etiam urbs Perinthus
                   condita est.

Michael 92:   Les villes de Camarina, Perinthe ... furent bâties.
Armenian 187:   Kamarina die Stadt ward gegründet.
Besides the joint entry in Jerome *M*, there is a separate entry on Perinthos in Jerome *F*, *D* and Q; *D* belongs to the tenth century and the
remainder to the ninth, contemporary with Synkellos and Dionysius.
The entry on Perinthos is not found in Jerome *T*; and the suggestion is
that the Perinthos notice is an interpolation into the Eusebian text. But
the number of east-west pairs makes this perhaps doubtful, at least until
Eusebius' source is identified for entries with this formula.

Date of the entry

Latin aA 1416   Syriac (i) 1416   Armenian 1417

29. MASSALIA: 598/7

Texts of the entry

Jerome 175:   Massilia condita.
Dionysius 25:   et urbs Massalia condita est.
Michael 92:   . . . et Ma⟨rseille⟩ furent bâties.
Armenian 187:   Massalia ward gegründet.

Date of the entry

Latin aA 1419   Syriac (i) 1419   Armenian 1423

The Armenian is depressed by the intrusion of the notice on Jeremiah
and Baruch into the right-hand column.

30. PHALARIS becomes tyrant: 571/0

Texts of the entry

Jerome 179:   Falaris tyrannidem exercuit an. xvi.
Armenian 188:   Phalaris führte die Gewaltherrschaft der Akragant
                   16 Jahre.

Date of the entry

Latin aA 1446   Armenian 1445

Again, no notice of the founding of Akragas precedes this entry.

ii. The formula-groups.   Examination of the formula-groups in the
Eusebian colony entries is of course beset by the difficulty that formulae may have changed in transmission. The example is 23, Sinope
II, which has the region of Pontos given only in Jerome T, and not
in the Greek, Syriac or Armenian. Clearly this region may have been
inserted by the learned T, or his may be the only record of its survival. Thus any inference from the formula-groups are necessarily
tentative, and the examination is simply a preparation for the later
consideration of other aspects of these entries.

Formula-group 1: colonies with founders named

2	Thebans at Kyrene	762/1
5	Milesians at Naukratis	749/8
12	Partheniai at Taras	
	Corinthians at Corcyra	706/5
22	Battos re-founds Kyrene	632/1

These four entries seem to be independent of the rest and perhaps of each other. The two foundations of Kyrene, if interconnected, show a highly idiosyncratic tradition, unknown to our other sources. The entry on the Milesians at Naukratis is part of a thalassocracy-entry; the entry on Taras and Corcyra is also idiosyncratic, for this synchronism has no other surviving record.

Formula-group 2a: Propontine singletons

10	Astakos-Nikomedeia	711/0
14	Kalchedon	685/4
16	Byzantium	659/8

These are all Megarian foundations in the Propontis: they are separated by intervals of 26 years. They form an interconnected group, with no obvious relation to any other group. But, over all, Eusebius shows a relatively large number of Propontine entries and for this group at least may share a source with the Περὶ Ἡρακλείας of Memnon of Herakleia Pontike, which has the same date for Astakos (434 F 1 §12).

Formula-group 2b: western singletons

19	Phalaris becomes tyrant in Akragas	652/1
24	Lipara founded	630/29
26	Phalaris overthrown	625/4
29	Massalia founded	598/7
30	Phalaris becomes tyrant	
	for 16 years	571/0–556/5

This seems to be (except perhaps for Massalia) a group concerned with a special problem of Sikeliote historiography. The polity of Lipara was founded by a Rhodian and Knidian enterprise which had failed to eject the Carthaginians from Motye. Our other sources give for its foundation the date of Ol.50, contemporary with one date for Akragas, itself settled from Gela, a Rhodian (and Cretan) colony. Thus whether at the early Eusebian dates, or at the date of Ol.50,

30

there seems to have been agreement that the foundations of Akragas and Lipara were connected.

The date of Ol.50 for Lipara seems to come from Timaios (Jac, 566 F 164), and Timaios (F 71) is also the only other authority who is known to have given a date for the foundation of Massalia— 120 years before Salamis, that is, 600/599 B.C.

The suggestion is therefore that in this formula-group of Eusebian entries, the dates for Phalaris and Lipara descend remotely from a polemical passage of Timaios; and that the date for Massalia also comes, with modification, from Timaios, but not necessarily from the same passage or by the same route.

Remoteness of derivation presumably accounts for the surprising fact that the group of entries includes no date for the foundation of Akragas. But possibly both of these controversial dates may be recovered from the information given under the name of Phalaris. In entry 30, Phalaris is said to have tyrannized for 16 years; entries 19 and 26 give him a 28-year reign. But if the earlier Phalaris also reigned for 16 years, ending in 625/4, he assumed power in 640/39; the year 652/1 is then the year of the foundation of Akragas for those who believed in an early date. Conversely, if Akragas was thus founded 12 years before Phalaris took power, for those to whom Phalaris usurped in 571/0 the year of the foundation of Akragas would be 583/2 B.C.

Thus it appears that the two sides to this historiographic controversy supported the following dates:

early

652/1	foundation of Akragas
640/39	usurpation of Phalaris
630/29	foundation of Lipara
625/4	overthrow of Phalaris

late

583/2	foundation of Akragas
580/79	foundation of Lipara (Timaios F 164)
571/0	usurpation of Phalaris
556/5	overthrow of Phalaris

One of the questions at issue in this debate was, no doubt, whether the failure at Motye was due to lack of Akragantine support, and if so whether this lack was due to the legal government or to the usurper.[8]

---

[8] See, further, Part Two below.

Formula-group   3a: Pontine   regional   singletons

17	Istros in the Pontos	657/6
21	Borysthenes in the Pontos	647/6
23	Sinope in the Pontos	631/0

These are all Milesian and Pontine, and apparently form an inter-connected group, independent of the other colony entries.

The preceding four groups of colony-entries may be independent of one another and of the following connected pair of groups. If the formula-grouping is to be trusted (which, as we have seen, is somewhat doubtful), Eusebius may have derived each of these four groups from different sources.

Formula-group   3b: western   regional   singletons

1	Pandosia and Metapontion in Italy	771/0
6	Naxos in Sicily	741/0
7	Syracuse and Katane in Sicily	736/5
9	Chersonesos in Sicily	717/6
20	Selinous in Sicily	650/49
27	Panaitios the first Sicilian tyrant	615/4

The differences between these entries and those of Thucydides are obvious and notorious: the Eusebian date for Selinous was however already known to Diodorus. If we can trust the way in which entry 27 refers to Panaitios, ignoring entirely the controversy which created formula-group 2b, the source for this group was independent.

Formula-group   4:   east-west   pairs   of   foundations

3	Megara and Zankle; Sinope	758/7
4	Kaulonia and Makalla; Kyzikos	757/6
8	Leontinoi [and Megara]; Maroneia	732/1
11	Sybaris and Kroton; Parion	709/8
13	Gela; Phaselis	691/0
15	Lokroi; Kyzikos	679/8
18	Akanthos, Stageira, Abdera, Kardia; Lampsakos	655/4?
25	Epidamnos; Prousia (Kios)	627/6
28	Kamarina; Perinthos	601/0

Gela and Phaselis are known from Aristainetos (771 F 1) to be a true pair of colonies, from one metropolis and with brother-oecists; the chief question about this formula-group is whether any of the other pairs are anything more than chronological coincidences.

32

Pairing of foundations *within* the west is an old feature of colonial historiography, first encountered in Antiochos (555 F 10), who synchronized Syracuse and Kroton: it also appears in synchronisms of Kroton and Sybaris (here, and Hippys 554 F 1), Syracuse and Corcyra (Strabo 6.2.4) and Kroton and Lokroi (Pausanias III 3.1, both in the reign of Polydoros at Sparta). Besides Sybaris and Kroton, the formula-group follows this tradition for Megara and Zankle, Kaulonia and Makalla[9] and the preceding group uses it also for Pandosia and Metapontion, Syracuse and Katane; it appears also in formula-group 1, for Taras and Corcyra. It is a question therefore whether this habit spread from western historiography perhaps by means of the Gela-Phaselis story, to the source for this Eusebian formula-group.

iii. The main Eusebian source for Sicily. Formula-group 3b must be supposed to belong to the same source as formula-group 4, on the ground that no source which dealt with Megara, Zankle, Leontinoi, and others would omit Naxos, Syracuse, Katane and conversely. The only Sicilian foundation not derived from this source by Eusebius is therefore Lipara in formula-group 2b.

If we tabulate the entries of formula-groups 3b and 4 together in a single chronological sequence, we have:

Pandosia and Metapontion	771/0?	
⟨Megara⟩ and Zankle	758/7	with ⟨Sinope⟩
⟨Makalla and Kaulonia⟩	757/6	with Kyzikos
Naxos	741/0	
Syracuse and Katane	736/5	
Leontinoi with Megarians	732/1	with ⟨Maroneia⟩
Chersonesos	717/6	
Sybaris and Kroton	709/8	with Parion
Gela	691/0	with Phaselis
Lokroi	679/8	with Kyzikos
	655/4?	Akanthos, Stageira, Abdera, Kardia, and Lampsakos
Selinous	650/49	

[9] As we have seen above, the Megara appearing with Leontinoi has probably arisen from the Megarians at Leontinoi with the Chalkidians.

Epidamnos	627/6 with Kios-Prousia
Panaitios tyrant	615/4
Kamarina	601/0 with Perinthos

iv. Doubtfully Eusebian entries. Because Perinthos appears only in the later manuscripts of Jerome, and Pandosia and Metapontion not at all, it has been held that these entries were introduced to the chronicle by a later interpolator of Eusebius. (The omission of Perinthos also from the Armenian means little, for in general that text is highly selective.) The presence of both entries in the Greek of Synkellos and in two Syriac sources is however, in favour of their having been in the Greek Eusebius, and omitted by error in Jerome.

If there can be doubt about these entries, there must be more about the Leontinoi entry, which is extant only in the Syriac. Its absence from Synkellos is not surprising, for he omits Syracuse also; its omission from Jerome is more serious. It is nevertheless difficult to believe in any reason which would move Eusebius, or any chroniclizing predecessor, to include Katane and exclude Leontinoi.

However, the main interest of these questions is that, if these entries were not Eusebian, they may not have come from the same source as the others. Perinthos in the Propontis is not of great interest to our present subject; of Pandosia and Metapontion there is hardly anything to say: Leontinoi is very likely to have been mentioned by a source which mentioned Panaitios of Leontinoi as the first Sicilian tyrant.

It is likely therefore that the foundation of Leontinoi was entered by Eusebius and omitted in error by Jerome; and that it derives from the same main source as the rest of these entries; Pandosia and Metapontion are more doubtful.

v. Relation to Thucydides' list. The intervals from Syracuse to Gela (45 years) and to Kamarina (135 years) are the same as the Thucydidean, and presumably this means that these three entries confirm one another's absolute dates. The manuscript tradition for Kamarina in Jerome is exceptionally good and confirmed by the Syriac, so that this group of absolute dates can presumably be taken as certain for the Eusebian text.

The interval from Syracuse in 736/5 to Akragas in 583/2, as implied by the later date for Phalaris in formula-group 2b, is also the

34

Thucydidean interval of 153 years. This should mean that the absolute dates are confirmed for more than the Eusebian text; that is, they are common to the main Eusebian source and the immediate source of formula-group 2b.

Since the ultimate source of formula-group 2b is probably, as we have seen, Timaios, these intervals in agreement with Thucydides, and the absolute dates for them, may go back to him. Whether they were also the absolute dates of Thucydides' source is not evidenced, but there is a certain presumption in favour.

The intervals from Naxos to Syracuse, and from Syracuse to Katane, Leontinoi, Selinous, and the implied early date for Akragas in formula-group 2b are however non-Thucydidean, and it is not necessarily to be presumed that the early date for Akragas comes from the same source as the others. Nor is the source for the others immediately identifiable. It was earlier than Diodorus, who uses the Eusebian date for Selinous.

The foundation of Chersonesos, and the tyrannies of Panaitios and Phalaris are not mentioned by Thucydides, and the first possibility is that Chersonesos and Panaitios came to Eusebius ultimately from the same historiographic source as his non-Thucydidean dates. The dating of Phalaris to 571/0–556/5 was probably earlier than Timaios, and may have been known to Thucydides' source; the dating of Phalaris to 640/39–625/4 is also probably earlier than Timaios, and an early date for Akragas might go with an early date for Selinous. It is therefore possible that the non-Thucydidean elements in Eusebius nevertheless derive ultimately from the classical Sikeliote historians.

vi. Historiography: a. *The Sicilian items.*   The reason why Thucydides embarks on his Sicilian excursus is to show his readers how mistaken the Athenians were in their estimates of the wealth, populousness, and natural Dorian hostility of the Sikeliotes. His mention of the Syracusan colonies of Akrai and Kasmenai, and failure to mention the Chalkidian Chersonesos-Mylai, Kallipolis, and Euboia are probably in themselves of no importance, but (therefore) points at which he permitted this intention to overmaster simple excerption from his source. It is a question, however, whether we can determine the historiographic intentions of Eusebius' main source from the fifteen entries we have attributed to him.

35

Within the Sicilian items, the chief difference with Thucydides is the early dating for Zankle, Megara, and her colony Selinous. According to Thucydides, Naxos was the first πόλις in point of time; Megara Hyblaia was not yet founded when the Megarians were at Leontinoi five years after Syracuse; and Zankle was at first a pirate settlement which became a πόλις—if we are to press Thucydides' sequence—after the reinforcement of Gela, that is, in the seventh century. It is possible that the Eusebian source did not differ so widely from this as appears at first sight. His Megara in 758/7 is probably the abortive settlement at Trotilon, given up in time for the Megarians to join in the colony at Leontinoi sixteen years later; if so, he agreed with Thucydides' source that Megara Hyblaia was not founded until some years after Naxos. Similarly, Zankle in 758/7 may be the pirate settlement. If these interpretations are correct, then Naxos is still the first πόλις to be founded in Sicily; the difference is that previous non-polis settlements are also not only recognized but dated.

According to Thucydides, Selinous was founded 100 years after Megara Hyblaia (which was more than six years after Naxos); according to Eusebius' source, Selinous is founded 108 years after the Megarians (on this interpretation) settle at Trotilon. According to Thucydides, the Megarians arrived in Sicily (at Trotilon) 'at the same time' apparently as the Chalkidians. Perhaps Thucydides' source had the same narrative as was used by Ephoros (F 137), which makes Theokles, founder of Naxos, also convoy the Megarians to Sicily, and so places the foundations of Naxos and Trotilon at the same time. If so, for Thucydides' source also Selinous must have been founded more than 106 years after Trotilon, and it is clearly likely that the figure of 108 years from Trotilon to Selinous was used by both historians. Then the difference is only that the Eusebian source allows a longer period for the Megarians at Trotilon than Thucydides' source did.

Within the Sicilian items, therefore, Eusebius' source differs from Thucydides in both a greater strictness in the meaning of the term πόλις, which suggests a time contemporary with or later than the rise and expansion of political science in the fourth century; and a greater confidence in the historiographic capacity to give precise dates, even for such irregular settlements as Trotilon and the early Zankle. These differences are substantial, but they are differences of historiographic method rather than of historical fact or evidence.

b. The Italian items. No surviving source other than Eusebius has anything to say about the foundation of either of the two cities named Pandosia. The one intended by Eusebius may have been that near Siris. Metapontion was said by Ephoros (F 141) to have been founded by Daulios tyrant of Krisa, that is, by Phokians. Makalla was perhaps Rhodian, and Kaulonia was Achaian, founded by Tryphon of Aigion. It would be interesting to know if this single colony from Aigion was connected, in Eusebius' source, with that sea-battle between Aigion and the Aitolians which led to the famous oracle comparing Pelasgikon Argos, Thessaly, Sparta, Chalkis, and Dorian Argos.[10]

The entry on Kroton and Sybaris is dated to *aA* 1308 by both Jerome and the Armenian, so it is one of the better-witnessed dates. As it is a date for three settlements named in alphabetical order, it is probably not the same date as is given by Dionysius of Halkarnassos[11] for Kroton alone at 710/09.

Eusebius' main source can hardly have failed to give a foundation-date for Taras, one of the most important of the Italian cities. The Eusebian entry however belongs to his formula-group 1, which names the founders of cities, in this case the Spartan Partheniai, at B.C. 706/5. But within formula-group 1, this is the only entry to pair cities, and thus is to be taken as independent of the rest of that group, and from the main source for the western colonies.

The last of the Eusebian items for Italy is Lokroi, founded from Lokris, again north of the Corinthian Gulf, like Metapontion from Phokis.

Thus Metapontion at the beginning, and Lokroi at the end of Eusebius' Italian items both come from north Greece, while Kaulonia, Sybaris and Kroton, and Taras, come from the south of the Gulf. Moreover the statement that Metapontion was founded by a tyrant of Krisa is hostile in tone; and there was a strong hostile tradition about Lokroi. The source of hostility to Lokroi may be revealed by an obscure tradition, known only in a romanticized form,[12] which connects the foundation with civil strife in Corcyra: at the date 679/8 we are approaching the time of the first war between Corinth and Corcyra mentioned by Thucydides.

If the source of hostility to Lokroi was Corinth and her depend-

---

[10] Ion of Chios FHG II 51, fragment 17; Peake and Wormell, *The Delphic Oracle*[2] (Oxford 1956) no.1.
[11] A.R. 2. 361.
[12] Konon 26 F 1.3.

encies and allies, her tradition may also have inspired the hostility to Metapontion, and the conception of a series of Achaian colonies between these two. On these grounds it is possible that the Italian items of Eusebius' source were arranged to display a historiographic thesis about the succession of powers in the Corinthian Gulf and their effects on western colonization.

This thesis would be, in general terms, that in the early years the peoples north of the Corinthian Gulf ruled it, and that western settlements were made either by them (Metapontion) or by colonists from the Aegean sailing round the Peloponnese (the Chalkidians at Zankle, the Megarians, the Rhodians at Makalla). Power in the Corinthian Gulf passed to the Achaians on the south with the defeat of the Aitolians by Aigion, whose colony at Kaulonia is synchronized with the last Rhodian colony of this period. The first πόλις in Sicily, nevertheless, was founded by Chalkidians and other Ionians; Corinthian power in the Corinthian Gulf is first signalized by the foundation of Syracuse. Chalkidian expansion in Sicily is rapid; then Achaian expansion in Italy. If the foundations of Taras and Corcyra in the same year belong to this historiography, then Corinth and Sparta are seen as acting in concert to secure the western route. After this, however, other powers make some recovery: Rhodes returns to the west with the foundation of Gela, and Lokris, north of the Corinthian Gulf, succeeds in planting Lokroi, not long before the first war between Corinth and Corcyra which, on the generally accepted ancient dates, shortly preceded the fall of the Bacchiad oligarchy and the rise of the tyranny in Corinth. At about the time of this convulsion, the colonies named are Akanthos and its associates; possibly, therefore, the weakness of Corinth was seen as resulting in the alliance of Chalkis and Andros for the foundation of Akanthos (and in that case, the Akanthos entry belongs to Eusebius' main source). Under the tyranny, however, Corinth with Corcyra founded Epidamnos, and with Syracuse sent an oecist to Kamarina.

If this, or something similar, was the historiographic thesis of Eusebius' main pre-chroniclized source, that authority was not Timaios, who was a determined critic of the tradition hostile to Lokroi. It is likely moreover that a historian exploring the consequences and effects of sea-power in the west would be contemporary with or later than Kastor of Rhodes (about 60 B.C.).

c. The eastern items. An early date for the foundation of Sinope would no doubt be an inference from the mention of a nymph Sinope by the Corinthian poet Eumelos (451 F 5), who was generally supposed to have lived about the time of the fall of the Bacchiad kings and the plantation of Syracuse: the early Kyzikos may come from the same source. Maroneia is undoubtedly an inference from Archilochos' reference to it (F 146 Bergk), and Parion also may come from his poems.[13] Phaselis was a subject of oracular poetry known to, or invented by, the local historian Aristainetos;[14] the later Kyzikos (in the time of Gyges) is probably a more historiographic entity. Akanthos has a memorable foundation-legend,[15] probably remembered in poetry attached to the cult of the hero-founder; Stageira was a sister-city. The early, and abortive, settlement at Abdera by Timesios of Klazomenai was commemorated by a hero-cult in the later city[16] which commissioned verses from Anakreon[17] and Pindar,[18] who no doubt recalled Timesios; Kardia (also from Klazomenai) is a sister-city.[19] Lampsakos has also a romantic foundation-story, attached to a cult of Lampsake,[20] and no doubt enshrined in verse. We know nothing of Kios (Prousia), but the tale of the founding of Perinthos survives,[21] and again we can assume hero-cult and poetry.

The eastern items of the east-west pairs thus seem fairly generally to be notable for song and story of rather various qualities. The purpose of the synchronisms may consequently have been literary: to provide poetic and romantic garnish to a rather prosaic historiographic thesis on sea-power.

vii. The problems of the historiographic original and the first chronicler. Since we do not know the principle by which Eusebius excerpted from his authorities, we must take the dimly seen and highly ten-

---

[13] These dates are probably to be connected with the Archilochan biography known to Cicero (*Tusc.* 1.1) dating the poet *regnante Romulo;* and with the date 720/19 for Thasos reported by Dionysius (251 F 3).
[14] Jac 771 F 1.
[15] Plutarch QG 30.
[16] Herodotus 1.168.
[17] Anakreon F 101 B[1].
[18] *Paian* II.
[19] Charon of Lampsakos (Jac 262 F 2) has a fine story of how the Kardienoi lost a battle to Naris of the Bisaltai.
[20] Charon 262 F 7.
[21] Plutarch QG 57.

tative inferences from his synchronisms with the utmost caution, and distinguish several separate problems.

A. There is some reason to suppose that Eusebius' source was late. First, parallel dates, or associated matter, are found in Diodorus, Dionysius of Halikarnassos, Cicero, and Konon (all of the first century B.C.), and in Memnon of Herakleia, at a later date. Secondly, 'sea-power' became a historiographic unifier, so far as we know, in the work of Kastor of Rhodes about 60 B.C., who, it seems, did not treat of the west. His work therefore has been extended by a later historian, who is Eusebius' main source for Sicily.

B. It appears that Eusebius' source was literary, if the eastern foundations among the east-west pairs were selected to provide poetic and romantic elements lacking in the western traditions. But there may have been one or more chroniclizing intermediaries between the source and Eusebius himself: Africanus at least, and possibly pagan predecessors like Phlegon.

C. If this source did original work on sea-power in the west, it does not follow that he also did original work on the colony dates; he may have adopted those to be found in earlier work which suited his thesis best.

D. The Eusebian entries which name more than one foundation divide into two groups according to whether the foundations are listed in alphabetical order or not. Alphabetical order is found in 4. Kaulonia and Makalla; 8. Leontinoi and Maroneia; 11. Kroton, Parion and Sybaris; 13. Gela and Phaselis; 15. Kyzikos and Lokroi; 18. Akanthos and Stageira in one region, Kardia and Lampsakos in others; 25. Epidamnos and Kios-Prousia (in Synkellos only); 28. Kamarina and Perinthos. It is not found in 1. Pandosia and Metapontion; 3. Megara, Zankle, and Kyzikos; 7. Syracuse and Katane, 12. Taras and Corcyra. In the case of Syracuse and Katane, we can see that the much greater importance of Syracuse may well have pre-empted first place; and the lack of alphabetical order in the other three instances may be accounted for either by the nature of the narratives concerned, or by the modes of excerption or transmission. The presence of alphabetical order in some certain cases speaks for rather careful excerption at some stage, perhaps for a more specialist chronicle or *Olympiades* than that of Eusebius.

Thus it appears that the Eusebian main source for Sicily may comprise the work of at least three authorities: one or more western

40

specialists; the 'sea-power' historian; and an excerptor, all of the later Hellenistic or Roman periods.

D. THE PROBLEM OF THE SINGLENESS OF THE SICILIAN TRADITION.

Thucydides and Eusebius share some of the intervals in the datings—from Syracuse to Gela, to Kamarina, and to Akragas; but Akragas has also other dates and other Eusebian datings are non-Thucydidean. The problem of the singleness of the tradition is therefore two questions:

(a) whether there was a recognized foundation-document for the historiography; disputed in detail (as for Akragas) but generally recognized as the starting-point of all controversies;

(b) whether there was an ante-historiographic single tradition, discussed and disputed by the historiographers.

On general grounds we should hardly expect to find in existence in the fifth century a single ante-historiographic tradition embracing all the Ionian, Dorian, and mixed Sikeliote cities. We should expect the ante-historiographic traditions to be numerous and particular, embracing at most the common history of Naxos and her colonies, or Syracuse and her colonies; and we should suppose that the general list was a product of learning. Nevertheless, the degree of agreement between Thucydides and Eusebius has often been taken as the basis for arguments to the contrary—that the historiographic agreement is founded on the singleness of an ante-historiographic tradition. Consequently our next task is to consider in general what may have been the primary sources of the historians, and their nature.

Meantime the Thucydidean and Eusebian dates are tabulated (Tables III and IV), on the assumption that they shared the absolute date for Syracuse at 736/5 B.C.

41

TABLE III

THE THUCYDIDEAN LIST IF SYRACUSE WAS FOUNDED IN 736/5 B.C.

737/6	Naxos founded, one year before Syracuse; 'at the same time', Megarians at Trotilon
736/5	Syracuse
731/0	Leontinoi with the Megarians, 5 years after Syracuse
?	Katane, after Leontinoi
?	Megarians, expelled from Leontinoi, encamp in Thapsos
729/8?	Megara Hyblaia founded 100 years before Selinous
691/0	Gela reinforced, 45 years after Syracuse
?	Zankle regularly constituted
666/5	Akrai, 70 years after Syracuse
646/5	Kasmenai, 20 years after Akrai
629/8?	Selinous (108 years after Trotilon?)
?	Himera
601/0	Kamarina, 135 years after Syracuse
583/2	Akragas, 108 years after Gela
484/3?	Megara Hyblaia destroyed after 245 years

TABLE IV

EUSEBIUS' SICILIAN DATES

758/7	Megarians (at Trotilon); (pirates? at) Zankle
741/0	Naxos (the first πόλις)
736/5	Syracuse and Katane
732/1	Leontinoi with the Megarians
?	(Megara Hyblaia founded)
717/6	Chersonesos
691/0	Gela
652/1	early date for ⟨the foundation of Akragas⟩
650/49	Selinous
630/29	Lipara
615/4	Panaitios of Leontinoi, the first tyrant
601/0	Kamarina
571/0	late date for the tyranny of Phalaris

PART TWO

EVIDENCE ABOUT PRIMARY SOURCES

A. ORACLES AND OECISTS. The use of Eumelos and Archilochos as contemporary witnesses for historical events mentioned or alluded to in their poems is an example of one kind of primary evidence used by the ancient historians. It is a question, especially for the Greek west, of how far oracular poetry about the foundation of colonies was also a source for historians.

Most oracles mentioned or quoted by historians are attributed to Apollo, and especially to Delphi. This is probably a highly selective convention, for there certainly were masses of other oracular material in existence. The bulk of popular oracles would of course be evanescent; but occasionally a competent verse or notable expression of sentiment would emerge from this and be incorporated into the institutional collections of oracles, which were made by states such as Sparta and Athens or by corporations such as the supposed descendants of Laios. There were also literary collections, such as those ascribed to Mousaios, Epimenides, and Abaris: we may suspect that such material tended to shade off into (i) the works and lives of wizards and seers (Amphiaraos, Melampous, Telchines, Kouretes and Korybantes, Arimaspians); (ii) religious and magical texts on Rites, Purifications, Healings, Omens, etc., overlapping with hymnography; and (iii) certain modified forms of this material suitable for incorporation into heroic epic, such as the Nekyia in the Odyssey, the Thesprotis in the Telegonia, and probably many stories of Medeia in the Argonautika. In various ways, the institutional and literary oracles approach the subject-matter of historiography; and *a priori* considerable use of oracular poetry as historical source-material might be expected. In particular, the cult of Apollo Archegetes at Naxos in Sicily is frequently taken to support the contention that Delphi had a close connection with the colonizing process there; that is, that not only was oracular poetry an important source for the historians of Sicily, but that they were right in using it.

But only two Sicilian cities have surviving foundation oracles: Syracuse and Gela. It may be coincidence that these are the two Deinomenid cities, and that the Deinomenid courts were literary centers; but the correlation is bound to arouse dubiety about both the age and the place of composition of these Delphic oracles.

In the most recent examination of the Sicilian foundation oracles, Parke and Wormell[1] take two, characterized by detailed geographical references, to be the oldest oracles for Syracuse (no.2) and Gela (no.3) respectively, and regard these as the authentic foundation oracles. The Syracusan oracles is probably incompletely quoted by Pausanias: in its full form it may have been the ultimate source for the name of Archias' father Euagetes, known to the Parian Marble (epoch 31), just as the Gela oracle, known from Diodorus, gives the name of Kraton, father of Antiphemos. These are the only two founders' patronymics which seem to have survived, and oracular verse is a very probable source for such details, publishing local cultic knowledge to the world of learning. Apart from their ventures into biography and geography, however, these oracles are dumb: they make no suggestions for, or confirmations of, the organization of the colony; nor do they incorporate any ritual recommendations, for example, to sacrifice to Apollo Archegetes on the first arrival in Sicily. That is to say, the interests of these oracles are the interests of learning, not of colonization nor of religion, and we should therefore suppose them to have originated in learning, as well as serving as source-material for learning later.[2]

The Syracusan oracle emphasizes that Ortygia is an island, and refers to the belief that the river Alpheus reappeared as Arethousa. Ortygia was joined to the mainland by a mole in the latter part of the sixth century, and about the same time the Sicilian poet Ibykos spoke of Alpheus and Arethousa. This suggests a context and date for the composition of the Syracusan oracle; and for the world of learning at

---

[1] *The Delphic Oracle* [2] (Oxford 1956).

[2] There seems to be no reason, other than habit, for supposing that the priests of Apollo were themselves these learned men. As priests, surely their primary interest was religious: had they also been learned, we should have heard of learned publications by them. But even the list of Pythian victors was published by laymen—Aristotle and his nephew Kallisthenes.

this time we should add the publication of the geography of Hekataios, and the visit to Syracuse in 504/3–501/0 of the Homerid Kynaithos (Hippostratos 568 F 5). The new temple at Delphi was recently completed at the time of this visit, and we may suppose a pre-disposition to welcome close association with the new splendor of the cult-center. Probably therefore we should take the date of the composition of the oldest Syracusan and Geloan oracles to be the latter part of the sixth century.

Other sources give no foundation oracles for other Sicilian cities, but another Delphic oracle for Gela, and three more for Syracuse. The Geloan oracle (no.410) is from Aristainetos (771 F 1) and probably of Hellenistic date: the joint Cretan founder has disappeared in the interests of the drama of the brother oecists of Gela and Phaselis. One of the Syracusan oracles (no.398) is also from a Hellenistic romance dealing with Archias and Aktaion. The third Syracusan oracle (no.229) is part of the famous story which brought Archias of Syracuse and Myskellos of Kroton together, and assigned wealth to Syracuse but health to Kroton: Antiochos (555 F 10) accepted the synchronism, but perhaps not the oracle, since he was careful to say that the two foundations coincided by chance. The oracle was quite probably therefore known to Antiochos (writing in the last quarter of the fifth century), and it alludes to the time when Kroton was famous for her athletes and doctors. In fact, it can probably be dated more closely. Astylos of Kroton won the stadion at Olympia in 488, 484, and 480; and it was a notorious scandal that in 484 and 480, in order to please the tyrant of Syracuse, he allowed his name and victory to be ascribed to that city. As the term 'oracle' included those genres of statement that we should call pamphlet, broadsheet, and brochure, this Syracusan oracle is probably to be taken as a broadsheet on the career of Astylos, and therefore be dated to 482 ± 2. If this is correct, an 'oracle' which began as a broadsheet in Gelon's time is already influencing the history of colonization for Antiochos some sixty years later, even if he rejected the oracle itself.[3]

So far as we can see, therefore, oracular verse on Sicilian foundation is not earlier than the later sixth century, and is confined to Syracuse and Gela. The two earliest oracles are compositions within the world of learning at that time, but preserve in the oecists' patro-

---

[3] The fourth Syracusan oracle is also on Deinomenid wealth, and purely a piece of moralizing: no.241 (from Porphyry).

45

nymics local cultic tradition, and publish it to the learned world.

For the Sicilian oecists in general, Thucydides is the source. He gives sixteen oecists' names, and all our other material taken together yields one more, and that probably corrupt (Philistos 556 F 3: Momnon(?) of Maktorion). Thucydides gives no patronymics, but remarks of Archias of Syracuse that he was a Herakleid. The question therefore arises, for Sicily, whether any of her historians attempted to trace the oecists in their metropoleis, and establish their genealogy and date, as Herodotus attempted for Battos and the foundation of Kyrene. It is worth while examining Thucydides' list of oecists with this question in mind.

Theokles, the oecist of Naxos and Leontinoi, is said by Thucydides to have arrived 'with Chalkidians', and Hellanikos, in his chronicle, The Priestesses (4 F 82), said that he came ἐκ Χάλκιδος. But for Ephoros he is an Athenian (70 F 137), and if it were Ephoros himself who was romancing here, we should expect him to have made Theokles a Kymaian. Probably then he is reporting an older statement (perhaps made during the preparations for the Sicilian expedition), by which time Chalkis was in no position to prevent such annexations.

Archias of Syracuse, son of Euagetes and a Herakleid, has a pedigree and, in Hellenistic romance, a biography in Corinth. But Corinth has no local historians, save for those who used the name of the 'prose Eumelos', and we cannot suppose that there was much local investigation there (though the statement that many of the colonists came from Tenea may mean that there was some enquiry into common cultic practices, hereditary priesthoods, and similar matters).

Euarchos of Katane has no patronymic or pedigree, nor, though oecist of a secondary colony, is he associated with an oecist from the original metropolis, Chalkis.

Lamis from Megara is the oecist of abortive settlements at Trotilon and Thapsos, where he died. He has no patronymic or pedigree, and he is not the oecist of Megara Hyblaia, for which the Megarian leader is not named. As giving the distinctive epithet to the settlement, the Sikel king Hyblon is in a sense the oecist.

Entimos of Crete and Antiphemos son of Kraton from Lindos are the joint founders of the reinforced settlement at Gela. Artemon of Pergamon (569 F 1) said that these two oecists spent considerable labor in gathering their colonists from Rhodes, Crete, and the Peloponnese; they then surmounted the hazards of the voyage and

46

the establishment of the colony and finally, in obedience to an Apolline oracle (the third—but not necessarily Delphic—for Gela) fought the Sikans. Another authority, however, Menekrates, brusquely dismissed this as nonsense, asserting that the oecists of Gela had an easy time. Artemon apparently had not heard of the story mentioned by Zenobius (1.54) that the oecists failed to pay attention to an oracle (the fourth for Gela), and were consequently destroyed by a Phoenician pirate.[4]

Rhodes had a flourishing school of local historians, and they had something to say about Antiphemos; but the reference to him that survives from their work (Xenagoras 240 F 15—the Lindian *Anagraphe*, Jac.532, entry 28) is confused, and though this is certainly the fault of the excerptor and not of Xenagoras, it may be that Xenagoras' account of Antiphemos had not made such an impression that the excerptor's mind was clear on his person and date. Either Aristainetos' oracle had not yet been invented or Xenagoras granted it no credence.

Thucydides mentions Zankle after Gela, perhaps intending to mean thereby that its transformation from a pirate's nest into a city-state occurred in the seventh century. There are two oecists, Perieres from Cumae and Krataimenes from Chalkis, the metropolis of Cumae. Zankle also has an oracle (no.384), not for the foundation, but about the hero-cult of the oecists, forbidding the use of their names. This is a ritual prescription, and by subject-matter is consequently a candidate for authenticity; but circumstances under which such a ban would be proper are disputable. Perhaps we should think of the time after Zankle had passed under the dominion of the Messenians and Samians, when there may have been pressure for the establishment of other oecist cults: Pausanias in fact calls Krataimenes a Samian (IV 23.7). The oracle would then date from the fifth century: it is possible that we can see one of its results in Thucydides' failure to date Zankle and Himera.

We now have a group of secondary colonies: Akrai and Kasmenai from Syracuse have no oecist named at all; Maktorion from Gela has the oecist Momnon(?), presumably from Gela and not associated with a colleague from the Geloan metropoleis; and Selinous from Megara Hyblaia, with an oecist, Pamillos, from old Megara but none from Hyblaia. On the other hand, the last three foundations, Himera,

---

[4] Unless this story originally referred to an early settlement reinforced by Artemon's laborious oecists.

47

Kamarina, and Akragas seem to follow the rule of having an oecist from both the mother and the grandmother cities, like Zankle. It is possible that the apparent irregularities of Akrai and Kasmenai (and Maktorion) are due to their not being fully independent political units; Selinous was the daughter of a city which seems to have had a Sikel oecist if it had one at all, and may therefore have suffered some ritual incapacity, made good only by bringing Pamillos from old Megara. But even with these possibilities in mind, there is still a notable difference between the first and second groups of secondary colonies, which bears on the question of the date of the regular constitution of Zankle in particular, and in general on the time when the custom of associating the grandmother city with a secondary foundation came into regular use.

Himera has three oecists, one of whom will represent the Myletidai, 'refugees from Syracuse', and the others presumably Zankle and Cumae: their names are Eukleides, Simos, and Sakon, and nothing is known of them. Kamarina has two oecists, Daskon and Menekelos, no doubt from Syracuse and Corinth; Akragas has two, Aristonoos and Pystilos, presumably from Gela and Rhodes. The name Aristonoos recurs at Gela as one of Gelon's brothers-in-law, but (as we shall see) the histories of the Emmenidai of Akragas change and develop in their own right, and there is little trace of any Geloan control material.

Taking together the oracles and the roster of oecists therefore we seem to find that the Sikeliotes began to take an interest in their own history late in the sixth century, and that oracles dating from that time contain and publish locally known cultic detail in the patronymics of oecists. A century later, Thucydides can list oecists for all the foundations he names except Akrai and Kasmenai, but the only oecist with a pedigree is Archias of Syracuse. In the later material— even that of Xenagoras of Rhodes—there is nothing to suggest that there was any metropolitan information available. This is not wholly an argument from silence, for those who invented more oracles for Syracuse and Gela could, obviously, have invented others for the other foundations, together with biographies of the oecists, however romantic (like that of Archias); and then we should have been bound to consider whether the Sikeliote historians, and those of their metropolitan cities, did not provide information, lost to us, on which such oracles and romances were formed. But the only oracle outside the eight for Syracuse and Gela is from Zankle, and is about ritual; it is

very likely to be authentic, and of fifth-century date. We have therefore to consider whether the early oracles and Thucydides' source
between them contain all that was still known about the foundation
period by the end of the fifth century. Whatever the answer to this
question may be, there are two noteworthy characteristics of the
information we do possess from these sources: first, the monopoly of
the oracular tradition by Syracuse and Gela; and secondly, the difference between the two groups of secondary colonies, the first consisting
of Akrai, Kasmenai, Maktorion, and Selinous and showing no regularity in their possession of oecists; and the second composed of
Zankle, Himera, Kamarina, and Akragas, all obeying the custom of
associating an oecist from the grandmother city with a new foundation. This suggests that, in Sicily at least, this custom can hardly be
older than the middle of the seventh century, but the reasons for its
invention or adoption do not appear.

Among the poetic sources for the early history we should not fail
to mention possible allusions in Stesichoros and Ibykos, and no doubt
other western poets, as well as the reference to the founding of
Syracuse by Archilochos (F 146) and similar allusions in other non-
Sicilian poets. Undoubtedly Hellenistic, if not Sikeliote, scholarship
collected all such references and made inferences from them about the
Sicilian foundation dates, and from those dates other inferences about
the dates of the poets. But so far as we can tell, poetry would always
give only relative dates, like Pindar's 'hundred years' from the
foundation of Akragas to Theron's victory: these were (so far as they
existed) translated into absolute dates by historiography.

B. *DEINOMENIDS AND EMMENIDS*. Other genealogical
material possibly relevant to the foundation period is preserved in our
sources. This concerns the families of Pindar's patrons, the Deinomenid tyrants in Gela and Syracuse, and the Emmenids in Akragas.

i. The Deinomenids. The greater part of our information on the
Deinomenids comes from the Sikeliote historians; before them, the
earliest account of their ancestry is found in Herodotus (VII 153),
and attributed by him to Sikeliote sources.

Herodotus says that the ancestor of the Deinomenids came to
Gela from the island of Telos, with Antiphemos and the Lindians.

49

This ancestor, unnamed by Herodotus,[5] is called Deinomenes by Xenagoras (240 F 15) and by the *Etymologicum Magnum* (225.1). A descendant of this Deinomenes was Telines, named by Herodotus as the first in the family who held the priesthood possessed by his descendants. This priesthood was described by Philistos (F 49) and Timaios (F 96) as that of hierophant of the goddesses, who are identified as Demeter and Kore by other Pindaric scholia (to *Ol.*6.158a and 160d), no doubt drawing on the same sources. Herodotus says he does not know how Telines came by this religious possession, and our sources do not discuss the matter, except that some scholar read in, or added, to *Pythian* 2.29 an allusion to a Cypriote origin.

The next member of the family mentioned is Molossos (Xenagoras 240 F 15), father of Deinomenes II. This Deinomenes dedicated a tithe of his war-spoils to Athena Lindia and is most probably the man after whom the Deinomenid tyrants were named. He had four sons and two daughters. His eldest son was Gelon, who became the cavalry commander of Hippokrates tyrant of Gela (Hdt.7.154), and when Hippokrates died he was left as guardian to Hippokrates' two sons. The guardianship may imply kinship to the boys, perhaps through their mother, or through a first wife of Gelon's. In time, Gelon superseded the boys and himself became tyrant of Gela; he married Demareta, daughter of Theron tyrant of Akragas (Timaios, F 93). This marriage probably occurred within the period 487 ± 2, and produced a son (Timiaios, F 21). Gelon died, in 478/7, while the boy was young, leaving as guardians his two brothers-in-law, the distinguished soldier Chromios son of Agesidamos, and Aristonoos, homonym and probably kinsman of one of the oecists of the Geloan colony at Akragas. These arrangements may suggest that Gelon and his two sisters were closer to one another than Gelon and his brothers—that Deinomenes married twice, and that the three younger sons were children of the second marriage.

Gelon's successor as tyrant and hierophant was his brother Hieron who (Philistos F 70, Timaios F 97) married three times. His first wife was daughter to Nikokles of Syracuse, and bore Hieron the son, Deinomenes III, who had been appointed king of Aitne by 470 (*Pythian* 1.111 ff.). This should mean that he was born at latest in 488, so that Hieron married the daughter of Nikokles while he—and

---

[5] Perhaps Herodotus assumed that it was obvious that he was named Deinomenes.

presumably Nikokles also—was still a Geloan. His second and third wives were the daughters of Xenokrates of Akragas and Anaxilas of Rhegion.

The third of the four brothers was Polyzelos, who married Gelon's widow Damareta, presumably in 478/7. A daughter of Polyzelos by an earlier marriage married Damareta's father Theron (Timaios F 93).

These intermarriages should enable us to make some reasonable estimates of the biographical dates of the Deinomenids. Theron was most probably the first husband of Polyzalos' daughter, who will have been at least fourteen years old when she married. If she went to Akragas at the time when Damareta first came to Gela within the period 487 ± 2, then she must have been born at latest in 501 ± 2. On this reckoning, Polyzalos can hardly have been born later than 526 ± 2; and his elder brother Gelon (especially if the two sisters came between) may have been five to ten years older—born, that is to say, between 536 ± 2 and 531 ± 2. Gelon would then be between 44 and 49 years old when he married Damareta; and Hieron, even if born as late as 528 ± 2, would be about 40 when his son was born.

If on the other hand, Polyzalos' daughter went to Akragas when Damareta married her father in 478/7 B.C., she could have been born as late as 492/1, and Polyzalos himself not later than 517/6. Gelon would then be born between 527 and 522, and be between 35 and 40 when he married Damareta; and Hieron, born perhaps as late as 519/8, would be 31 (or less) when his son was born in 488 or earlier. This dating is genealogically much more reasonable and it may be supported by a very muddled and (apparently) lacunose scholium (to Ol.2.29b): it is speaking about Damareta's second marriage when the words appear γαμβρῶν οὖν γεγονότων αὐτῶν and apparently the reference is to the exchange of daughters between Theron and Polyzelos.

On this second dating, Gelon would be in his later twenties when Hippokrates became tyrant of Gela and Gelon joined his bodyguard; in his middle thirties when he became tyrant of Gela himself; in his early forties when he became tyrant of Syracuse, and approaching fifty when he died. Hieron would be in his early forties when he succeeded Gelon, and approaching his middle fifties when he died. Polyzalos died before Hieron, who was succeeded by the youngest brother, Thrasyboulos, who abdicated before his first year was complete. We know nothing of his marriages, children, or death; and

51

nothing is known of the biographies of Gelon's and Hieron's sons, nor of the children, if any, of Gelon's sisters.

Our knowledge of the Deinomenid genealogy is not extensive, but it comes from early sources and seems sound. The line of descent is probably continuous from the time of the establishment of the priesthood by Telines, who (if Gelon was born about 527) may have been active in public life in the years around 585. It is thus probable that our informants give us a continuous record from the time when the state of Gela recognized Telines' priesthood down to the expulsion of Thrasyboulos from Syracuse. Before the upper limit the record is partial and below the lower limit non-existent.

TABLE V

THE DEINOMENID GENEALOGY

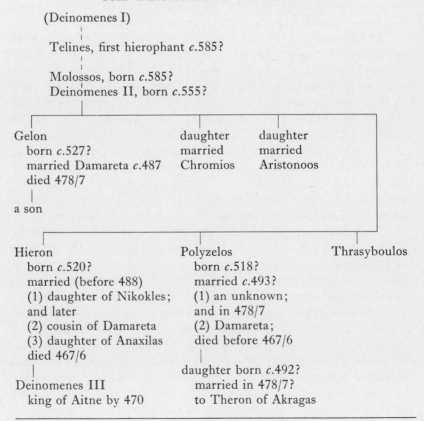

(Deinomenes I)

Telines, first hierophant *c.*585?

Molossos, born *c.*585?
Deinomenes II, born *c.*555?

Gelon
  born *c.*527?
  married Damareta *c.*487
  died 478/7

a son

daughter
married
Chromios

daughter
married
Aristonoos

Hieron
  born *c.*520?
  married (before 488)
  (1) daughter of Nikokles;
  and later
  (2) cousin of Damareta
  (3) daughter of Anaxilas
  died 467/6

Deinomenes III
  king of Aitne by 470

Polyzelos
  born *c.*518?
  married *c.*493?
  (1) an unknown;
  and in 478/7
  (2) Damareta;
  died before 467/6

daughter born *c.*492?
married in 478/7?
to Theron of Akragas

Thrasyboulos

This suggests that the information about the Deinomenids was taken, by Herodotus and the Sikeliote historians, from exact living memory—the elders and experts who were the oral equivalent of archival material in Gela and Syracuse. If this material did not reach (in any detail) beyond the time of Telines' priesthood, then the upper horizon, before the middle of the sixth century, is much the same as Herodotus' informants show elsewhere. But this means that material of this kind cannot have been used to determine a historical date for the foundation of Gela. Moreover, the modern historian naturally suspects a connection between the secession to Maktorion (during which Telines became famous), the admission of Telines to the priestly nobility of Gela, and the colonization of Akragas from Gela. But so far as we know these events were not connected by the ancient historians – in other words, the Deinomenid genealogical information was not, apparently, used to fix the foundation date even of Akragas.

ii. The Emmenids: the controversies. The surviving genealogical material for the Emmenids comes from a tradition of very different quality: late, legendary, and controversial. It is astonishing that our information about two contemporary families who closely inter-married, and both of whom employed Pindar, should have been of such different calibers. Both traditions begin with Pindar's (and for the ancients, other) odes which sketch, in their allusions, the state of contemporary information, and were presumably primary sources; yet the Deinomenid information, firmly placed within historiographic limits by Herodotus, breaks away from the poetic and is, apparently, historical, while the Emmenid continues and enlarges the poetic or romantic down to a fairly late period of Hellenistic learning.

The chief authorities for the Deinomenids are Herodotus, Philistos, and Timaios; those named for the Emmenids are Aristotle (Kallisthenes), Timaios, Hippostratos, 'the early commentators' on Pindar (i.e. Aristophanes of Byzantium) Aristarchos, Artemon of Pergamon, and his critic Menekrates.

The non-controversial statements about the Emmenids are few: they were descended from Laios (Σ *Ol.*2.39b) and Oidipous (Σ *Ol.*2 *inscr.*, 65c); Theron was the son of Ainesidamos (Σ *Ol.*2 *inscr.*, 8a, 3.16); his children were his heir Thrasydaios (Σ *Pyth.* 2.132a) and Damareta wife of Gelon (Timaios F 93); his second wife was the daughter of Polyzelos of Syracuse (Timiaios F 93). Beyond this, the material is devoted to the pursuit of four controversies.

a. The Emmenid name. Pindar uses the name of the Emmenidai in *Ol.*3.69 and *Pyth.* 6.5; and we should probably infer from this that 'the Emmenidai' is what Theron called his lineage.

'The 'early commentators', Aristophanes of Byzantium, derived the name from an Emmenes who destroyed the tyranny of Phalaris (*Σ Ol.*3.68a). We should attribute to this same source statements given anonymously in our scholia:

(i) that the Emmenidai were a φατρία (*Σ Ol.*3.67b, 68b)—that is, some kind of descent-group or kindred;

(ii) the genealogy Telemachos father of Emmenes, father of Ainesidamos, father of Theron, father of Thrasydaios and Philokrates (*Σ Ol.*3.68a).

Aristarchos on the other hand (*ΣPyth.* 6.5a) held that the Emmenid name was οὐκ ἀπὸ φυλῆς, not from a tribe (?), which should mean he denied it was the name of any kind of descent or kinship-group;[6] the reference goes on to give his explanation of the name as a poetic plural of the personal name Emmenides. With this there belong:

(i) Hippostratos 568 F 2(a): Telemachos had two sons, Emmenides and Xenodikos; Emmenides was head of the lineage of Theron and Xenokrates, Xenodikos of the line of Hippokrates and Kapys.

(ii) An anonymous genealogy in *Σ Ol.*3.68d: Telemachos destroyed the tyranny of Phalaris and was father of Emmenides, father of Ainesidamos, father of Theron and Xenokrates; Theron's son was Thrasydaios, and Xenokrates' son was Thrasyboulos. This is probably also Hippostratos, for Aristarchos (*Σ Isth.* 2 *inscr.*), in contrast, held that Thrasyboulos was αδελφ⟨ιδ⟩ο⟨ῦ⟩ς nephew and not son to Xenokrates.

Aristophanes of Byzantium was the author of Kinship Terms, and we cannot exclude the possibility that the controversy on the φατρία was anthropological rather than historical. If it was historical, then Aristophanes must have presented some evidence which called the Emmenidai a φατρία, and Aristarchos must have rejected this evidence. If the controversy was anthropological, then Aristophanes recognized in the genealogy of the Emmenidai those characteristics which corresponded to his definition of a φατρία, and therefore applied that term to the Emmenidai. And in that case Aristarchos rejected

---

[6] Other descendants of Oidipous were known as Aigeidai.

54

both the term φατρία and part of the genealogy to which it was applied. The genealogy used by Aristophanes included the name of Emmenes, and made him the destroyer of Phalaris' tyranny. The genealogy used by Aristarchos must, from his argument, have included the name Emmenides for the same person; and at least Hippostratos' version of this genealogy makes Emmenides' father Telemachos the destroyer of Phalaris' tyranny.

It is a reasonable hypothesis that these different genealogies are connected with the controversy, evidenced by Eusebius' entries in his formula-group 2b, on the dates of the foundation of Akragas and Phalaris' tyranny. Apparently, according to Aristophanes of Byzantium, Phalaris was overthrown by Emmenes, presumably at or near the Eusebian date of 556/5; while according to Aristarchos and Hippostratos he was overthrown by Telemachos, presumably at the Eusebian date of 625/4. It is improbable that either Aristophanes or Aristarchos created this controversy, though each may have marshalled new arguments; it is probable that, in some form, it goes back to the Sikeliote historians themselves.

b. The genealogical position of Xenokrates. According to *Σ Isth.* 2 *inscr.*, the 'early commentators', Aristophanes, held that Xenokrates was brother to Theron, and this statement is repeated anonymously in several scholia (*Pyth.* 6.44b, c, *Ol.*2.87b, 89a). It is also represented erroneously in the scholia which assert that Theron won his Pythian victory jointly with 'Hieron his brother' (*Ol.*3.67b, 2.82c, 2.87a), although Aristotle (Kallisthenes) in the Register of Pythian Victors named only Theron (*Ol.*2.87c).

But Artemon of Pergamon (569 F 6) held that Xenokrates was not brother to Theron, but συγγενής, kinsman only; to him therefore we should also attribute the statements that
(i)   Theron's brother was Praxandros (*Σ Ol.*2.89e);
(ii) Xenokrates was the son of a Thrasyboulos (*Σ Isth.* 2 *inscr.*).

Thus we have three versions of the relationship of Xenokrates and Thrasyboulos to Theron, which all seem to be inferences from the allusions in Pindar's *Pythian* 6, and Simonides' poem on the same victory in 490 B.C.

It may be suspected that one of the reasons why the allusions of Pindar and Simonides were thus differently interpreted was that different kinship terms for the same relationships were used by the two poets. Xenokrates' daughter (who married Hieron), the niece of

55

Theron, is described in the scholia both as Theron's ἀδελφ⟨ιδ⟩ῆ and as his ἀνεψία.. The first term means 'niece' in Attic and standard Greek; the second (which means cousin in Attic) means 'niece' in Ionic (cf. the masculine in Hdt. VII 5 for a sister's son) and Byzantine. The Ionian Simonides may therefore have used the term ἀνεψιός of Thrasyboulos' relationship to Theron, just as Pindar uses πάτρως for its reciprocal (*Pyth.* 6.46).

Similarly, the scholium on *Ol.*2.173g reports anonymously that Hippokrates and Kapys were ἀνεψιοί of Theron, and this may mean either that they were nephews or that they were cousins. They are mentioned in the surviving scholia only in a genealogy attributed to Hippostratos, but other genealogists probably mentioned them also, and Artemon of Pergamon may have used ἀνεψιοί in the Ionian sense. If he did, he made them sons of Praxandros, and replaced Hippostratos' collateral line of Xenodikos by his own collaterals Thrasyboulos, Xenokrates, and the younger Thrasyboulos.

c. The origin of the Emmenids. The third controversy was on the question whether Theron's ancestors came direct from Rhodes to Akragas or whether they settled first in Gela. In the original sources, these arguments can hardly have been conducted without mentioning dates for the planting of Gela and Akragas, and the controversy must have had some relation to the disputed dates.

The tradition began with Pindar's Encomium on Theron which was held (*Σ Ol.*2.15d) to show that the Emmenids came directly from Rhodes; and Timaios (F 92) and Aristarchos (*Σ Ol.*2.16a) apparently believed the same. Artemon of Pergamon, however, with his usual independence thought they came through Gela (*Σ Ol.*2.16b and anonymously in 15c). Hippostratos (F 3) seems to be quoted in agreement with Artemon, saying that the family had worked for hire in Gela, ἐπὶ φυλακῇ τῆς πόλεως. This tale of a mercenary origin may be a construction after the model of the mercenaries of the Deinomenids who became citizens of Syracuse, while the belief in a Geloan origin for the Emmenids may be founded on the existence of a Geloan homonym for Theron's father Ainesidamos (Hdt. VII 153: Ainesidamos son of Pataikos), who became a member of Hippokrates' bodyguard at Gela and is probably the same person as Ainesidamos tyrant of Leontinoi. But Menekrates (*Σ Ol.*2.16c) returned to what was apparently the older view and brought the Emmenids direct from Rhodes to Akragas.

d. The heroic ancestry. All our sources agree that the Emmenids were descended from Laios and Oidipous; in the second *Olympian* Pindar names Polyneikes and his son Thersandros. In the scholia 76a–82d this is taken as meaning descent from Oidipous through Polyneikes, by way of Thera and the royal Aigeid lineage there. This genealogy is given anonymously, and names Theron's grandfather as Chalkiopeus (not Emmenes or Emmenides): it will not therefore come from Aristophanes, Aristarchos, or Hippostratos. Nor does it come from Menekrates who (Σ *Ol.*2.16c and anonymously in Σ *Ol.*2.70) gives the Emmenid descent through Eteokles, brother of Polyneikes, from Kadmos in 27 generations. The Chalkiopeus genealogy is therefore probably due to Artemon of Pergamon.

iii. The Emmenids: doctrines of the disputants. We should certainly or probably attribute to Aristophanes of Byzantium the doctrines that

(i) Emmenes destroyed Phalaris (in or near 556/5 B.C.);

(ii) the φατρία of the Emmenidai took their name from him;

(iii) Theron was the father of Thrasydaios and Philokrates;

(iv) Xenokrates was the brother of Theron and father of Thrasyboulos and Hieron's wife;

(v) the Emmenidai were descended from Polyneikes and came direct to Akragas from Rhodes.

Aristarchos seems to have agreed with Aristophanes except that

(i) the Emmenid name was not of phylic origin, but a poetic plural of the name Emmenides;

(ii) Thrasyboulos was son of Theron and nephew of Xenokrates.

The controversies become extreme with the work of Hippostratos in his Sicilian Genealogies. The doctrines which are certainly or probably his are:

(i) the lineage of Emmenides has a collateral line, descended from his brother Xenodikos, and represented in Theron's time by Hippokrates and Kapys;

(ii) Telemachos destroyed the tyranny of Phalaris in 625/4;

(iii) the ancestors of Telemachos served as mercenaries in Gela.

It is possible that, in support of this doctrine, Hippostratos adduced the names of Hippokrates and Ainesidamos as common to Gela and the Emmenids.

Artemon agreed with Hippostratos that the Emmenids came from Gela, but otherwise seems to have thoroughly reconstituted the Sicilian part of the genealogy;

(i) Emmen(id)es is replaced by Chalkiopeus as son of Telemachos: this probably means that Artemon took Telemachos as the destroyer of Phalaris. Presumably he required the name Emmen(id)es for an earlier ancestor, perhaps the head of the lineage in Gela.

(ii) Theron's brother was not Xenokrates but Praxandros, who was perhaps the father of Hippokrates and Kapys.

(iii) Xenokrates was the son of an elder Thrasyboulos (who may have been son or nephew of Chalkiopeus).

Menekrates seems on the whole to have reverted to the older tradition against Artemon's innovations, and to have carried his polemic so far as to deny the doctrine—apparently undisturbed from Pindar to Artemon—that the Emmenids were descended from Polyneikes. Menekrates traced them instead from Eteokles.

iv. The Emmenids: periods of controversy. It seems clear that a number of different controversies in Pindaric scholarship became entangled through the generations, and that we should distinguish between the quarrel between Aristophanes and Aristarchos, which is about critical methods; and the differences between the other three authorities, who have their pet interpretations of the Pindaric and Simonidean data.

Aristophanes apparently introduced into his commentary on Pindar an anthropological interpretation of the genealogy of the Emmenidai; Aristarchos not only rejected this but held that 'the Emmenidai' was a purely literary invention. In other words, literary criticism must remain within literary limits, and not call upon external speculations. This is a controversy of method—the development of a social science versus the integrity of scholarship; both principles are respectable, and their conflict is still familiar.

Hippostratos' main belief appears to have been that genealogical inference from the available data (personal names, for instance) could be carried much further than previously. This principle is also still familiar; what is not clear is whether Hippostratos was aware of the dangers.

58

These dangers become clear in the works of Artemon and Menekrates, who are mere constructionists. Presumably, however, they were the latest authorities at the time when Didymos was finalizing the Pindaric commentaries, so that their doctrines received far greater attention than they deserve.

The questions of interest which arise out of these controversies are the general historiography presupposed by the 27 generations detailed by Menekrates; material in the Sikeliote historians (in addition to the evidence from Pindar and Simonides) which the controversialists could have used. But perhaps the most interesting of all, and the least capable of answer, is the question whether Hippostratos in his Sicilian Genealogies, was in any way influenced by the development of anthropology in the hands of Aristophanes and his predecessors.

C. THE DEINOMENID DATES. The history and chronology of the Deinomenids is often mentioned in our immediate sources but the original treatments are all lost to us and the extant references are usually in very second-rate and erroneous authorities.

The tradition begins, for us, with Herodotus' statement (VII 166) that the battles of Salamis and Himera were fought on the same day, that is, late in the campaigning season of 480, or early in the Olympic year 480/79. Deinomenid dates must have been given by Hellanikos in the Priestesses, and by Antiochos, but do not survive. Hellanikos' long life overlapped with the time of the Deinomenid tyranny, and Antiochos' father and grandfather must have known a great deal about it, but we know nothing of how much or how little information was given by either.

The last authority of the fifth century to be concerned with Deinomenid dates was probably Hippias of Elis, in his list of Olympic victors. Fragments of this list appear in the papyri, in Dionysius of Halikarnassos, and in the Pindaric scholiasts, with an extraordinary number of errors. *Pap. Oxy.* 222 (Jac 415 F 1) and the scholiasts (*Ol.*1 *inscr.*) agree that Hieron won in 472/1; the papyrus names him also at 476/5; the scholia add 468/7 (where the papyrus has [Hiero]nymos) and are supported by Pausanias (VIII 42.8), who quotes the dedicatory inscription put up by Deinomenes son of Hieron after his father's death. Hieron thus had a victory at each of the Olympiads held during his reign—but the scholia date his first victory to 488/7 which Pausanias (VI 9.4) ascribes to Gelon from evidence of the inscription. Pausanias however refuses to follow the *communis opinio* that this Gelon was the tyrant, because Gelon was described in the inscription as of Gela, and Pausanias believed that the tyrant had taken power in Syracuse in 491/0. It is, naturally, universally believed that Pausanias has confused the date for Gelon's accession to power in Gela with the date for the beginning of his rule in Syracuse. This is confirmed by Dionysius of Halikarnassos (*AR* 7.1.4) who reports, under the year 491/0, that Gelon had recently (that is, before harvest-time and the shipping of corn to Rome) taken over the tyranny from Hippokrates. Dionysios makes the error of supposing that Hippo-krates and Gelon were brothers, but his date is nevertheless clear.

These sources therefore report:

491/0   Gelon takes power in Gela;
488/7   Gelon's victory at Olympia;
476/5   Hieron's first victory at Olympia;
472/1   Hieron's second victory at Olympia;
468/7   Hieron's third victory at Olympia.

An indirect piece of evidence for Deinomenid dating from Hippias' victor list is given by the victories in the stadium of Astylos, who gave his correct style as a Krotoniate in 488, but 'to please Hieron' was proclaimed a Syracusan in 484 and 480. Pausanias (VI 13.1), who is our source for this scandal, presumably names Hieron here because of his belief about the date of Gelon; but the story is evidence that in Hippias' time it was believed that Deino-menid rule in Syracuse began before August 484 B.C.

The treatment of Deinomenid chronology by Philistos and Ephoros is unknown to us; the state of the tradition in the fourth century is represented only from several passages in Aristotle. In the *Poetics* (23.2) he mentions the coincidence of Himera and Salamis as a mere fact of no artistically usable significance. In the *Politics* (5.12) he gives some figures: the Deinomenid tyranny lasted only 18 years, of which Gelon ruled seven (dying in the eighth); Hieron ruled 10 years while Thrasyboulos was deposed in his eleventh month. Aristotle is clearly drawing on an exact and detailed source here—we shall discuss his figures in comparison with those given by Diodorus below.

Aristotle-Kallisthenes must also have dealt with some Deino-menid dates in the Register of Pythian Victors. Hieron, presumably entered as of Gela, would appear in this list in 482 and again in 478; and as of Aitne, his new foundation, in 470.

Timaios' treatment of the Deinomenid dates is again unknown; either he or (more probably) Philistos will have given them their Olympic year formulae by which they appear in later sources.

In the third century, the Parian Marble does not let slip the opportunity for error which the Deinomenid dates seem to have offered to our sources. In epoch 53, the Parian dates the tyranny of Gelon 215 years since, in the archonship of Timosthenes; this archon-year is 478/7. Apparently the Parian was here expanding his notes, and in his draft for the mason wrote ἐτυράννευσεν where he should have had ἐτελεύτησεν. Consequently, he proceeded to allow 7 years for Gelon's reign (as does Aristotle), and to calculate the date for Hieron's accession. His table of synchronisms did not agree with his source for his notes, and consequently he dates Hieron to '208 years since in the archonship of Chares' which was 472/1: his 'years since' allow Gelon the proper seven years, but the archon synchronism allows only six. This is the earliest surviving evidence for the year 478/7 in the Deinomenid dates; but the two entries throw far more light on the Parian's methods and equipment than they do on Sicilian history.

From the second century we have fragment 69 of Apollodoros, quoted by Didymos to show that the foundation of Aitne (the old Katane) occurred in 476/5, but after the Olympic Games with which that year opened. Here again we seem to have a glimpse of the exact tradition, which knew whether Aitne was settled before or after August 476.

From the first century we have the evidence of Diodorus, which is detailed from the year 480/79 onwards. Under the year 478/7 he reports (11.38.7) that Gelon died after a seven-year reign, and Hieron reigned 11 years 8 months. Under the year 467/6 he reports (11.66.4) that Hieron reigned 11 years and Thrasyboulos one ἐνιαυτός which probably means 'the greater part of a year' (as in Ath. Pol. 13.2 *ad fin.*). Under the year 466/5 he reports (11.68.4) the deposition of Thrasyboulos. It is Diodorus also (11.24.1) who gives the alternative to the Salamis tradition when he says that Himera was fought on the same day as Thermopylai, a few weeks before Salamis, but (because of the slight shift of time) in the Olympic year 481/0.

From the statement that Hieron reigned 11 years 8 months we see that Diodorus is drawing on an exact chronological tradition. The question is whether this exact chronology was single, or whether Aristotle and Diodorus represent two versions of it or two stages in its development. If they do, then the exact tradition was controversial; yet we find plenty of evidence of error but none of controversy in our sources. If there had been controversy we should expect it to be traceable in the Pindaric scholia, or in Pausanias' remarks on Gelon.

On the other hand, the figures as they stand are irreconcilable, and Diodorus is very clear on Hieron's exact duration, while his statements for Gelon and Thrasyboulos may easily be taken as the same as Aristotle's. Thus if there is textual error, it must be in Aristotle's figures, and in two of them—the 18 years for the whole tyranny, and the 10 years for Hieron. In view of the early history of the Aristotelian corpus, we cannot exclude such textual change, even though the group of figures contains no difficulties in itself. We have to choose between attacking a text which there is no apparent reason to suspect, and supposing a chronological controversy where there is no evidence for one. Moreover, Aristotle's other figures for tyrannical chronology are not always pellucid; so we must not suppose that in this one instance the editors have made a special endeavour to make sense of them. And any endeavor that was made must have been occasioned not by the sense but by the text itself. There is however one simple way in which a text, intended to agree with Diodorus' chronology, could have become what we now find in Aristotle without any special efforts. In the lines so ran that the words in two of them were related:

... ἀλλὰ τὰ σύμπαντα εἴκοσι ...
... ἐτελεύτησεν, δέκα δ'Ἱέρων ...

and if above and after the δέκα there was written a β′ or ‖ to correct the figure for Hieron to 12 years (a rounding from 11 years 8 months), but this was taken by an editor copyist with the εἴκοσι of the line above, the lines would then yield the δυοῖν δέοντα εἴκοσι of our text, thus providing the 18 and 10 years instead of the 20 and 12 years required for agreement with Diodorus. This is textually only a possibility, but the alternative of a chronological controversy which has disappeared without trace, is perhaps the more difficult to believe, when the evidence on the tradition of Deionmenid history is that it was very exact.

If, then, we are to take the exact chronological tradition as single, the durations for the three tyrants at Syracuse are as follows:

Gelon: seven years and a little more. This is given by Aristotle, and for the seven years confirmed elsewhere. If Astylos called himself a Syracusan in August 484 to please the tyrant of Syracuse, then the Deinomenid tyranny was established there before that date.

Hieron: eleven years and eight months. This is given by Diodorus, who agrees with our other sources that Gelon's death and Hieron's accession fell within the archon-Olympic year 478/7. Diodorus also places the death of Hieron in 467/6, so that the eleven years eight months must have extended from early in 478/7 to late in 467/6.

Thrasyboulos: eleven months according to Aristotle, from late in 467/6 to nearly as late in 466/5.

Thus if we take strictly the exact durations given, in relation to the Olympic years in terms of which they are stated, we have the following dates for the ancient exact chronology:

(Gelon takes power in Gela, early summer 491/0);
Gelon takes Syracuse within the period August to October 485/4.
Hieron succeeds, within the period September to November 478/7.
Thrasyboulos succeeds, within the period April to July 467/6.
Thrasyboulos is deposed, within the period February to May 466/5.

If such an exact chronology of the Deinomenid tyranny once existed, it would of course be part of the historiography which also produced the exact genealogical detail and for which the oldest authorities quoted are Philistos and Timaios. The state of the tradition by the time it reached Jerome is however:

487/6 Gelon at Syracuse; Pindar and Simonides
478/7 Hieron at Syracuse
475/4 Hieron succeeds Gelon; Pindar
462/1 Democracy in Sicily

Obviously at least two sources on Hieron are represented here, and one of these (with its note on Pindar) will be the same as that of the first date, with its note on Pindar and Simonides.[7] The other source is from political rather than literary history and has the right date for Hieron; the date for democracy in Sicily is presumably for

---

[7] These dates, in some remote original 'Ολυμπιάδες, no doubt referred to the victories of 488/7 and 476/5.

more than Syracuse and refers to the final post-Deinomenid conference and the resettlement of the populations.

D. *GENERAL OBSERVATIONS.* The whole of the preceding discussion on the primary sources for Sikeliote history seems to show that (in the genres mentioned) almost no information about the foundation period originating earlier than the sixth century survived, and that all the written material before Herodotus was poetic. The second important point is that Herodotus' treatment of the Deinomenids fixed the historiographic and non-speculative tradition of treating their genealogy and chronology with exactitude. Herodotus does not treat of the Emmenids, and their tradition (and that of Akragas) remained speculative and controversial down to Eusebius' time.

This seems to mean that when Herodotus gathered his Deinomenid material from the experts and elders, and published it, he set a standard below which his Sikeliote successors would not allow each other to fall. No doubt his remarks on Sikeliote history were felt to be grossly inadequate, and the purpose of the first Sikeliote historian, Antiochos of Syracuse, was primarily to remedy this insufficiency. Care in the collection of the information available from local elders and experts in the fifth century characterized Thucydides' source on the colony foundations, where the names of the oecists were undoubtedly sought out from local cultic material; and this must mean that, as between Hellanikos and Antiochos for Thucydides' source, we must choose Antiochos. His history will in turn probably have provoked local or familial reactions, and this additional material from the experts and elders may have been absorbed by Philistos in the early fourth century. After this we can expect no other survivals of oral tradition; thenceforward every fresh statement about colonial foundations must have been an inference from, or construction upon, material already written.

In the fifth century, as we have seen, cultic and other oral information could provide exact dates for the Deinomenid tyranny and exact if limited genealogical information about the Deinomenids. It could also provide names, and at least in some cases patronymics, of oecists. One question is whether it could also provide lineage genealogies reaching back to foundations earlier than Akragas. The evidence is all indirect and somewhat confusing.

The Gamoroi, rulers of Syracuse until 485/4, were—if we are to

64

press the evidence of their name—descended from the original colonists who 'portioned the land' between them. It was therefore to some extent at least a legal necessity for a Gamoros to know his lineage. In the other cities we have less information but we should expect that in some at least the descendants of the hero-founder had some privileges (for example, an annual dinner in the Prytaneion or its equivalent) for which a genealogy would be a legal necessity. Side by side with these considerations we should put the fact that some fifth-century historians claimed to be able to give lineage genealogies: Hekataios that of his own descent, Herodotus the Agiad and Eurypontid lines in Sparta, Pherekydes that of Miltiades, and so forth.

Yet these claims are not earlier than the beginning of prose-writing. Considerable fragments of the once vast mass of genealogical epic survive and they have a rather different subject-matter. Homer's Lykian genealogy is an account of the different branches of descent from Bellerophon; Hesiod deals either with different branches of a genealogy or with descent through a female. There are few lists of successive male generations like those in the Trojan genealogy in Homer, or Herodotus' Spartan lists.

There thus appears to be (with few exceptions) a marked difference between the genealogical subject-matter of genealogical epic, and that of prose.

What is interesting is that this difference could imply complementarity. If a man of birth normally learnt in childhood his *legal* genealogy back to his eponymous ancestor, the genealogical epic could be the place where that ancestor himself was set in his genealogical context; the first kind of knowledge could be expected of every individual of birth, the second only of the experts.

A parallel can be quoted: 'At as young an age as five or six years children are capable of reciting their full genealogy to their clan-family ancestor. Knowledge of the complete genealogy tree of any large group, however, is restricted to old men and elders for whom such information has direct political importance.' This is the practice among the northern Somali;[8] the genealogical span of the clan-family varies between twenty and thirty named generations.[9] In the same system, each clan-family is segmented into 'clans', with fifteen to

---

[8] I. M. Lewis, 'Historical Aspects of Genealogies in Northern Somali Social Structure', *Journal of African History*, III 1 (1962) 35 ff.
[9] I. M. Lewis, 'Force and Fission in Northern Somali Lineage Structure', *American Anthropologist* 63, 1 (1961) 94 ff.

twenty named generations, these into 'primary lineages', and these again into 'dia-paying groups' which are small lineages or sets of small lineages, some four to eight generations in span.[10]

This oral learning has its own structure: 'when one asks the names of sons of a clan founder, for example, those given first are almost invariably the eponyms of important lineages. Other sons whose descendants are few, or whose lines have disappeared entirely, are only dimly recalled by clan elders and Sultans expert in the history of their clan. They are not common knowledge. In explaining their relationship and giving their genealogies, moreover, Somali usually follow through the main lines of descent first, concentrating upon the "long branches" at the expense of subsidiary "short branch" descent lines. Thus, usually it is the ancestor whose descendants are most numerous, and who is therefore most important structurally, rather than the first-born, whose name is mentioned first.'

This is a situation of genuine learning, none the less genuine for being oral; and like other kinds of learning it gives important people most attention and has its general and specialist levels. If we replace the sultans by the genealogical epics, and add in the Greek case the emergence of historical enquiry in these poems and continuing into historiography, we have a situation which would well explain the difference between our poetic and prose sources as a complementarity.

Such a tradition would also go far to explain the controversy on the Emmenid name. Eponyms in the Greek genealogies normally occur either in the very early generations, or where a female link intervenes. For example, the Asklepiadai have as their eponym Asklepios, of the generation before the Trojan War, and Asklepiads remained Asklepiads over the centuries and in whatever states they were citizens. Similarly the descendants of Kadmos seem to have called themselves Aigeidai in Thebes, Sparta, Thera, and Kyrene. Thus to say that their branch in Akragas had the name of the Emmenidai, and was a φατρία, was untoward; it is the more likely to have been true (and indeed is the natural inference from Pindar, so far as the name is concerned), but it is not surprising that it was controversial.

---

[10] This smallest Somali lineage would correspond to that of the Bouselidai in Athens, whose two sections were at feud about an inheritance, ownership of which was uncertain because the identity of a grandmother of the deceased was disputed. But a Greek *legal* lineage record ignored females: see Broadbent *Studies in Greak Genealogy* (Leiden 1968).

We thus may have, for men of birth, a general Greek situation of legal genealogical general knowledge complemented by epic expertise, and within this a colonial situation, at least in Akragas and perhaps generally in Sicily, where new segments of metropolitan lineages were truly or falsely formed. We should expect that the majority of foundation-members of colonies were obscure people in their home-lands; but once they were translated into the Gamoric nobility of a colony, genealogical segmentation was an obvious mode of stating their extraction. It is therefore probable that in the fifth century the Gamoroi were able to recite their legal lineages, and that other nobilities in other Sicilian cities, before the great transportations, were able to do so too. But such lineages would not give year-dates for the colony foundations any more than the other possible sources we have examined. We must therefore have recourse to the internal evidence of the dates, and examine their numerical relations to one another.

PART THREE

THE CHRONOGRAPHIC HYPOTHESIS

A. ARITHMETICAL RELATIONSHIPS IN THE COLONY DATES. If we examine the intervals given by Thucydides between his colony dates, we observe that several of them share the factor 9: there are 45 years from Syracuse to Gela, from Gela to Kasmenai, from Kasmenai to Kamarina, and 18 from Kamarina to Akragas.

Moreover, if we are right in assigning the Eusebian date of 736/5 to the foundation of Syracuse in Thucydides, and, to the Thucydidean list, the Eusebian interval of 108 years from Trotilon to Selinous, then also: there are 99 years from Akragas in ⟨583/2⟩ to the fall of Megara in ⟨484/3⟩, 108 years from Naxos and Trotilon in 737/6 to Selinous in 629/8, and 144 years from Selinous to the establishment of Gelon at Syracuse in 485/4; and 63 years from Megara Hyblaia in 729/8 to Akrai in 666/5. The only exception is the foundation of Leontinoi in 731/0.

If then we look in the same way at the Eusebian dates for Sicily given in his main source, we see: 45 years from Syracuse to Gela, 36 years to Akanthos and its associates; 54 years to Kamarina; 9 years from Naxos to Leontinoi and 117 years to Panaitios; 108 years from Trotilon to Selinous; 108 years from the first attempt at the colonization of Abdera in the same year as Akanthos in 655/4, to the fall of Lydia and the colonization of Abdera from Teos in 547/6.

Thus even if our assignment of Eusebian absolute dates and intervals to Thucydides is wrong, it seems nevertheless to be a patent fact that Thucydides and Eusebius both share in demonstrating that some Sicilian colony dates were calculated by methods which involved the use of the factor 9.

i. Calculations with the factor 9. Thus it appears certain that the source of Thucydides and the main source of Eusebius for Sicily made calculations involving the factor 9: there is uncertainty how far

68

these calculations extended for Thucydides' source. Judgment on whether the assignment of the Eusebian absolute dates, and the Eusebian interval from Trotilon to Selinous, to Thucydides is correct depends to a considerable extent on whether any convincing explanation can be given on why Thucydides (with these assignments) no less than Eusebius shows more than one calculation (from Naxos, from Syracuse, from Megara); why in both cases some foundations are not in the series; and why Thucydides speaks of some foundation-dates as approximate.

The obvious first hypothesis is that the multiples of nine years represent some kind of generation-reckoning, counting in generations of 27 or 36 years. For example, the calculation for Syracuse in 736/5 would be that it was founded seven 36-year generations before the fall of Megara. But if this is so, several questions arise:

(1) Why, in Thucydides, is Naxos one year before Syracuse when generation-reckoning was using units of the size of 36 years? The answer could be either (a) that the tradition of the elders and experts in the fifth century held that there was one year's difference in the ages of Naxos and Syracuse, and this tradition was incorporated in the calculations; or (b) two calculators have been at work, one of whom dated Naxos, and the other respected this date but placed Syracuse in relation to the fall of Megara. For example, since we know that Hellanikos (4 F 82) in the Priestesses dated the foundation of Naxos, it might be that Antiochos accepted this date, but made his own calculations for Syracuse and other cities. We shall examine the evidence more fully in Part Four.

(2) Why are nearly all the intervals not of 36 years or multiples of 36, but of 45 ($=36 \times 1\frac{1}{4}$), 18 ($=36 \times \frac{1}{2}$), 99 ($=36 \times 2\frac{3}{4}$), or 63 ($=36 \times 1\frac{3}{4}$) years? The answer is perhaps that they are approximations to such statements as 'in the course of the next generation' or 'midway through the (same or next) generation' or approximations using the factor 9 to such numbers as Pindar's hundred years. In other words, the ancient calculators (unlike modern historians faced with such statements) insisted on *arithmetical consistency* in their numbers. This may also explain Thucydides' insistence that the dates for Kasmenai, Kamarina, and Akragas, the three latest of his dated foundations, are approximate. In the case of Akragas we know from Pindar that there was older and uncalculated evidence, and it is possible that the poets had mentioned Kasmenai and Kamarina in much the same way (and

that their statements were quoted by Antiochos and so known to Thucydides).

(3) Why does Eusebius differ in some dates (Trotilon, Naxos, Katane, Leontinoi, Selinous) from Thucydides?

The probable answer here is that new evidence or new arguments were brought to bear and therefore new calculations made: the evidence will be examined, so far as it survives, in Part Four.

ii. Calculations with the factor 13. If we now look at Eusebius' other colony dates, we find also an extensive use of numbers with the factor 13.

formula-group 1:
762/1   first settlement of Kyrene by Thebans,
                130 years;
632/1   Battos in Kyrene.

formula-group 2a:
711/0   Astakos,
                26 years;
685/4   Kalchedon,
                26 years;
659/8   Byzantium.

Formula-group 3a:
657/6   Istros,
                26 years;
631/0   Sinope.

formula-group 3b:
736/5   Katane,
                260 years;
⟨476/5   Hieron refounds Katane as Aitne.⟩

formula-group 4 (main series):
757/6   Kaulonia, Makalla, Kyzikos,
                78 years;
679/8   Lokroi, Kyzikos,
                52 years;
627/6   Epidamnos, Kios-Prousias,
                26 years;

70

601/0 Kamarina,   Perinthos,
             117 years;   260 years
⟨484/3 fall of Megara;⟩   ⟨340/1   Siege of Perinthos.⟩

formula-group 4 (earliest dates):
771/0? Pandosia and Metapontion,
              13 years;
758/7 Trotilon, Zankle, Sinope,
              273 years;
⟨485/4 Gelon at Syracuse.⟩

With a factor of 13 years, the generation-length would be of either 26 or 39 years, and the last series above seems to show that it was of 39 years (for $273 = 39 \times 7$), so that the date 758/7 means the same number of generations before Gelon as the date (in 36-year generations) of 737/6.

The first question raised by the existence of both 36-year and 39-year generations is of course why both exist. The hypothetical answer is that they were, in the first case, invented to date a genealogy consisting of two lines of descent from a common ancestor, with different numbers of generations in the two lines, but a known (or believed) synchronism between the last generations in each line. Then

$$36 \times 13 = 468 \text{ years} = 39 \times 12$$

would be a mathematical model of the genealogical data.[1]

The second question is whether these methods of attributing dates were widely used, and for which periods. From the Sicilian evidence, we have seen that historiography preferred exact dates to poetically 'rounded' ones. Of the three known dates for Akragas, that of 583/2 belongs to the 36-year generation calculations common to Thucydides and Eusebius; that of 652/1 is 39 years, or one generation, after the foundation of Gela in 691/0; and that of 580/79 is 104 ($= 39 \times 2\frac{2}{3}$) years before Theron's Olympic victory in 476 B.C. The three dates obviously represent different historiographic assertions: Akragas is founded one (652/1) or three (583/2) generations after Gela; or 104 years is the nearest *arithmetically consistent* number to Pindar's 'hundred years'. If three calculations were made for a single Sicilian foundation, and that the latest, it is clearly probable

---

[1] We shall have evidence to refine this preliminary guess in Part Five below.

71

that such methods were very widely used and for all periods before the middle of the sixth century.

B. GENERAL HYPOTHESIS. 1. At some time before Thucydides wrote his Sicilian excursus, there was conceived and invented a method for creating mathematical Models of genealogical information. Once the Model for any area of historiographic subject-matter was decided upon, it was applied with arithmetical consistency throughout, even though some of the events so dated had historically superior (but less precise) dates already. For example, the modern rendering of Pindar's date for Akragas would be *c.*575 B.C., but the ancient arithmetically consistent renderings were 583/2 and 580/79 according to the calculation used.

2. The observation of such arithmetical consistency defines the ancient discipline of chronography.

3. All dates given in precise years before the middle of the sixth century are to be *presumed* chronographic; exceptions have to be proved.

4. The ancient arithmetical consistency imposes on the modern student an exactitude of textual study, but offers in return an additional and powerful means of discriminating sources and pedigrees of our information. For example, the entry-formulae used by Eusebius distinguish four entries on *colonies with founders named* from the rest of his colonial entries; within these four the first and second foundations of Kyrene might, from Jerome's evidence, be from different and hostile sources. From Synkellos' language we could infer either that both entries came from an otherwise unknown historiography of Kyrene, or that the two entries had been modified (from the Greek translated by Jerome) into an apparent compatibility. The chronography of the dates shows that the first inference is more probable. Moreover, the chronography is not shared with the other two entries, so that taking the formulaic and chronographic evidence together we should divide formula-group 1 into three: (a) the two entries of Kyrene, (b) the thalassocracy entry with Naukratis, and (c) the western pair, Taras and Corcyra.

Again, the three Megarian colonies in the Propontis (formula-group 2a) are confirmed by their chronography to be a group, while the three Milesian colonies in the Pontos (formula-group 3a) are

72

divided into Istros and Sinope on the one hand, and Borysthenes on the other.

5. It must be a principle of modern study that textual questions are to be settled textually, and chronographic questions chronographically. The two studies can be exceedingly helpful to one another, but only on condition that they do not trespass on each other's domains. Just as in studying the (non-chronographic) Deinomenid dates we had to recognize both that Aristotle's text shows no disturbance and that the tradition shows no controversy, and decide to which fact the greater weight should be given, similarly in dealing with chronographic dates any such conflict must be fully exposed. To emend chronographic texts for chronographic reasons without such exposure is merely to create a modern chronography.

6. The purposes of chronographic study are (a) the study of the origins, development, and end of the ancient discipline; (b) the determination of the sources and pedigrees of our information, and (c) the recovery of the unchronographized form of our information so that it can be used for modern historical studies. For example, the fact that both 758/7 and 737/6 mean 'seven generations before 485/4' transforms the whole situation of the controversy between the 'archivists' and the 'generationists' on the Sicilian colony dates. The question now is *how* did the ancient experts and elders know (or come to believe) in their oral archives that there were seven generations?

7. Just as no date before the middle of the sixth century can be assumed historical, so sequences of events relative to one another in our sources cannot be assumed trustworthy. Before we can use a statement that an event happened 'before the conquest of Messenia' we have to know how the date of the event, and the date of the conquest of Messenia, were chronographized, in relation to that particular statement.

8. The problem of generational oral historiography is by no means confined to ancient Greece, but now forms one of the more rapidly advancing subjects in modern anthropology. It is recognized that societies differ in the types of such historiography that they practise: some deliberately manipulate the genealogies to represent not the past but the present balance of political relationships,[2] thus creating

---

[2] L. Bohannan, 'A Genealogical Charter', *Africa* XXII (1952) 301 ff.

legal rather than historiographic documents; in others (where the society provides different means for legal statements) the genealogies are by intention historiographic, but the presently less important lineages have shorter 'branches', and the legal element enters into statements about eponyms.[3] In others again, different types of historiography are used in different groups or classes of the population.[4] There is thus no *a priori* principle which can be assumed for the Greeks, or for all the Greeks.

9. But the Greeks may have been unique among the peoples using generational historiography in that they developed the mathematical Models of chronography. Study of their historiography consequently has close links with two other disciplines, the history of mathematical ideas, and the anthropology of generational historiography in general.

---

[3] I. M. Lewis, 'Historical Aspects of Genealogies in Northern Somali Social Structure', *Journal of African History* III 1 (1962) 35 ff.
[4] I. G. Cunnison, *The Luapula Peoples of Northern Rhodesia* (Manchester 1959).

PART FOUR

EVIDENCE FROM FRAGMENTARY TEXTS

A. THE PREDECESSORS OF THUCYDIDES. So far as we know, there were three writers on Sicily before Thucydides: Hekataios the geographer, Hellanikos the chronicler, and Antiochos of Syracuse, author of a Sikelika and an Italika. Besides these, Herodotus had published an excursus on the Deinomenids, and mentioned such western events as Dorieus' expedition.

i. Hekataios (Jac. 1). Very little survives of Hekataios' work on Sicily, and the fragments (F 72–79) are not informative. Only F 73: μετὰ δὲ Κατάνη πόλις, ὑπὲρ δὲ ὄρος Αἴτνη suggests that the method of exposition was a geographical order; and there is no trace of any dates in any of his fragments.

Thucydides reports that the Sikanoi of Sicily came from a river Sikanos in Iberia; Hekataios (F 45) on the other hand is reported for a city Sikane in Iberia, whose inhabitants were, for him, presumably still living there. What he said of the origins of the Sikanoi of Sicily is lost, but he may be the source of the statement that they were the aboriginal inhabitants, a statement mentioned but rejected by Thucydides.

ii. Hellanikos (Jac. 4). Hellanikos is certainly more important for the historiographic tradition and is quoted for Sicilian dates—though unfortunately not so that they can be identified. He held that the Sikanoi were Iberian (F 79), with which Thucydides agrees; and that the Elymoi and Sikeloi were from Italy, the former settling five years before the latter who arrived in the 26th year of Alkyone's priesthood at Argos, in the third generation before Troy. Thucydides has a different origin for the Elymoi, and a different date for the Sikels, some 300 years before the arrival of the first Greeks.

Hellanikos (F 199) also provides a heroic eponym for Gela, who is

75

Gelon the son of Aitne and Hymaros (?Hykkaros). This may have been taken from a poetic source after the settlement of Aitne in 476/5 B.C. Thucydides disagrees, saying that the town was named from the river Gelas, and that the first fortified settlement was called Lindioi.

The third fragment (F 82), like the first, comes from the second book of Hellanikos' great Chronicle, the Priestesses of Argos. It says Θεοκλῆς ἐκ Χαλκίδος μετὰ Χαλκιδέων καὶ Ναξίων ἐν Σικελίᾳ πόλεις ἔκτισε, and must have been entered under a specific year which is not reported. The 'cities' also are not named, though one of them must have been Naxos; Theokles was also (according to Thucydides) the oecist of Leontinoi, and (according probably to Thucydides and certainly to Ephoros F 137) the Megarian foundation of Trotilon was contemporary with that of Naxos.

The third volume of the Priestesses of Argos seems to have ended about 423 B.C., and was probably published soon afterwards. We have no information on the publication date of the second volume from which the Sikel and Theokles fragments are taken; it may have been some years earlier. There is no extant evidence that the Geloan fragment comes from the Priestesses, nor that Hellanikos dated other Sikeliote foundations.

One question about Hellanikos' work on Sicily is the form of his entry or entries in the Priestesses. The possibilities seem to be two: that he entered each foundation under the year to which he assigned it, or that he gave all the foundations together in an excursus in Theokles' year, as he gave[1] all the mythical trials by the Areopagus together under Orestes' year in F 169. In the first case, of course, he must have given all dates in years; in the second case he may have given all but Naxos in generations, as he does for the Areopagus trials.

This is a question to be borne in mind when we come to the chronographic details of Thucydides' list. Here we should raise a larger question: had Thucydides any predecessors in the use of the list form for these foundations? If Hellanikos entered the foundations at appropriate years in his chronicle, then any successor would have to excerpt them in order to make a list; and if Antiochos in his Sikelika similarly followed chronological order, giving the event and politics of each foundation at its appropriate place, then also any later historian would have to excerpt them to make a list. If on the other

---

[1] In the Priestesses (Jac. on 323a F 22) not the Atthis (as on 4 F 169).

hand Hellanikos gave a list of foundations under his Theokles entry, he could himself have assembled such a list from Hekataios, and his successors could have abstracted it easily, either for replacing generation-dates by year-dates, or for quotation.

That is to say, on formal grounds and ignoring for the moment the details of the chronography, the simplest hypothesis for the origin of the list method of treating the Sicilian colony dates is that Hellanikos excerpted the list from Hekataios and gave it, with a year date for Theokles and perhaps generation-dates for some other foundations, at Theokles' year; Antiochos took this same list, working out additional year-dates, in his introduction to his Sikelika, and Thucydides quotes from him.

iii. Antiochos (Jac. 555) Antiochos (T 3) began his Sikelika with the murder of Minos by the daughters of Kokalos, king of the Sikanoi, and ended it with the Pan-Sikeliote peace conference of 424/3 B.C.

His account of the Sikanoi does not survive, but he may have agreed with Hellanikos against Hekataios. We have several fragments on the Sikeloi (F 2, 4, 5, 6, 9) whom he made a section of the Italoi, an Oinotrian people, who were driven out by other Oinotrians and the Opikoi. Dionysius of Halikarnassos complains that he did not 'make the date clear' (χρόνον μὲν οὐ δηλοῖ) of this event—perhaps by comparison with Hellanikos' 26th year of Alkyone. Thucydides also mentions the Opikoi, and Italos king of the Sikels, and dates the invasion of Sicily only approximately.

Some modern scholars have argued from Dionysius' comment that Antiochos gave no dates at all, and therefore cannot have been Thucydides' source. If, however, we look at the fragments from Antiochos' Italika we see that he is continually relating colony-foundations to other events: Kroton is contemporary with Syracuse (F 10); Zankle is earlier than Rhegion, and Rhegion's own foundation is connected with the conquest of Messenia (F 9); Taras is later than the conquest of Messenia (F 13); Sybaris is founded before Kroton (F 10), and before Taras (F 12); Metapontion is later than Taras (F 12). In other words, Antiochos in his Italika is working with synchronisms and sequences in time, and it is most unlikely that he did not have dates of some kind. If he 'did not make clear' the date of the Sikel invasion, this may only mean that he gave the approximate date quoted by Thucydides; and his refusal to be more precise may have been a matter of principle – the absence of sufficient genealogical

77

information for a purely barbarian event. Thucydides' query on the story that the Sikels crossed the straits in rafts may reflect Antiochos' doubts not only about the date but even about the narrative. Hellanikos' date in the 26th year of Alkyone—of which no trace appears in Thucydides—would then be regarded by both historians as an inference altogether outrunning the evidence.

The claim of Antiochos to be Thucydides' immediate source rests principally upon the richness of local detail in the names of oecists given by Thucydides, which can only have been collected from local cultic sources; and upon the resemblances in the two accounts (so far as Antiochos' survives) of the barbarian background. Negatively, various details exclude Hekataios and Hellanikos as Thucydides' main sources. On the other hand, it seems likely that Antiochos knew both Hekataios and the second volume of Hellanikos' Priestesses, accepting or rejecting their doctrines by comparison with his local sources of information – the 'most trustworthy and lucid of the ancient narratives' (F 2).

a. His chronological detail. The following discussion assumes that the absolute dates assigned to Thucydides' source in Part One above are correct, and that Thucydides is quoting from Antiochos.

1. Naxos and Trotilon 737/6; Selinous 629/8. Naxos and Trotilon are $261 = 36 \times 7\frac{1}{4}$ years before Hieron's depopulation of Naxos and Katane in 476/5; and Selinous is three generations younger than Megarian Trotilon.

The date of Hellanikos' entry on Theokles of Naxos in the Priestesses is unknown. Antiochos will have accepted or reworked it, and perhaps translated a generation-date for Selinous into years. He will also have sought out such local detail as the oecist of Selinous.

The sources here are therefore perhaps Hellanikos, and certainly local detail, and Antiochos' own working over of this material.

2. Leontinoi (with Megarians) 731/0; Katane undated; Megara 729/8. This group of statements, with the detail about Lamis and Thapsos, Hyblon, Euarchos, and Theokles, comes from local informants and is therefore to be attributed to Antiochos. The dates, or lack of them, are probably the best he could do (as with the Sikel invasion); later chronographers were more confident. Antiochos' account of the early Megarians seems to have been, 6 years at Trotilon, $1\frac{1}{2}$ years at

Leontinoi, winter in Thapsos,[2] refuge with Hyblon and establishment of Megara Hyblaia in 729/8, a century before Selinous was founded.

The source here seems to be local detail, in so far as this was still available after the Deinomenid transportations.

3. Syracuse 736/5, with dependent calculations. The year assigned to the foundation of Syracuse is 36×7 years before the fall of Megara in 484/3. At this time according to Herodotus (VII 156, no year-date given), Gelon transferred to Syracuse the nobility of Kamarina, Megara, and Euboia, and part of the nobility of Gela, and made them citizens. This action destroyed the Gamaroi of Syracuse as the privileged holders of full political rights. Two dates together give Antiochos his main Sikeliote framework; no foundation is earlier than 737/6, but dates are generally related to the era of Syracuse in 736/5.

The following also seems to belong to the main framework: Antiochos (T 3) began his history with the death of Minos at the hands of Kokalos' daughters, and in Jerome this event is dated to 1204/3 B.C., without mention of the name of the source. But from 1204/3 to 736/5 is $468 = 39 \times 12 = 36 \times 13$ years; and from 1204/3 to the Pan-Sikeliote conference with which Antiochos ended his History in 424/3 is $780 = 39 \times 20$ years. It seems therefore likely that Antiochos dated the death of Minos to 1204/3 B.C., and to do this he presumably relied upon genealogies making Herakles (ancestor of Archias of Syracuse) contemporary with Theseus, who married the daughters of Minos.

Diodorus reports, apparently immediately from Timaios, that Lipara was colonized in 580/79 as the result of an expedition led by Pentathlos, a descendant of Hippotes the Herakleid. This Hippotes is no doubt the same as the father of Aletes of Corinth, ancestor of Archias of Syracuse; and 580/79 is $156 = 39 \times 4$ years after 736/5. Archias and Pentathlos were therefore reckoned as remote relatives, and it is likely that Timaios is here using Antiochos' dating.

The dates for Kasmenai in 646/5 and Kamarina in 601/0 are either dependent upon that for Syracuse, or brought into harmony with it, being respectively $90 = 36 \times 2\frac{1}{2}$ and $135 = 36 \times 3\frac{3}{4}$ years later.

Antiochos synchronized the foundations of Syracuse and Kroton (F 10), probably on the evidence of the Astylos oracle (see Part Two above).

---

[2] Polyainos (*Strat.* V 5) says winter in *Trotilon*, presumably a slip.

The sources here, therefore, include probably some written material besides Hellanikos' date for Naxos: the Astylos oracle, possibly a mention of Kamarina or Kasmenai by Sappho, and other poetry which has not survived. Whether the Herakleid genealogies upon which Antiochos also relied were already written down seems uncertain.

It would appear certain that the only reason why Antiochos used both 36 – and 39 – year generations must have been that his genealogical data—the numbers of generations—did not agree. His Archias is the (thirteenth or) fourteenth from Herakles, and Pentathlos the seventeenth; yet—Antiochos must have argued—Archias in Syracuse was more than three generations before Pentathlos in Lipara. He may have stated this argument in terms of his general base-date in 424/3, saying that Pentathlos was four generations earlier, but Archias more than eight generations earlier, for the availability of information in this form is more probable. Even this form of the data is probably derived, that for Syracuse being originally seven generations before 484/3, seven generations of the rule of the Gamoroi. In that case, the seven generations of the Gamoroi was not a general statement derived, from a comparison of lineages and taking the average, but specific, relying upon Herakleid generation-counts among the Gamoroi; and this is very probable.

4. *Gela 691/0; Akragas three generations later.* There may also be an inheritance from Hellanikos here, if F 199 comes from the Priestesses. Moreover, there could be a Hellanikan chronographic reckoning, suitably simple for an independent calculation: 691/0 is $180 = 36 \times 5$ years before the expedition of Dorieus in 511/0 B.C., and this expedition opened that struggle with Carthage which led to the Geloan and Syracusan tyrannies.

The date for Dorieus is known to us from Diodorus (XI 90), but may have been first published by Hellanikos who must have dated the fall of Sybaris. Antiochos (F 10) also dealt with the foundation of Sybaris, which he placed sometime before Kroton in 736/5. Antiochos' Kroton is thus $225 = 36 \times 6\frac{1}{4}$ years before the conquest of Sybaris, and it is obviously in this context overwhelmingly probable that his date for Sybaris was $9 \times x$ years before 736/5, so that Sybaris existed for a number of 36-year generations (745/4 is an attractive guess, allowing $234 = 36 \times 6\frac{1}{2} = 39 \times 6$ years).

There is no reason to believe that Hellanikos gave a year-date for

Akragas; this will have been supplied by Antiochos, who is also probably the source for the dating of Phalaris to the years 571/0–556/5. By this time we are reaching the usual beginning of historical chronology, and these dates for Phalaris may be more or less accurate.

They are, however, perhaps unlikely to be exact and to have passed from archives into historiography, for we must notice that in Antiochos' dates there is a tendency to emphasize events which are 45 years apart: Syracuse in 736/5, Gela in 691/0, Kasmenai in 646/5, Kamarina in 601/0, Phalaris' death in 556/5, Dorieus' expedition in 511/0, the end of the Deinomenid tyranny in 466/5. While the last two dates are certainly historical (and from Antiochos' point of view a very pleasing coincidence), the first four dates are chronographic, and consequently that for Phalaris is of uncertain kind. In general the close chronographic relations between Geloan and Syracusan dates in Antiochos' scheme show a strong historiographic tendency to look at pre-Deinomenid history in the light of Deinomenid achievements; but there is in fact no reason to connect Gela and Syracuse closely before the time of Gelon.

5. Zankle and Himera. These foundations are undated in Thucydides, although Antiochos probably gave dates. The sequence of the mention of Zankle by Thucydides, after Gela in 691/0, suggests that the regular settlement with oecists was dated to the seventh century; we should expect this refoundation (and the original 'pirate settlement' when it was dated) to be placed a recognizable number of generations before Zankle became Messene in the early fifth century. Unfortunately, the date for this change of name does not survive in our sources.

6. Leontinoi and Akrai. These two foundations are 65 years apart, and Akrai is 65 years earlier than Kamarina. Megara Hyblaia is 63 years before Akrai, and also 9 years before the Olympic victory of Orsippos the liberator of Megara, a date which presumably goes back to Hippias' list of Olympic victors, compiled a generation after Antiochos was writing.

Antiochos therefore seems to have some parallel calculations here: Kamarina is founded $39 \times 3 = 36 \times 3\frac{1}{4}$ years before Gelon's reconstitution of Syracuse; Akrai is founded $39 \times 1\frac{2}{3}$ years earlier still; from Akrai back to Chalkidian and Megarian Leontinoi is another $39 \times 1\frac{2}{3}$ years, while from Akrai back to Megara Hyblaia is $63 = 36 \times 1\frac{3}{4}$ years.

Leontinoi is thus $247 = 39 \times 6\frac{1}{3}$ years before Gelon's reconstitution of Syracuse, and this point of the history may have been that around which the other Megarian details were organized by Antiochos. It is not at all clear why Akrai is so deliberately connected with Leontinoi and Megara; we might almost suspect Megarian participation in the foundation of Akrai.

b. *Antiochos' chronography and historiography.* The examination of Antiochos' dates thus seems to show that his main calculation used the base-date 484/3, and that this was the year of the reconstitution of the citizen-body in Syracuse, when the Megarians and others were brought in by Gelon. However, it is also apparently the case that Antiochos made an independent calculation for Naxos and Trotilon, using the base-date of 476/5. This admitted variability of base-dates, however, is no more than the expression in chronography of localism within the history of the Sikeliote region; and in considering Antiochos' chronography we should rather remember that his was the first regional history than emphasize the incomplete unity of the chronographic construction.

The main calculation began with the death of Minos in 1204/3, and reckoned $39 \times 12 = 468 = 36 \times 13$ years from that date to the foundations of Syracuse and Kroton in 736/5, while the whole History covered 39×20 generations. If we endeavor to relate the other calculations to the central scheme as simply as possible, the result is Table VI. Here both the links between the calculations, and the hypothetical dates, are reduced as much as possible to the minimum consonant with an attempt to obtain a synoptic view of this side of Antiochos' work.

Most of the dates have already been discussed: the first column, for example, represents the Hellanikan starting-point of Antiochos' datings.

This is linked to the second column at the historical date of 485/4. The head of the second column is formed by the hypothetical Antiochine date for Sybaris, which we have already discussed, and which, with the date 511/0, forms the link with the third column. I have inserted in the second column Jerome's date for the foundations of Taras and Corcyra, tentatively, because it fits both the arithmetic and the information available for Antioches' dating of Taras (F 12, 13).

The third, fourth, and fifth columns represent Antiochos' main scheme from the foundation of Syracuse to her reconstitution, from

Leontinoi to the same date, and from the death of Minos to the Peace Conference. All these dates have already been discussed.

To make the reading of Table VI easier, I have written hypothetical dates with double queries, and dates which may be Antiochine but are only evidenced in Jerome (and have only convenience to recommend them) by single queries.

The Table shows the absolute centrality of Geloan–Syracusan unity, as formed by the Deinomenids, to Antiochos' historical view. Outside it we find (so far as survival permits) only the Hellanikan inheritance (which provides an upper limit of possible dates for Syracuse), and outstanding events closely connected with Syracusan history, such as early attempts at Lipara and by Dorieus against the barbarians. Of course Antiochos will have treated of much more in his History, but it seems likely that this balance would not be upset if we had more information.

Chronographic schemes on their formal side are most interesting if they are used to express the historian's periodization of his subject-matter, and Antiochos seems to have attempted something of this kind. His whole purely chronographic period, from the death of Minos to that of Phalaris, is 36×18 years; the archaic period, from the fall of Phalaris to that of the Deinomenids, is $36 \times 2\frac{1}{2}$ years. Within the purely chronographic period, there are 36×13 years of barbarism, and its ending is foretold by the appearance of Naxos and Trotilon just before the next sub-period begins. This consists of 36×5 years of the Hellenization of Sicily up to the death of Phalaris; and once more the ruling theme of the next period is foretold, by the clash with Carthage which led to the foundation of Lipara. It seems therefore that Antiochos had a fairly clear notion of the periods of his history, or at least a well-developed historical sensibility, which found expression in his chronography.

B. *BETWEEN ANTIOCHOS AND TIMAIOS.* During the fourth century two notable authors worked on Sicilian history. One was the specialist Philistos, famous in ancient times for his political ideology, and in modern because he was the first to use Olympic years for dating. The other was Ephoros, the first to attempt a general history of Greece, based on the many local histories written since Herodotus' time. Ephoros remained the standard general authority for many generations, and much in later sources rests on his general outlines.

i. Ephoros (Jac. 70). Ephoros seems to have discussed the Sicilian

TABLE VI

DATES ATTRIBUTABLE TO ANTIOCHOS

	I	II	III	IV	V
		1204/3 death of	Minos		
		459 years			
		??745/4 foundation of Sybaris??			
		39 years			
Chronographic	737/6 foundations of Naxos and Trotilon		9 years		736/5 ERA DATE
	108 years		736/5 foundations of Syracuse and Kroton		156 years
			45 years		
				731/0 foundation of Leontinoi; of Megara Hyblaia	
				729/8 foundation	
				65 years	
				720/19 Olympiad of Orsippos	
				54 years	
		706/5 foundations of Taras and Corcyra?	691/0 foundation of Gela	666/5 foundation of Akrai	
		195 years	45 years	65 years	
Dates			646/5 foundation of Kasmenai		
			45 years		
	629/8 foundation of Selinous			601/0 foundation of Kamarina	

84

144 years   18 years   117 years

583/2 foundation of
    Akragas   27 years

556/5 death of

580/79 foundation of
    Lipara?
    156 years

Phalaris
    45 years

511/0 expedition of
    Dorieus
    27 years

511/0 fall of
    Sybaris
    26 years

484/3 reconstitution of Syracuse

485/4 Gelon conquers Syracuse
    9 years

476/5 Hieron
    depopulates
    Naxos

424/3 Pan-Sikeliote
    Peace
    Conference

Historical

Dates

colonies in the fourth book of his history, entitled Εὐρώπη, but the surviving fragments are meagre. In F 137 he says that Theokles was an Athenian who led an expedition of Chalkidians and Ionians to Sicily, and at the same time convoyed a Dorian enterprise, most of whose members were Megarian. The Chalkidians founded Naxos, the Megarians Megara Hybla. The date is given in generations, and the figure is restored from the poetic geographer Pseudo-Skymnos who on Sicily seems to follow Ephoros; it is the tenth generation after Troy.

Pseudo-Skymnos (*Periegesis* 270 ff.) gives the same information, then proceeds to report that Dorians (other than the Megarians) left the expedition in Italy, at Zephyria. Here they were found by Archias of Corinth as he voyaged to the foundation of Syracuse. After these events, the Naxians founded Leontinoi, and other Ionian settlements were Zankle, Katane, Kallipolis, Euboia, Mylai, Himera, and Tauromenion. The remaining Dorian settlements in Sicily were Megarian Selinous, Gela and Akragas, Messene (with Ionians from Samos), and Syracusan Kamarina, destroyed by Syracuse after an existence of 46 years.

The last statement is perhaps further detailed in a Pindaric scholium (*Ol.*5.16), which reports that Kamarina was founded in Ol.45 (600/599–597/6) and destroyed by the Syracusans in Ol.57 (552/1–549/8).

The only other relevant fragment from Ephoros (F 138) says that Lokroi Epizephyrioi was founded soon after Syracuse and Kroton; this account was presumably linked with the story of the Dorians left behind by Theokles at Zephyria.

The first problem is clearly what year or period Ephoros meant by the 'tenth generation after Troy'. His date for Troy is nowhere stated, but is believed to be the source of Strabo XIII 1.3 who says that Troy fell sixty years before the Return of the Herakleidai. We have two statements of Ephoros' date for the Return:

F 233: from the Return to the archonship of Euainetos (335/4) was, according to Ephoros, 735 years. This means that Ephoros dated the Return to 1070/69 B.C.

T 10: Ephoros began his history with the Return, and continued for almost 750 years to the siege of Perinthos. Since this was in 341/0 B.C., this report means that Ephoros dated the Return to about 1090 B.C.

86

It does not necessarily follow that one or the other of these inadequate testimonies is false. Ephoros' narrative of the Return was obviously extended, and contained much local detail in Corinth, Sikyon, Achaia, Argos, and the Argolic Akte (F 18, 19); Crete (F 29); Arcadia (F 112, 113); Elis (F 115); Messenia (F 116); Sparta (F 117, 118); Boiotia (F 119). It is clear in fact that for him 'the Return' was not the name of an event so much as of a protracted convulsion, and that the two dates given for 'the Return' in our sources are the dates of two events within it. The earlier date, that about 1090 B.C., is probably the date from which we should reckon back 60 years to Troy; then the later date, in 1070/69, is Ephoros' main historiographic or chronographic date, at the orthodox interval of 80 years after Troy.

Thus Ephoros dated Troy about 1150 B.C., and the foundation of Naxos and Trotilon in the 'tenth generation' thereafter means either the last 36 of 360, or the last 39 of 390 years (if he used the generation-lengths already established). Thus, for Ephoros, Naxos and Trotilon were founded either before about 790 or before about 760—in either case considerably earlier than the date of 737/6 given by Hellanikos and Antiochos.

At the other end of the colony list, Pseudo-Skymnos and the Pindaric scholium may represent Ephoros on Kamarina. A period of 46 years beginning within Ol.45 and ending within Ol.57 can only mean the years of which 597/6 was the first and 552/1 the forty-sixth; this date for the foundation of Kamarina is thus 597/6, four years later than the date of Antiochos.

ii. The Parian Marble (Jac. 239). The thirty-first entry in the Parian Marble states that it is (a lost number of) years since Archias the son of Euagetes, being the tenth from Temenos, led a colony from Corinth and founded Syracuse in the 21st year of Aischylos king of Athens.

Since the number of 'years since' is lost, determination of the date depends upon the identification of the 21st year of Aischylos.

All our later authorities except Synkellos agree that Aischylos ruled for 23 years (even the Barbarian, who gives this figure to Thersippos by mistake). In most sources Aischylos' successor Alkmeon rules for 2 years; the Barbarian gives him ten, which is probably an error caused by the proximity of the decennial archons; and Eusebius in the *Chronographia* gives him twelve, an error arising from a dittography—when the first Olympiad became ἐν τῶι ιβ′ year of

87

Aischylos, instead of ἐν τῶιβ΄, the years attributed to Alkmeon had to be changed from two to twelve to keep the beginning of the decennial archons (after Alkmeon) at the same absolute date as before. This was 753/2 for Eusebius. The decennial archons ruled for seventy years and were succeeded by the annual archons who in the next entry of the Parian Marble are dated (if the figures are right) to 683/2 B.C., and so also in the best of our later sources.

It is thus probable for the Parian that the decennial archons began in 753/2, and were preceded by two years of Alkmeon, 755/4 and 754/3. The 23-year reign of Aischylos then comprises the years 778/7 to 756/5, and the 21st year, when Syracuse was founded, is 758/7 B.C.

This date is $273 = 39 \times 7$ years before Gelon took power in Syracuse in 485/4, and was used by Eusebius' source for the first settlements in Sicily, Trotilon, and Zankle. The Parian's source on the other hand follows more nearly upon Antiochos' historiography, holding that it was Syracuse that was founded seven generations before Gelon, and, presumably, that this was not the first settlement.

It is probable therefore that the Parian's source for Syracuse was Ephoros, and if this is correct, Ephoros dated Naxos and Trotilon before 760 B.C., and Syracuse in 758/7. This date will have been shared with Kroton (F 138). Ephoros thus differs from Antiochos on Syracuse only in that he uses a different generation-length (and prefers the year 485/4 as his base-date). That is, the dates 736/5 and 758/7 are due to different treatments of the same fundamental information: that there were seven generations of the Gamoroi before Gelon.

Another connection between Ephoros and the Parian Syracuse is provided by the fact that Ephoros' later date for the Return, 1070/69, is $312 = 39 \times 8$ years before Syracuse in 758/7 B.C. This raises the question of what the Parian meant by saying that Archias was the 'tenth from Temenos'. According to Ephoros, the founder of Dorian Corinth was Aletes, while the founders of Dorian Argos were Temenos and his son Kissos. According to later authorities, when the Herakleids occupied Argos and other cities, they set aside Corinth to be given to Aletes when he should return from his wanderings. It is likely therefore that Ephoros dated the Dorization of Argos to about 1090, and the handing over of Corinth to Aletes in 1070/69. Thus the Parian's Temenos seems to stand for the Ephoran period from about 1090 to 1071/9, then there come the eight 39-year generations from 1070/69 to 759/8, and the tenth generation begins in 758/7 with Archias.

Ephoros as a universal historian treated the Sicilian foundations no doubt cursorily, and certainly as part of the introduction to his History proper in the Εὐρώπη. His main chronographic concern would be to attach the most important of the foundations to a more general framework, and this agrees with the evidence for the placing of Syracuse in relation to Corinth. But it also follows that there may have been little direct relationship between Ephoros' dates and those of his Sikeliote predecessors, either in criticism or imitation; and that a modern study of Ephoros, restricted to his Sicilian dates, may not comprehend either his problems or his intentions. Nevertheless, it does seem that the seven generations of the Gamoroi at Syracuse, established by Antiochos, was also accepted by Ephoros; and modern study is almost certainly right in holding that the Corintho–Syracusan scheme in Ephoros was central to his Sicilian history, as the Syracusan–Geloan scheme was central to Antiochos.

iii. Philistos (Jac. 556).   Part I of Philistos' history of Sicily 'covered more than 800 years' (T 11a): in fact, it ran from the foundation of Carthage in 1215/4 (F 47) to the year 406/5, and thus covered 810 years.

Like Ephoros, Philistos (F 136) agreed with the earlier authorities that the Sikanoi came from Iberia but on the Sikels he disagreed with his predecessors, saying that they were Ligyan, driven out of Italy by the Umbrians and Pelasgoi, 80 years before Troy (F 46).

One date for the colonial period survives, and the date only—the event is lost. This is 'the Olympiad at which Oibotas of Dyme won the stadion' (F 2), that is, the sixth Olympiad, 756/5–753/2 B.C.

But whatever the event, this year seems to have been Philistos' era date. From 1215/4 up to and including 406/5 is $810 = 27 \times 30$ years, while from 1215/4 to 756/5 is 27×17 years, so that from 756/5 up to and including 406/5 is $27 \times 13 = 351 = 39 \times 9$ years. Philistos thus introduces to the chronography of the west a new generation-length of 27 years, using the same factor of 9 years as did the 36-year generation employed by Hellanikos and Antiochos.

A number of dates given anonymously in our later sources seem to be connected by 27- and 39-year reckonings with Philistos' era-date of 756/5. Of these, two secondary foundations from Zankle are the earliest, and suggest that the year 756/5 was the date of the foundation of Zankle. Chersonesos (if the same as Mylai) is the elder, dated by Eusebius to 717/6, which is 39 years (one generation) after

89

756/5; while Himera is dated by Diodorus (XIII 62) to 648/7, which is $108 = 27 \times 4$ years after 756/5: it is also $182 = 39 \times 4\frac{2}{3}$ years before the repopulation of Himera in 466/5. The Eusebian date for Lipara, in 630/29, is $18 = 27 \times \frac{2}{3}$ after Himera.

Although Chersonesos and Lipara both appear in Eusebius at these dates, they belong to different formula-groups: Chersonesos to the main source, and Lipara to the source on the controversy about the dates of Akragas and Phalaris. It is noteworthy therefore that, arithmetically, Philistos could have used Antiochos' date for Gela in 691/0, since this year is $65 = 39 \times 1\frac{2}{3}$ years after 756/5; and that the early date for Akragas, in 652/1, continues this 39-year reckoning by one generation. Thus the early dates for both Lipara and Akragas seem to be traceable to Philistos, quoted from him by Timaios and so handed on to Eusebius' source on the Akragas controversy.

Since the foundation of Lipara was connected with the existence of Selinous (Diod. V 9), it is also likely that Philistos is the source for the date of 650/49 for this foundation (Diod. XIII 59, and Eusebius). This should mean—if our previous inferences are correct—that he dated Trotilon (or Megara Hyblaia, possibly) $108 = 27 \times 4$ years earlier, in 758/7, the year of Ephoros' Syracuse and Kroton.

On these arguments, the dates shown in Table VII are attributable to Philistos. When we compare them with the dates attributable to Antiochos (Table VI) some further considerations emerge:

(1) The period of $459 = 27 \times 17$ years which Philistos places between his Carthage and his era date of 756/5 is parallel to the 459 years between two dates attributed to Antiochos – Minos' death in 1204/3 and the foundation of Sybaris hypothetically dated to 745/4. It seems therefore that Philistos has taken an arithmetical by-product of Antiochos' scheme, and used it centrally in his own.

(2) The era date of 756/5 and the date for Himera belong to a set of years which was possibly already used by Antiochos, and which is fairly crowded with events known to us from many different sources. If Antiochos, Hippias, and Philistos all used this series, it is clearly likely that the Corinthian dates which fall upon it (747/6 and 657/6) are due to Ephoros; and that there was some reason common to all these historians for the use of these inter-related dates. Probably the reason did not lie in Sicily: possibly it was found in Megarian and Corinthian history.

90

(3) If we apply to Philistos' dates for Zankle, Chersonesos, and Himera the usual assumption that quotations or survivals from an author are quoted or survive precisely because they are part of his characteristic thesis, then we are to infer that 756/5, 717/6, 652/1, and 648/7 are central to Philistos' work; that Zanklaian history was in some sense of special concern to him, that he had something important to say on the history of the straits, possibly as the link between the Sikeliotes and the Italiotes. This would imply that while Antiochos wrote the history of two regions in his Sikelika and Italika, for Philistos this history was that of one region, of which Zankle was the hinge. The contrast between Antiochos and Philistos in this respect would be essentially the difference between fifth and fourth century views of the Greek west and its development.

(4) The early dates for Carthage, Himera, Lipara, Akragas, and Selinous contrast at some points with Antiochos, and at others with the general later tradition (such as Carthage at 814/3). The Akragas controversy bulks large in ancient learning, and the date of Selinous in modern archaeology; both disputes seem to go back to the early dates given by Philistos. Since Philistos dated Carthage very early, it seems probable that he believed the great Sikeliote conflict with Carthage began early, in the middle of the seventh rather than in the opening years of the sixth century. He perhaps shared Thucydides' view that in the first century of the Sikeliote period the conflict was less organized, the Carthaginian activity in Sicilian waters being confined to coastal trading and sporadic piracy which retreated before the Greek advance. An important date quoted from Timaios (see below) may have come to him from Philistos, and if so helps to explain the early dates for the Greeks in western Sicily: this is the Carthaginian colony of Ebesos in the Balearics dated to 654/3 B.C. Such a Carthaginian move would give the reason for the rapid succession of Greek foundations: 652/1 Akragas, 650/49 Selinous, 648/7 Himera, 630/29 Lipara. It is very possible also that Philistos commanded much more Etruscan material (especially in relation to the straits) than Antiochos had used.

Among the particular early dates, we have most information from the ancient sources on that of Akragas, for the ensuing controversies fill the Pindaric scholia and are still alive in Eusebius. The Pindaric

91

TABLE VII

DATES ATTRIBUTABLE TO PHILISTOS

1215/4 foundation of
Carthage
459 years

756/5 ERA DATE: 756/5 foundation of
Zankle?
9 years   39 years

747/6 oligarchy of the
Bacchiad
kindred in
Corinth
18 years

758/7 foundations of Trotilon and Naxos?
26 years   108 years

732/1 Leontinoi
founded, with
Megarians
26 years

729/8 foundation of
Megara Hybla
9 years

720/19 Orsippos
Olympionikes
54 years

717/6 foundation of
Chersonesos
26 years

706/5 foundations of Taras and Corcyra
26 years   52 years

691/0 foundation of
Gela
39 years

679/8 foundation of

Chronographic Dates

92

666/5 foundation of Akrai
9 years
657/6 Kypselos in Corinth
9 years
648/7 foundation of Himera
18 years
630/29 foundation of Lipara
18 years
612/1 foundation of Kamarina
——— 81 years
531/0 foundation of Dikaiarchia
126 years
405/4 Beginning of Philistos' Part II

Lokroi
27 years
652/1 foundation of Akragas
27 years
625/4 Telemachos destroys Phalaris
135 years
490/89 destruction of Kamarina
9 years
481/0 Battle of Himera

654/3 Ebesos founded by Carthage
143 years
650/49 foundation of Selinous
511/0 expedition of Dorieus
26 years
485/4 Gelon takes Syracuse

Historical Dates

93

scholars who followed Philistos were probably Hippostratos and Artemon, who respectively attributed the destruction of Phalaris to Telemachos (and not to his son), and named that son Chalkiopeus instead of Emmen(id)es. The starting point of the arguments which issued in these assertions would always be the primary sources, Pindar and Simonides; and Pindar's statement in 476 B.C. that Akragas had not seen a man like Theron for a century could obviously be taken in two ways—either he is saying that the destruction of Phalaris (in 556/5) was not so great as the total of Theron's achievement, or he is saying that the destruction of Phalaris was earlier than 576/5. The late dates for Akragas and Phalaris take the first view of Pindar's meaning (whether they agree with his judgement or not); the early dates take the second view and thus give more weight to the poet's judgment. To accept Pindar as a historical or political authority in this sense meant for the ancients some kind of acquiescence in his philotyrannical sentiments: and Philistos' own political viewpoint would exactly agree.

The corollary of this interpretation of Pindar, however, would be that Philistos was under the necessity of providing a narrative of Emmenid history. It is therefore of interest to note that Philistos may have found no reason (if we assume certain conditions) to make any changes in the Emmenid genealogy. Let us assume, for example, that the *akme* date of the last generation of the Emmenids is midway between their first appearances (Thrasyboulos in the Pythian victory of 490 B.C.) and their last (Thrasydaios' death in 472/1), that is, in 481/0; and that their generations are reckoned in 36-year units. We can then construct the following table.

akme *date*   *generation*

625/4   Telemachos (destroys Phalaris 625/4)
                     /
589/8   Emmen(id)es (destroys Phalaris 556/5)
                     /
553/2   Ainesidamos
                     |_____
                     /   /
517/6   Theron   Xenokrates
                     /   /
481/0   Thrasydaios   Thrasyboulos

Here, the shift backwards from 556/5 to 625/4 is from a destruction

94

of Phalaris by Emmen(id)es late in his life to a destruction by Telemachos in his youth, so that without any alteration of the genealogy a number of implications could be clarified. If Emmen(id)es destroyed Phalaris in 556/5, there is nothing *in these imputed dates* to prevent his presence at the foundation of Akragas and his acquiescence in the establishment of Phalaris' tyranny. If, on the other hand, Telemachos in his youth is the destroyer of Phalaris, then *on these imputed dates* he was not old enough to have any say in these earlier affairs, and the Emmenid reputation was cleared.

As we have seen, there are several strands in the Akragantine controversy, not all of which are closely interdependent. The statements quoted from the later authorities seem (so far as we can judge) to be frivolous, and it is in accord with this—if Philistos worked in the way just suggested—that the question of the imputed dates does not seem to have been raised. A 36-year generation for a direct line of descent is certainly much too long; historically it is very likely that the year 556/5 fell towards the end of Telemachos' life, and that the earlier man destroyed Phalaris at the later date. But the Eusebian entries seem to witness that this solution occurred to no authoritative historians. It is of course possible, in view of the state of our sources, that this is an unfair judgment: there may have been other points in the tradition which ruled out such a solution, but the Telemachos version so well suits what is known of Philistos' attitude to tyranny, that it is not necessary to suppose that these other points, if they existed, were used by him.

The datings attributable to Philistos therefore suggest that he attained a unified view of his subject-matter: that Sicily and Italy formed for him a single region; that the central problem of this region was the conflict with Carthage; that to meet this problem tyranny was necessary. The revisions of Antiochos' dates are consequently part of the revision, reorganization, and unification of Antiochos' subject-matter, and probably owe far more to this development of method than to any access of new information.

Ephoros thought highly of Philistos (70 F 220=556 T 23a), and probably used him as his main source for Sikeliote history, but not without modification, even chronographically. Ephoros' main calculation was in 39-year generations from Aletes to Gelon through the year 758/7 for Syracuse; Philistos' main calculation was in 27-year generations from Carthage up to and including 406/5, and through 756/5, probably for Zankle. It is likely enough that Philistos dated

95

either Trotilon or Megara Hyblaia to 758/7, but it is not clear that he had any other immediate contact with Ephoros' datings. If this is correct, what Ephoros obtained from Philistos was not any specific dates but a licence to reckon Sicilian dates in 39-year generations, that is, to raise the dates of the earliest foundations by more than twenty years.

iv. Hippys of Rhegion (Jac. 554). The existence of two such contrary authorities for the early history of Sicily as Antiochos and Philistos would not worry the most general reading public, who would rest upon Ephoros; but the western public, and others with special interest in the west, would seek for judgment between them. The first specialist attempt to provide an alternative may have been made in three works attributed to Hippys of Rhegion: the Sikelika in five volumes; the Foundation of Italy; and a Chronicle. From this opus hardly anything survives: the synchronization (at an unknown date) of the foundations of Kroton and Sybaris (F 1); and the foundation in 636/5 of a shrine of the Palikoi in Geloan territory (F 3).

Estimation of the work of Hippys is difficult because the fragments reveal a mixture of conventions: the division of the histories into separate works on Sicily and Italy is nearer to Antiochos than to Philistos; the use of Olympiad and archon in a dating formula (F 3) is Hellenistic. The ancient critics accounted for this mixture by dating Hippys in the fifth century, and giving him a later editor named Myes. Both names recall those of Pythagoreans, and the opus may in fact have represented the Pythagorean historiography of Sicily and Italy. The production of such a school may consequently have shared characteristics of the 'lay' historians of several periods: a generally conservative organization of the subject-matter, and modernity in technical details like dating formulae.

The synchronization of Sybaris and Kroton is a tidiness conformable with a Pythagorean history, enabling a writer to treat of the relations between the two cities over a long period. Eusebius preserves a date for this synchronism, in 709/8, which is $198 = 36 \times 5\frac{1}{2}$ years before the destruction of Sybaris in 511/0, and also $180 = 36 \times 5$ years before Cicero's date for the arrival of Pythagoras in Kroton in 529/8. It may be that both 709/8 and 529/8 come ultimately from Hippys, whom some could well take as being especially informed on these matters. It is clearly most unlikely that Hippys also synchronized Kroton with Syracuse in the tradition of Antiochos and

Ephoros: he presumably criticized and rejected the Astylos oracle as evidence for the foundation date of Kroton, and brought forward local witnesses instead.

The dating formula for 636/5 reports Epainetos *basileus* in Athens (for the archon), and Arytamas of Sparta for the Olympic victor. Although neither name is known in other sources, the formula has resisted attempts at emendation, and it has been noted that the Eusebian Olympic victor for this Olympiad, Phrynon of Athens, is said to have won the *pankration*, not the *stadion*, by Diogenes Laertius. It is likely therefore that the Eusebian text is wrong here, and that Arytamas was the stadionikes in 636/5. We should consequently take the *basileus* Epainetos more seriously, and consider why a *basileus* should appear in the Athenian archon-list. This is the same question as asking why an archon should be excluded from that list, and at this date only one answer seems possible: that 636/5 was the year of the accursed Megakles, whose eponymous function was given to his colleague. That is to say, Kylon was Olympionikes in 640/39, and his *coup d'état* failed in 636/5, according to the official Athenian archon-list.

C. *TIMAIOS* (*Jac. 566*): *i. The fragments*. The more important outcome of the incompatibility of Antiochos and Philistos was the work of Timaios: his Histories in 38 volumes, and a volume of chronological tables entitled Olympic Victors, which gave parallel lists of Spartan kings and ephors, Athenian archons, priestesses of Argos, and Olympic victors. This great chronological activity is ill-represented in the fragments, where eight dates survive, some of them in vile texts and with very different dating formulae.

Fragment 71 gives perhaps the most certain date, reported in verse by pseudo-Skymnos, so that the verse-form protects the figure and the formula: Massalia was founded 120 years before Salamis. This dates Timaios' Massalia firmly to 600/599 B.C., and introduces a new chronographic computation, for 120 years is $36 \times 3\frac{1}{3}$. This is the first known time in western chronography that thirds of a 36-year generation are used.

Fragment 80 contains a figure which may be illuminated by this computation: Timaios' date for the foundation of Corcyra is said to have been six hundred years after Troy. Since Timaios' Troy was in 1193/2 (Fragment 125), this statement dates Corcyra to 593/2, which

97

is incredible (even as a confusion in the text, for it is perfectly clear that the subject is the foundation of Corcyra by the Bacchiad Chersikrates, and there is no sign of confusion with the Corcyrean affair in Periandros' time). Either the figure or the upper terminus must therefore be wrong in this report. But $600 = 36 \times 16\frac{2}{3}$ years, which is the method of computation that Timaios used for Massalia.

The figure is therefore likely to be right, and we should suppose a lacuna in the text: μετὰ ἔτη χ′ ⟨τοῦ upper terminus, καὶ – – –⟩ τῶν Τρωικῶν.

Timaios therefore seems to have reckoned both Massalia and Corcyra in 36-year generations divided into thirds: Eusebius enters Massalia at 598/7 and Corcyra (with Taras) in 706/5, that is, $108 = 36 \times 3$ years apart. The Eusebian entries belong to different formula-groups, but the interval looks as though it is relevant to Timaios. If we use it, it yields:

480/79	Salamis
	$120 = 36 \times 3\frac{1}{3}$ years (F 71)
600/599	Massalia
	$108 = 36 \times 3$ years (Eusebius)
⟨708/7⟩	Corcyra (and Taras?)
	$600 = 36 \times 16\frac{2}{3}$ years (F 80)
1308/7	upper terminus

Fragments 60 and 164 also contain dates which seem certain. The foundations of Rome and Carthage in 814/3 is very well evidenced, and the year is $728 = 39 \times 18\frac{2}{3}$ years after 1308/7. Lipara in 580/79 is $234 = 39 \times 6 = 36 \times 6\frac{1}{2}$ years later than Rome and Carthage, so that we seem here to have a computation running from the same upper terminus, but in 39-year generations. That Timaios also used the 27-year (or 36-year generation divided into quarters) seems also to be witnessed by the date for Ebesos in the Balearics in 654/3: this is $54 = 27 \times 2 = 36 \times 1\frac{1}{2}$ years after Corcyra in ⟨708/7⟩.

Fragment 126 seems also to show this kind of generation, for the Return of the Herakleidai in 1155/4 is $153 = 36 \times 4\frac{1}{4}$ years after 1308/7. We can therefore identify the missing upper terminus as the generation of Herakles himself:

1308/7	Herakles	36 years
1272/1	Hyllos	36 years
1236/5	Kleodaios	36 years

98

1200/1199	Aristomachos	36 years
1164/3	Temenos, etc.	9 years, before
1155/4	The Return	

The lacuna in the text of Fragment 80 can consequently be filled:

μετὰ ἔτη ἑξακόσια ⟨τοῦ 'Ηρακλέους καὶ υπε'⟩ τῶν Τρωικῶν.

Fragment 125 shows yet another kind of generation. At the year 1308/7, Herakles is $828 = 36 \times 23$ years before Salamis in 480/79. It will therefore not be coincidence that the fall of Troy in 1193/2 is $115 = 23 \times 5$ years after 1308/7. Here again, Timaios is, for a western chronographer (and so far as we know), innovating: the 23-year generation had earlier been used for the Lydian 'Herakleids'.[3]

Fragment 19 is the worst of the texts. It gives the date for the foundation of Kamarina. The history of this small town was catastrophic: it was founded from Syracuse (in 601/0 according to Antiochos or in 597/6 according, probably, to Ephoros); destroyed by Syracuse (in 552/1, which is most likely to be a historical date); captured by Hippokrates of Gela (Philistos 556 F 15); destroyed by Gelon (Hdt. VII 156, Philistos F 15); and refounded in 461/0 (Diod. XI 76.5) largely by the efforts of Psaumis, who was an Olympic victor in 452 B.C. Pindar's fourth and fifth *Olympians* are in his honor, and at V 19 Pindar calls Kamarina a new foundation. The two versions of the scholium on this 'new foundation' are:

A:

   (1) νέοικαν ἕδραν εἶπε τὴν Καμάριναν ὁ Πίνδαρος,
   (2) σαφηνίζει Τίμαιος ἐν τῇ δεκάτῃ.
   (3) εἰσὶ δὲ οὗτοι οἱ Καμαριναῖοι ⟨οἱ⟩ ὑπὸ τῶν Γελω ⟨— — —⟩ τυράννου ἀνηρέθησαν, εἶτα ὑπὸ Γελω ⟨— — —⟩
   (4) συνῳ κίσθησαν ἐπὶ τῆς ⟨— — —⟩ ὀλυμπιάδος
   (5) ἡ δὲ ἅλωσις ἐγένετο κατὰ τὴν Δαρείου τοῦ Πέρσου διάβασιν.

CDEHQ:

   (1) 'Ιπποκράτης
   (2) ὑπὸ τοῦ τῶν Γελώων τυράννου ἀνηρέθη, εἶτα ὑπὸ Γέλωνος.
   (3) συνῳκίσθη ἡ Καμάρινα κατὰ τὴν μβ' ὀλυμπιάδα (612/1—609/8) ὥς φησι Τίμαιος
   (4) διὸ καὶ νέοικαν ἕδραν εἶπε τὴν πόλιν.
   (5) ἡ δὲ ἅλωσις αὐτῆς ἐγένετο κατὰ τὴν Δαρείου τοῦ 'Υστάσπου στρατείαν.

This muddle apparently once began by saying that an explanation of the 'new foundation' could be obtained in Timaios' tenth book[4] which

---

[3] See 'Herodotus as Chronographer' *Klio* 46 (1965) pp.109 ff.
[4] This dealt with Pythagorean systematics, then resumed the historical narrative and treated Gelon's reign (Jac. Komm. 3b, 544).

dated the destruction of old Kamarina to 490 B.C. This older city was founded in Ol.42 (E says Ol.22), had passed into subjection to Gela under 'the tyrant of the Geloans' Hippokrates, and was destroyed by Gelon.

There is no chronographic objection to 612/1 B.C. for the foundation of Kamarina: the year is $96 = 36 \times 2\frac{2}{3}$ years after Corcyra, $12 = 36 \times \frac{1}{3}$ years before Massalia, and $60 = 36 \times 1\frac{2}{3}$ years before the conquest in 552/1. This last interval of $60 = 36 \times 1\frac{2}{3}$ years is parallel to the $45 = 27 \times 1\frac{2}{3}$ years given by the Pindaric scholiasts and pseudo-Skymnos, apparently from Ephoros. It is likely therefore that Ephoros has taken the generation-count, and Timiaios the absolute date, from Philistos.

The major difficulty in this scholium is the dating of the capture by Gelon to 490 B.C., for Herodotus clearly understood from his sources that Gelon destroyed Kamarina after he took power in Syracuse in 485/4. Consequently, the date of 490 B.C. has been taken to be that of the capture by Hippokrates. But as we have seen, the exact tradition of the Deinomenid dates made Gelon usurp power in Gela in 491/0 when Hippokrates was dead. And in spite of many errors in our immediate sources it is clear that for the ancients the Deinomenid dates were very exact and not capable of manipulation.

Consequently, we must suppose that Timaios disagreed with Herodotus' informants, and held that Gelon destroyed Kamarina in 490 B.C., removing the inhabitants to Gela; and that after he took power in Syracuse he brought them there, together with a number of other Geloans. This means that the destruction of Kamarina, in September 490 B.C. is the first recorded event of Gelon's reign after his usurpation.

ii. The dating formulae. According to our sources, every one of Timaios' dates is expressed in a different formula: before Salamis, after ⟨Herakles and⟩ Troy, before Ol.1, after Carthage, before the archonship of Euainetos, before the Return, at the time of Marathon, in Ol.42. Some of this variety (e.g. the archonship of Euainetos) is due to our informants, but it is likely that some of it also reflects something in Timaios' own work. Consequently we cannot rely upon any dating formula to indicate authorship of a date by Timaios; and therefore we may be right in taking the Eusebian evidence, from two different Eusebian formula-groups, of an 108-year interval between

Corcyra and Massalia (even though the Eusebian dates are two years lower).

iii. The genealogical framework. The chronographies of Antiochos and Philistos show arithmetical Models of $36 \times 13 = 468 = 39 \times 12$ and $27 \times 13 = 351 = 39 \times 9$ years respectively, and these are Models of genealogies. But while we cannot do more than guess what these genealogies may have been for these two earlier authors, we have a little information from Timaios: that his upper terminus was Herakles, that Pentathlos, the oecist of Lipara, was a descendant of Herakles through Hippotes, the father of Aletes of Corinth (F 164), that the founder of Corcyra was Chersikrates, a Bacchiad and Herakleid like Archias of Syracuse (F 80). Consequently it is probable that Timaios' genealogical framework was Herakleid.

From Herakles in 1308/7, there seem in the surviving dates to be three series of computations, one in 23-year generations through Troy to Salamis; one in 36-year generations through the Return to Salamis; and one in 39-year generations through Rome and Carthage to Lipara. If we examine these series for their genealogical implications and interrelationships we obtain the following 'pedigree' shown in Table VIII.

This is chronographically compact and rational, except that the 39-year series does not share in the lower terminus common to the other series. Genealogically, it shows a phenomenon of interest: the 'descendants' of Herakles segment into three chronographic series; the 'descendants' of Temenos and his brothers into two; the 'descendants' of Aletes into two; and the 'descendants' of Corcyra into two. This suggests that the phenomenon of segmentation, well-known to anthropology, was part of Timaios' genealogical assumptions.

A similar importance should be attached to the coalescence of two lines among the 'ancestors' of Corcyra: this represents the same phenomenon (in Timaios' terms) as the statements by the lexicographers to the effect that a *genos* was united not by descent, but by organization. In fact, this chronographic coalescence almost certainly means that Timaios placed both Corcyra and Taras (from Sparta) at this date, as they are paired in Eusebius – Phalanthos, the oecist of Taras, is said to have been a Herakleid. (But Timiaos also had a special interest in Sparta – he said there were two Lykourgoi F 127 – which is not reflected in the surviving named dates.)

The deliberation of Timaios' use of genealogical phenomena

101

TABLE VIII
PEDIGREE OF TIMAIOS' SURVIVING DATES

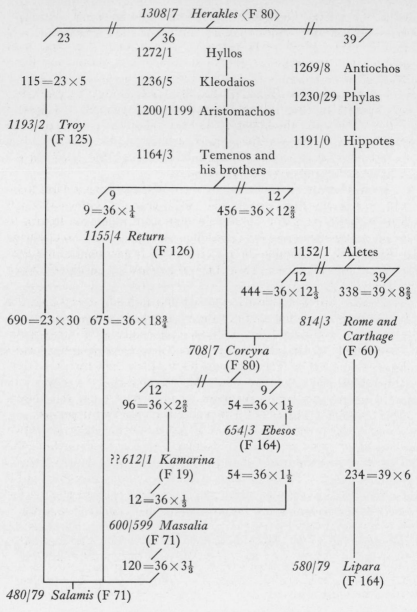

1308/7 *Herakles* ⟨F 80⟩

/23   //   /36   //   39/

1272/1 Hyllos

1269/8 Antiochos

115 = 23 × 5   1236/5 Kleodaios

1230/29 Phylas

1193/2 *Troy*
(F 125)   1200/1199 Aristomachos

1191/0 Hippotes

1164/3 Temenos and
his brothers

/9   //   12/

9 = 36 × ¼   456 = 36 × 12⅔

1155/4 Return
(F 126)   1152/1 Aletes

/12   //   39/

444 = 36 × 12⅓   338 = 39 × 8⅔

690 = 23 × 30   675 = 36 × 18¾   *814/3 Rome and
Carthage*
(F 60)

708/7 Corcyra
(F 80)

/12   //   9/

96 = 36 × 2⅔   54 = 36 × 1½

654/3 Ebesos
(F 164)

?? *612/1 Kamarina*
(F 19)   54 = 36 × 1½   234 = 39 × 6

12 = 36 × ⅓

600/599 Massalia
(F 71)

120 = 36 × 3⅓   *580/79 Lipara*
(F 164)

480/79 Salamis (F 71)

could mean that by his time, or in his mind, these phenomena had been transformed by the development of social science into concepts available for use in the construction of chronographic and other Models. Certainly, Timaios' chronography shows no trace of the purely arithmetical pictures given by Antiochos and Philistos; and—if this is truly part of our meagre evidence—it may be due to the availability of these genealogical concepts, rendering the purely numerical abstractions unnecessary, and replacing them by what would seem to be more solidly historiographic material. Timaios, for example, seems to have possessed a pedigree for the oecist of Lipara, and on this basis to have abandoned Philistos' date for that foundation and reverted to what may have been Antiochos' date. At the same time, his date for Ebesos suggests that he acknowledged some part of Philistos' argument for the early dates of Akragas, Selinous, Himera, and Lipara.[5]

Thus although Timaios' dates for Syracuse and most of the other Sicilian foundations are not given—at least with his name—in our sources, we should expect that they were not the same as Philistos', but that some at least reverted to the older tradition; but we should also expect that they would be divided among several chronographic segments, and not show the simple arithmetics of the older authorities.

The question of the attribution of unnamed dates is therefore much more difficult than in the cases of Antiochos and Philistos. We should of course endeavor to err on the conservative side, and therefore only attribute dates which are in one of the segments or series of numbers evidenced by the named dates.

The only exception is the possibility that Timaios' Spartan segment is not represented by the $456 = 36 \times 12\frac{2}{3}$ years from Temenos and his brothers to Phalanthos in Taras. We are not told that Phalanthos was Agiad or Eurypontid, only that he was Herakleid, and his date of 708/7 is not connected chronographically (the interval of 197 years is a prime number) with the expedition of Dorieus the Agiad in 511/0 B.C. This date is chronographically connected (among those that can be inferred) with the Herakleid ancestors only at 1200/1199 for Aristomachos; this suggests that Timaios' date for

---

[5] The expression of the date of Ebesos as 160 years after Carthage has been held to show an archival source for the interval, with erroneous absolute dates (Rhys Carpenter *AJA* 68 (1964) 178); but as we have noted above, no evidence can be extracted from the formulae in which Timaios' dates are reported.

103

Aristodemos of Sparta was 39 years later, in 1161/0, and not at the year of Temenos in 1164/3. But apart from this possibility, dates should be attributed to Timaios only when they fall on one of the lines of calculation evidenced by the named dates.

D. THE LATER TRADITION. The representatives of the later tradition of the colony dates are for us the Pindaric scholia, various authors and possible connections in the first century B.C., and Eusebius. Our general problem is to consider whether, on chronographic, historiographic, or other grounds, as we can attribute the dates to their originators.

If these originators were the classical Sikeliote historians, we have now some guiding ideas on the nature of their work. Whatever other concerns Antiochos and Philistos may have had, one of their interests was certainly politics; whatever other matters may have been treated by Hippys, one of his concerns was religion; the breadth of Timaios' treatments certainly included what we may call the social—the use of genealogical and kinship information and concepts. But for the authorities on Sikeliote history after Timaios we have little information. We hear, for example, of Hippostratos' Sicilian Genealogies, but the fragments are not sufficient even to tell us whether that work was, in principle, romantic or scientific; we know even less of Polemon's Foundations of the Italian and Sicilian Cities. Among the general historians, we know something of Diodorus—that he was a compiler; but hardly anything of Eusebius' other general history mentioned in his bibliography, Kephalion's Nine Muses; we know something of the annalist Phlegon of Tralles, nothing of the Olympiads of Cassius Longinus. In particular, we are ignorant of the sources of possible chronographic originality in these periods of Hellenistic and imperial learning; are we to look to Hippostratos and Polemon or—as we should for mainland Greece—to Eratosthenes, Apollodoros, Sosikrates, and their followers? In this condition of ignorance, it is impossible to say whether or not it is more likely that new dates proposed after Timaios' time are dependent on general or specialist historiography; and our own starting-point is as narrow an examination as possible of what was done.

i. Anonymous dates reported by the Pindaric scholiasts. Besides the date of 612/1 reported from Timaios for Kamarina, the scholiasts and pseudo-Skymnos report 597/6 for the same event. This date is (1) not

104

from Antiochos, who placed the foundation at 601/1; (2) is not from Philistos if Timaios took 612/1 from him; (3) is related to the date 612/1, for that year is $36 \times 1\frac{2}{3}$ years before the Syracusan conquest in 552/1, while 597/6 is the parallel $27 \times 1\frac{2}{3}$ years before the same conquest. This arithmetic points to the fourth century for the origin of the date; and its use by pseudo-Skymnos points (as we have seen) to Ephoros, the geographer's authority for Sicily. It seems, therefore, that Ephoros here as elsewhere is modifying Philistos' datings.

The date of 580/79 for Akragas is also given anonymously by the scholiast, in the context of a discussion of the rounding of figures in Pindar. The originator of this date may or may not be the same person as the authority for the discussion on rounding. The latter seems more suitable to a Pindaric commentator explaining why 580/79 is a better date for Akragas than Antiochos' 583/2 or Philistos' 652/1—a historian scrupulously quoting his primary sources would surely have discussed rounding versus chronographic precision before reaching 580/79. In this context, we cannot quite exclude the possibility that a Pindaric commentator himself proposed the date 580/79 to exemplify the nearest possible chronographic computation to Pindar's century, but it is perhaps more likely that he took it from a historian, possibly, once more, Ephoros.

ii. Anonymous dates reported by Diodorus. Ebesos in 654/3 and Lipara in 580/79 are attributed to Timaios (F 164) for the usual reasons of context and traceable influence. We have already seen reason to believe that Timaios himself took Ebesos from Philistos and Lipara from Antiochos. Diodorus' dates for Selinous in 650/49 and Himera in 648/7 presumably also are due directly to Timaios, who will have taken these also from Philistos. If Philistos taught that Ebesos in 654/3 provoked a Greek reply consisting of Akragas in 652/1, Selinous in 650/49, Himera in 648/7, and Lipara in 630/29, Timaios probably accepted Ebesos, Selinous, and Himera, but returned towards the Antiochine tradition for Akragas and Lipara.

Diodorus (XI 24.1) is also our authority for the dating of the Battle of Himera to 481/0, which should form part of the exact chronology of the Deinomenids, and is therefore attributable to Philistos, as in Table VII above. It would be accepted by Timaios and reach Diodorus through him.

iii. Other scattered references. Strabo (VI 2.4) says that the two

105

Bacchiads, Archias and Chersikrates, founded Syracuse and Corcyra at the same time. This appears in Strabo as an addition to the classical synchronism of Syracuse and Kroton by Antiochos and Ephoros; and since Strabo mentions Ephoros' name shortly afterwards, and his story of Archias includes the non-Megarian Dorians of Zephyrion whom Ephoros also knew, it is generally supposed that the synchronism of Syracuse and Corcyra is Ephoran. This would mean that Ephoros' date for Corcyra was 758/7, whereas Timaios' date seems to have been 708/7, and the Eusebian date is 706/5, synchronized with Taras: this may be very much older, going back to Antiochos. Both Timaios and Strabo name Chersikrates as the Corinthian founder; Timaios says he drove out Kolchians (presumably descended from the pursuers of the Argonauts) from Corcyra, Strabo says that the expelled were Liburnians. Nothing in these accounts prepares us for Plutarch's statement (QG 11) that the people driven out or under by the Corinthians were Eretrians, though this may be connected with the Eusebian date of 706/5 for the Corinthians, $216 = 27 \times 8 = 36 \times 6$ years before the destruction of Eretria in 490/89 B.C.

Corcyra had no known local historians, and her history was therefore dependent either upon the authorities for Sicily and Italy, or—like that of Corinth—upon the universal historians, for whom the bitter struggles of the fifth century may have provided a number of highly ideological reports. That the pre-Corinthian (or non-Corinthian) inhabitants were barbarians (either factual and Liburnian, or mythical and Kolchian) may well be such a report. But it seems more important that the wide variation in dating bears upon Corinthian history. In 758/7 the Bacchiad monarchy was (according to our later authorities) still in being and Telestes had recently recovered his throne; at this date therefore the exiles Archias and Chersikrates are presumably to be taken as supporters of the previous usurpation. In 736/5 the Bacchiad oligarchy had already begun, so that a personal reason for their departure had to be proposed, and this is provided by the Archias horror-story for Syracuse in 736/5 and by Timaios' outlawry of Chersikrates in 708/7. But the synchronism of Taras and Corcyra probably means that even for the late dates for Corcyra a political context was not lacking: Sparta and Corinth act jointly to secure the way to the west, and at the same time deliver themselves of unwanted persons. This political context probably refers to the Lelantine War, which otherwise does not appear in the remaining

106

information about Sikeliote foundations, though it must have been mentioned by all the specialist historians.

Another scattered reference is given by Stephanos of Byzantium under his entry on the Sicilian Enna, which he says was founded 70 years after Syracuse. He gives no absolute date nor the name of his source. It is very likely that his figure is wrong, for Enna is much too far from Syracuse to have been colonized at so early a date. The Ennaioi are mentioned about 550 by Philistos (F 5) as allies of Syracuse with the Megarians against Kamarina and the Sikeloi, but these Ennaioi need not have been Greeks.

iv. The Eusebian chronography. In the study of the Eusebian formula-groups in Part Two above, the simple verbal patterns of sources were displayed. We now come to the study of simple numerical patterns in the datings, which (in so far as the state of the texts allows) may be a more reliable means of analysing the Eusebian sources and their historiographic intentions.

All the Eusebian western foundation dates, except that for Chersonesos (717/6) and those for Akragas and Lipara, fall into a pattern of three interrelated pairs of dating series, as shown in Table IX; and this pattern is open-ended, leading through Trotilon and Selinous to the dates of the Megarian colonies in the Propontis (formula-group 2a). This pattern includes therefore: Naukratis, and Taras and Corcyra from formula-group 1; all formula-group 2a; all formula-group 3b except Chersenesos, and all formula-group 4.

We have therefore two Eusebian sources for the Sicilian colony dates, one minor and concerned with the Akragas controversy, the other the major source. The minor source would seem to be derived, in a scrappy and incomplete way, from some specialist work on Sicilian history, and the pedigree from the classical historians to Eusebius for this minor tradition may therefore be hypothetically traced: Hippostratos was interested in the Akragas controversy (F 2); his work was used by the annalist Phlegon of Tralles (556 F 1, 257 F 36), to whose carelessness the omission of dates for Akragas may well be due, and whose Olympiades is named as a source in Eusebius' bibliography (257 T 4, F 8 16).[6]

The major source seems to be much more substantial, and its

---

[6] He confused Thaletas of Crete and Thales of Miletos (F 33), in which error Eusebius followed him.

107

TABLE IX

EUSEBIUS' MAJOR SOURCE

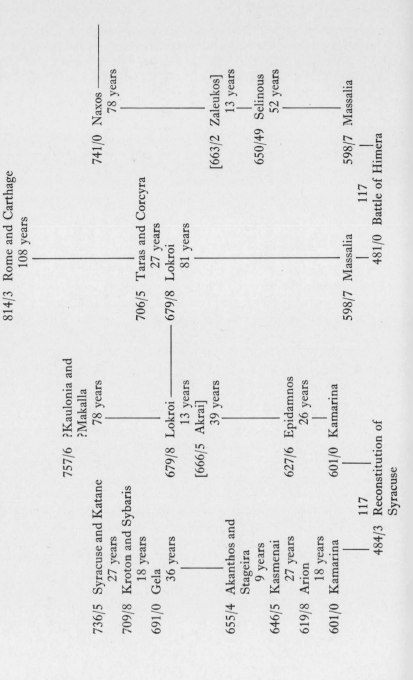

736/5 Syracuse and Katane
       27 years

709/8 Kroton and Sybaris
       18 years

691/0 Gela
       36 years

757/6 ?Kaulonia and
       ?Makalla
       78 years

814/3 Rome and Carthage
       108 years

741/0 Naxos
       78 years

655/4 Akanthos and
       Stageira
       9 years

646/5 Kasmenai
       27 years

619/8 Arion
       18 years

601/0 Kamarina

679/8 Lokroi
       13 years

[666/5 Akrai]
       39 years

706/5 Taras and Corcyra
       27 years

679/8 Lokroi
       81 years

[663/2 Zaleukos]
       13 years

650/49 Selinous
       52 years

484/3   117   Reconstitution of
                  Syracuse

627/6 Epidamnos
       26 years

601/0 Kamarina

598/7 Massalia

481/0 Battle of Himera

598/7 Massalia

117

Battle of Himera

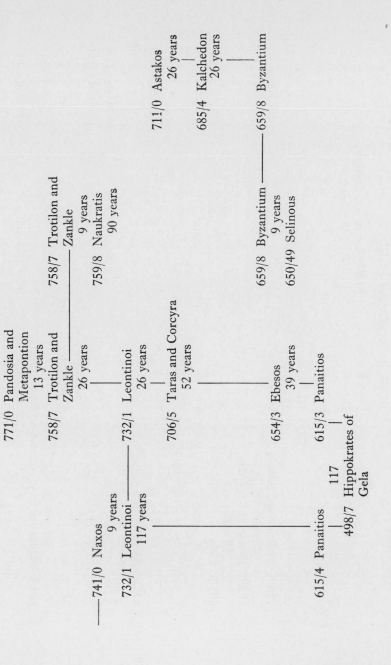

tradition probably requires two writers of some authority: a western specialist who originated the numerical patterns of the chronography in Table IX on the basis of the classical historians – and the author of the 'sea-power' thesis who extended Kastor's notion to the western Mediterranean on the foundation laid by the first authority. A candidate for identification as the first authority is Polemon, author of (*inter multa alia*) Foundations of the Sicilian and Italian Cities; the sea-power historian, with his literary leanings, is probably one of the writers of the Hadrianic age, among whom Kephalion is named in Eusebius' bibliography.

The pairs of date-series have both traceable ancestries and historiographic intentions. The first pair uses multiples of 9 and 13 years back from Antiochos' base-date at 484/3 (the reconstitution of the Syracusan policy by Gelon), and contains the dates derived from Antiochos: Syracuse in 736/5, Gela in 691/0, (Kasmenai in 646/5), Kamarina in 601/0; (and Akrai 65 years before Kamarina, in 666/5). To these are added:

(1) Katane in 736/5 and coeval with Syracuse, while Antiochos made it more than five years later. The reason for this date is presumably that 736/5 is $260 = 39 \times 6\frac{2}{3}$ years before Katane was refounded as Aitne by Hieron in 476/5. Thus Syracuse is seven generations before 484/3, and Katane $6\frac{2}{3}$ generations before 476/5: Antiochos expresses this relative dating by making Katane later than Syracuse, while Eusebius' source uses generations of different lengths and so arrives at a single absolute date for one of those pairs of cities so common in western historiography.

(2) Kroton and Sybaris in 709/8. This date was certainly chosen to fit the chronographic pattern, for several others were available: 758/7, 736/5, and 710/09 for Kroton; ?745/4? and 721/0 for Sybaris. As we have seen, the Antiochine ?745/4? for Sybaris and 736/5 for Kroton were most probably reckoned from Dorieus' date of 511/0: Sybaris is $36 \times 6\frac{1}{2} = 39 \times 6$ years, Kroton is $36 \times 6\frac{1}{4}$ years, earlier. The Eusebian date of 709/8 probably derives ultimately from Hippys of Rhegion, who thus places both foundations $36 \times 5\frac{1}{2} = 27 \times 7$ years before Dorieus. This close connection with a local base-date (already weakened by Antiochos' synchronism of Kroton and Syracuse on the oracular evidence) becomes more tenuous with Ephoros, who carries the Syracusan synchronism back to 758/7, though this is still $247 = 39 \times 6\frac{1}{3}$ years before

110

Dorieus. The Kroton of Dionysius of Halikarnassos in 710/09 is $225 = 36 \times 6\frac{1}{4}$ years before 485/4: this is a revision of Ephoros in the light of the rejection of the oracular evidence used by him and Antiochos. The dates for Sybaris in ?745/4? and 709/8 could also be reconsidered after Timaios introduced the 36-year generation divided into thirds: then ?745/4? can be taken as $36 \times 7\frac{1}{3}$ years before 481/0, and 709/8 as $36 \times 6\frac{1}{3}$ years before: some unknown chronographer has consequently proposed 721/0, recorded by Pseudo-Skymnos, which is $36 \times 6\frac{2}{3}$ years before 481/0.

The Eusebian source has thus rejected dates for Sybaris and Kroton which do not fit his chronographic pattern and also the Antiochine dates which would fit the chronography but rest on a synchronism derived from oracular evidence which did not survive criticism by Hippys of Rhegion.

(3) The seventh century dates really need to be considered together, for they show a historiographic thesis. As we have seen, there was a tradition, known to us only in a romantic version, which connected the foundation of Lokroi with Corcyrean enmity to Corinth; the Syracusan Akrai has no oecist in Thucydides, which may mean an absence of good communications with Corinth; Akanthos and Stageira show Chalkis in concert with other Ionian powers, not with Corinth; Kasmenai, like Akrai, has no oecists. But the next entries show a change: Epidamnos is founded jointly by Corinth and Corcyra; Arion's famous western voyage is no doubt the event selected for his Eusebian *akme* date; and Kamarina has Syracusan and Corinthian oecists. Thus the series of dates express a Corinthian weakness in the middle fifty years of the seventh century, and a recovery in the last quarter. The traditional picture of Corinthian history at this period is of a political decline under the Bacchiad oligarchy, ended by the usurpation of power by Kypselos, who takes the vigorous but ungoverned economy in hand and, by tithing it for ten years, builds a wealthy state which rises to pan-Hellenic influence under Periandros by the end of the century.

(4) ?Kaulonia and ?Makalla in 757/6 may refer to a tradition which held that these towns had been connected with Lokroi before the rise of Kroton. Kaulonia was Achaian; Makalla may be the same as Petelia, of Aegean origin (Thessalian or Rhodian). Their appearance in Eusebius is probably due rather to the 'sea-power'

111

historian, who will have selected them from among the available data to emphasize the emergence of Achaia as a colonizer of the west. The date is the orthodox 'seven generations before Gelon' so often used for the introduction of political organization to western areas.

The second pair of date-series goes back in multiples of 9 and 13 years from 481/0, Philistos' date for the Battle of Himera, and includes Philistos' date for Selinous at 650/49: it could also include either Philistos' date for Akragas in 652/1 or the anonymous date recorded by the Pindaric scholiast at 580/79, which we have attributed to Ephoros. Taras and Corcyra at 706/5 and Massalia at 598/7 are, however, modifications of Timaios rather than of Philistos, while Naxos at 741/0 agrees neither with Ephoros nor Antiochos.

The placings in this pair of date-series form, as it were, a commentary upon and enlargement of the historiography of the first pair. There the main subjects were the rise of Achaia, the weakness and recovery of Corinth. In the present series, the synchronized foundations of Taras and Corcyra show Bacchiad Corinth at its most powerful, in alliance with the Spartan conquerors of Messenia, and connects these scandalous foundations with that of the no less scandalous Lokroi, whose date is the chronographic link with the first pair of date-series. But the recovery of Corinth is now contrasted with the Phokaian foundation of Massalia: the Greek frontier has passed beyond Corinthian horizons.

Ephoros paired Syracuse and Corcyra, it would seem, by guessing that the two Bacchiad oecists were contemporaries; the Eusebian source probably had in mind the expulsion of the Eretrian settlement in Corcyra, $216 = 36 \times 6 = 27$ years before the destruction of Eretria herself. It is difficult to think of such an expulsion without reference to the Lelantine War: and if this is intended, we see that the historiography of the first pair of date-series is now expanded here also: the rise of Achaia (Kaulonia, Kroton, Sybaris), Corinth (Syracuse), and Chalkis (Naxos, Katane) is followed by the Lelantine War, which results in, or at least is followed by, the political weakness of Corinth in the west.

The date for Naxos links the second pair of date-series with the third.

The third pair of date-series is concerned with the Chalkidian colonies, which came into the ambit of the Geloan tyranny in Hippokrates' reign. Since Hippokrates reigned for seven years and died before harvest-time 491/0, he will have taken power in 498/7, and the Chalkidian dates in this pair of series seemed to be reckoned on this base-date. Naxos in 741/0 is $243=27\times9=36\times6\frac{3}{4}$ before Hippokrates, or enjoyed that period of independence. Leontinoi is nine years later, and her tyrant Panaitios (the first Sicilian tyrant, since Akragas is not founded until 580/79) usurps power $117=39\times3=36\times3\frac{1}{4}=27\times4\frac{1}{3}$ years after the foundation of Leontinoi and the same period before Hippokrates. At this date his rule should represent the influence of Periandros in Sicily. The chronographic relationship of his date to that of Carthaginian Ebsesos in 654/3, however, also emphasizes Philistos' thesis that the Sicilian tyrants were a response to the Carthaginian challenge, while the appearance of Taras and Corcyra also in this series recalls the preceding period of Corinthian power and its weakening by the Lelantine War.

In this series also Megarian Trotilon and Chalkidian Zankle replace Ephoros' Syracuse, Corcyra, and Kroton at 758/7. For Ephoros, this was seven generations before Gelon at Syracuse in 485/4; for Eusebius' source, it is $6\frac{2}{3}$ generations before Hippokrates, and the seven-generations date is apparently 771/0, occupied by the Italian Pandosia and Metapontion. Pandosia here may stand for Siris, and these foundations in 771/0 are surely part of the 'sea-power' thesis. Zankle in 758/7 is, in this context, probably not an error for Philistos' 756/5 (in spite of Chersonesos in 717/6), but one of the Chalkidian cities chronographically related to their conqueror Hippokrates. This early date, before Naxos in 741/0, will belong to the pirate pre-political settlement. Similarly Trotilon, 26 years before the Megarians join the Chalkidians at Leontinoi, is presumably not a πόλις, and the historian must have stated that the Megarians came to Sicily independently, not in Theokles' convoy.

The open end of this chronographic system is found mainly through Megarian history: Trotilon in 758/7 is $108=36\times3=27\times4$ years before Selinous in 650/49; Byzantium in 659/8 belongs both to this series and also to formula-group 2a, the three Megarian colonies in the Propontis. This chronographic linkage confirms the inference from the east-west pairs (formula-group 4) that the Eusebian source was interested in more than the Sicilian cities, however much he may have relied upon a specialist authority. Similarly, at this open end we have evidence of his 'sea-power' interest: for example, Naukratis in 749/8 is on the Trotilon-Selinous series of figures but is part of an entry on the thalassocracy of Miletos. The Eusebian main source for

113

the colony entries is therefore probably the same as his source for the thalassocracies in the *Canons*. Exactly how much of the chronographic pattern and how many of the details are to be attributed to the 'sea-power' historians, and how much to his specialist western source (who may be Polemon), is, and is likely to remain, uncertain.

This chronographic examination of the material which we formerly studied in formula-groups has revealed inadequacies in that study. Formula-group 1, colonies with founders named, contributes Naukratis and Taras-Corcyras, to the main source; its two entries on Kyrene, chronographically connected with one another, may be independent, but also may be linked with the open end of the system, as in the columns below.

771/0	Pandosia and Metapontion 9 years		
762/1	Thebans at Kyrene—————	762/1	Thebans at Kyrene 13 years
	45 years	749/8	Naukratis 13 years
		736/5	Syracuse, Katane 104 years
717/6	Chersonesos in Sicily 81 years		
636/5	(Palikoi shrine near Gela; Kylon's conspiracy in Athens during the tyranny of Theagenes in Megara) 9 years	632/1	Battos in Kyrene 52 years
627/6	Epidamnos founded from Corinth and Corcyra 36 years		
591/0	fall of Krisa 9 years		
582/1	First Pythiad		
		580/79	(Akragas and Lipara)

If this is properly attributable to the Eusebian major source, then it is likely that the 'Thebans in Kyrene' are somehow connected with the Phokians of Metapontion and 'Boiotos son of Metapontios', in the remote period before the Euboians of Zankle constituted a πόλις and

114

established its granary at Mylai-Chersonesos. Megarian history appears again at 636/5, which will be a date fixed in the fifth century by the Athenian archon-list: it is also $91 = 39 \times 2\frac{1}{3}$ years before the Eusebian date for Theognis' *akme* in 545/4.

It may be therefore that all the entries in formula-group 1 belong to Eusebius' main source; the Megarian entries which constitute the whole of group 2a also belong to the open end. Group 2b, however, contributes only Massalia: Lipara and the Akragas controversy come from the minor source. Group 3a, the Pontine colonies, seem to be quite independent; groups 3b (if Chersonesos belongs to the open end) and 4 belong to the main source. The formula-groups thus fall into three classes: the differences among groups 1, 2a, 3b, and 4 are apparently irrelevant to the question of source; but the differences between these groups and group 2b (except Massalia) on the one hand, and group 3b on the other are apparently significant.

E. CHRONOGRAPHY AS HISTORIOGRAPHY. In the investigation of the chronographic work of Antiochos, Philistos, Timaios, and Eusebius' main source, we have so far been observing the development of historiography, the formation of its concepts and its methods of constructing a narrative. Antiochos forms a regional history of Sicily out of a set of particularist traditions, and in some cases we can see what these particularist traditions were, like the seven generations of the Gamoroi at Syracuse. Philistos enlarges the scale of the single region to include Italy, as was natural to a fourth-century historian; more important, he selects a single chain of cause and effect as the unifier of his history: Carthage and tyranny. Timaios is a universal historian and chronicler, and so brings Sicily and the west in general into a universal chronographic scheme based on Herakleid genealogies: he thus introduces to historiography the notions of segmentation and coalescence of descents which were formed in the nascent anthropological studies. The Eusebian main source comprises almost certainly the work of two men, a western specialist work and the 'sea-power' historian. The western specialist is probably responsible for the basic chronographic pattern which sets out the learned *traditio* for each set of details, judiciously considers the proposals of the various authorities, and produces a smooth and orthodox sequence of events in the west related, apparently, closely to the accepted history of metropolitan Greece – at a guess, this is Polemon, resting on the labors of Eratosthenes and Apollo-

115

doros. His work is used by the 'sea-power' historian to create a new kind of history, in which the principal period of Greek colonization is seen as part of the much longer period of thalassocratic history but followed out in detail (especially for the west) which Kastor is perhaps not likely to have included.

If the first chroniclizer in the Eusebian ancestry was responsible for the alphabetic order of the names in some of the colony entries, he was probably a person of some care in his own presentation of the material, and in the use of his sources; it is unlikely that he omitted Akragas and Lipara. If the Eusebian tradition on these foundations comes from the minor source, and that source is Hippostratos for the facts and Phlegon for the chronicle form, then either Africanus or Eusebius himself is responsible for rejecting Akragas and Lipara at 580/79, and inserting instead the entries from the minor source. The influence responsible may be that of literary history and Pindaric scholarship, from which point of view it is obviously possible that the 'sea-power' historian's account of these foundations may have been held inadequate. We have seen that some of Eusebius' entries on the Deinomenids probably come from a literary history, and some comments in such a history may have moved Eusebius or Africanus to look up the Akragas entries in Phlegon.

Our enquiry must now, however, turn to chronography, in which field we are faced with two problems: the meanings of the different generation-lengths, and the original information about numbers of generations on which all this ancient work was based.

---

[7] This hypothesis will be modified in *The Thalassocracies*.

116

PART FIVE

KINDS OF GENERATIONS

THE CHRONOGRAPHIC HYPOTHESIS, as so far proposed, takes us only halfway to an understanding of this field of work by the ancient historians. We can with its aid relate various dates to one another in chronographic systems and observe something of the relationship of various systems to one another; but these observations only serve to raise still more fundamental questions. One set of such questions leads us out of chronography into problems of the original information, which we shall discuss later; there are many questions within chronography itself to be considered first. Of these, some relate to the history of chronography: by whom was it invented and when and why; for what purposes was it designed and did it meet them, well or badly; did it, in either technique or purpose or both, develop beyond its original form, and so forth.

All these questions can hardly be tackled until a group of systematic questions have been examined: what were the basic ideas from which this quantitative and model discipline arose, and what were the relations of these ideas to any historical reality. In this systematic field, perhaps the best approach is to begin with the questions why the chronographers used different generation-lengths at all and why they chose the lengths of 23, 27, 36, and 39 years.

The last of these questions is quantitative, and therefore likely to be the best starting-point for enquiry into a quantitative discipline. If, however, we wish to discover not only the system of ideas, but also the relation of these ideas to historical reality, we must have some external evidence about the historical reality. This, in view of the state and kinds of our sources, cannot be obtained from the ancient writings.

What we are demanding is quantitative evidence on the historical reality by which we can measure the relations of the chronographic quantities to historical fact. No such quantitative evidence stands

117

ready to hand in an immediately usable form, but there exists a mass of material out of which usable quantities could be created: the number of skeletons from ancient and medieval populations is by now very large, and from these it is conceivable that average vital statistics could be derived. These statistics would give us a measure for the historical reality or otherwise of the generation-lengths used by the chronographers; and from this comparison we could proceed to the other questions.

The techniques required to derive statistics from the skeletal material are those of the demographer, and the discussion which follows is conducted by Mr. J. A. Newth, with interpolations from the ancient written evidence as required.

A. AN ANCIENT DEMOGRAPHIC MODEL: i. Direct skeletal evidence. The ancient and medieval skeletal material now available has recently been collected and considered from the physician's point of view by Dr. Calvin Wells, in *Bones, Bodies and Disease* (London, 1964). Among other matters, he discusses age at death as shown by the skeletons from various populations, over a very long span of prehistoric and historic time, and summarizes his findings as in the table below.

| Population | Percentage of Persons Dead by Age: | | |
	30 years	40 years	50 years
Neanderthalers	80.0	95.0	100.0
Cro-Magnons	61.7	88.2	90.0
Mesolithics	86.3	95.5	97.0
Tepe Hissar	48.3	78.9	99.3
Caister	57.4	81.8	97.5

From the demographic point of view, we may start with these physicians' figures, and examine their interrelations. To do this, we need to express Dr. Wells' percentages in other rates as follows:

(1) If 80 percent of the Neanderthal skeletons are those of persons dead by their thirtieth birthday (or so), then 20 percent are those of persons who survived to their thirtieth birthday. For the convenience of our future arithmetic, this can be expressed as 200

118

per mille; and we can similarly translate Dr. Wells' other figures to give:

Population	Survival Rates to Age:		
	30 years	40 years	50 years
Neanderthalers	200	50	0
Cro-Magnons	383	118	100
Mesolithics	137	45	30
Tepe Hissar	517	211	7
Caister	426	182	25

(2) From these survival figures we can derive death-rates specific to the two decades of life 30–40 and 40–50 years. If 200 per thousand Neanderthalers are alive at age 30, and 50 per thousand at age 40, then 150 per thousand die in the decade 30–39 years, and the ten-year specific death-rate for this decade is 150/200 or 0.750. Similarly for the remaining cases:

Population	Ten-year Death Rates for Ages:	
	30–39 years	40–49 years
Neanderthalers	0.750	1.000
Cro-Magnons	0.692	0.153
Mesolithics	0.672	0.333
Tepe Hissar	0.611	0.967
Caister	0.573	0.863

It is these ten-year death-rates which tell most about the figures in relation to one another. We observe that the specific death-rates for the decade 30–39 decline steadily through historical time over a relatively narrow range. Their consistency with one another in respect of this trend is remarkable in itself, and wholly in accord with the kind of improvement in longevity that we should expect from improvements in farming, diet, and related matters. That is to say, the historical trend is both arithmetically rational and historically reasonable, and since the physicians' figures show these two qualities, those figures may be accepted as giving something of a real picture of the populations concerned for that decade of life.

For the 40–49 year decade however the specific death-rates are quite different. Those for Tepe Hissar (in the fourth millennium

119

B.C.) and Caister agree fairly closely around 0.900, but the figures for the earlier populations are very divergent—in fact, their divergencies are so great that we cannot suppose the physicians' figures to represent anything real in the actual behaviour of these populations, and must presume that only a misleadingly small number of skeletons exist.

Thus the physicians' figures contain relationships which can be made explicit, and hence translated into words: from Neanderthal to medieval times the specific death-rates for the decade 30–39 years of life move gradually from about 0.750 to about 0.575; and for the last five millennia of this period the rate for the decade 40–49 years of life was around 0.900. Consequently, we may cautiously assume as reasonable that in the second to first millennia B.C. (the period with which the chronographers were concerned) the general death-rate for ages 30–40 was 0.600 and for ages 40–50 it was 0.900 – a majority of the population was dead by the age of 40, and nearly all by the age of 50.

If this is true, or anywhere at all near the truth, we must consider fairly narrowly what we, and the ancients, meant by a 'generation'.

ii. Demographic and historical generations. In the first place, the 'generation' of history, and the 'generation' of demography are different concepts, and—leaving entirely aside loose and popular usages —each discipline has minor variants of its own concept, used for specific purposes.

The demographic generation is the average period of time from the births of a set of people to the births of those children who replace them in a stable population. Obvious variants are found by narrow definitions of the set of people concerned, for example, persons of one sex (succession of mother by daughter) and so forth; but essentially the demographic generation is a reproduction period.

The generation of history, on the other hand, is a period not from birth but from succession to succession: for history is interested in the activities of adults from the time at which they succeed their parents in the conduct of affairs. Essentially, therefore, the historical generation is a survival period.

Applied to individuals, the demographic generation requires that they live long enough to reproduce themselves: if on the average (let us say) this occurs at the age of 25, it does not affect the demographic concept of a generation if the parent usually dies a year later; and

120

the demographer can assume that, since the society he is investigating exists under these circumstances, it has successfully made provision for the survival of orphans.

But the historian faced with a population in which people usually died at the age of 26 years would not believe his informants; and his first, unconsidered, reason would be the inference that a series of people dying at the age of 26 must reproduce themselves at the age of 13 years. This inference derives from the assumption that the survival period is a derivative of, and equal to, the reproductive period. To see that this has been assumed, we need only recall how often the Herodotean 'three generations to a century' (for hereditary reigns and priesthoods, that is, survival periods) has been applied indifferently to citizens and dynasties without enquiry into laws of succession and other relevant matters.

Both demography and history therefore make, or may make, assumptions around these concepts of 'generations'; and since one of these assumptions is that the reproductive and survival periods are, on the average, equal, we have in the present enquiry to examine these periods quantitatively. We should then examine these quantities in relation to laws of succession and any other matter which may illuminate the provisions made for the survival of orphans.

We begin with an attempt to construct a picture of the age-structure overall of a stable population in which the figures already obtained find their place—that is, in which the ten-year death rate is 0.600 for the decade 30–39 years of age, and 0.900 for the decade 40–49 years of age.

iii. The life-table from ten years of age. It is known that, from medieval times onwards, the lowest ten-year death rate is that of the teens, followed by that of the twenties. It is difficult to think of any reason why this general pattern should not apply to earlier times, and therefore it seems right that we should extrapolate backwards into our period.

For that period, however, we have no evidence of the magnitudes involved, and for an assignment of quantities we must guess, then test against indirect evidence.

Reasonable guesses for populations of our period would be figures of the order of 0.300 for the death-rate of the 10–19 years age group, and 0.400 for the decade 20–29 years. We can write these guesses together with our skeletally derived figures as a single series thus:

Age in Years	Number of Survivors	Specific Death-Rate	Number of Deaths
10	100	0.300	30
20	70	0.400	28
30	42	0.600	25
40	17	0.900	15
50	2		

From this series we can derive expectation of life figures. Similarly, expectation of life figures for some ancient and medieval populations can be derived from some of Dr. Wells' data; and comparison of these two expectation figures provides an indirect check upon our guesses for the death-rates.

To derive expectation of life figures we proceed thus: each of the 100 ten-year old children in the series above can on the average expect to live for one-hundredth of the total time they all live. This total time may be estimated as follows:

of 100 persons aged 10 with a death-rate of 30 per cent for the decade 10–19 years of life, 70 will reach age 20 and in that time live 700 man-years;

of the same 100 persons, 30 will die in the ten-year period, or 3 every year on the average. Suppose that these deaths are evenly spaced, so that one person lives 2 months, another 6 months, another 10 months, and so forth; summated, these fractions yield $30 \times 10/2$ or 150 man-years.

Thus the whole group of 100 persons will live 850 man-years in this decade.

Similarly, the 70 survivors of this group at age 20 will live $420 + 140 = 560$ man-years in the decade 20–29 years of life; and similarly for the remaining decades.

Hence the total of all man-years lived from age 10 by 100 persons with these death-rates will be 1,810; so that the expectation of life at age 10 is 18.1 years.

Similarly the expectation of life at age 20 for members of this population will be 13.9 years; and therefore at age 18 the expectation of life will be of the order of 14 or 15 years. This figure can be compared with expectation of life figures derived from Dr. Wells' skeletal data.

These data (*Bones, Bodies and Disease*, p. 179) are the ages at death of persons buried in such groups as reflect the life of a community— village cemeteries and so forth—and Dr. Wells' numbers may be translated into expectation of life figures thus:

Population	Expectation of Life at Age 18* in Years
Chalcolithic Anatolians	13.9
Ancient Romans	13.0
Early Texas Indians	19.4
Norfolk Anglo-Saxons	16.3
Aebelholt Medievals	12.9

*Mean of the two sexes.

This range of figures from 12.9 to 19.4 years suggests that our model figure of 14 or 15 years is very reasonable and that therefore so are the estimated death rates on which it is based.

It is therefore reasonable to suppose that our series of estimated death-rates from 10 years of age onwards is a serviceable model for ancient populations, and in different parts is either derived from or supported by the skeletal evidence: that is to say, for these age-groups we have now that measure of external evidence which we desire.

To make this measure fully useful, however, we need to complete it by finding figures for the first ten years of life, and here the skeletal material deserts us, for the fragility of young bones means that there are few remains, while social habits in the disposal of children's corpses are often very different from those common in the disposal of adults, so that any remains may not be found together with those of adults of the same population. This last part of our model therefore has to be constructed out of demographic material only, that is, out of assumptions proper to our model as so far constructed, and general demographic regularities applied to our model quantities.

iv. The death-rate up to age 10 (the birth rate): a. Assumptions. In our model population so far, the number of persons who survive their fiftieth birthday is negligible. This means that, for our population as

123

a whole, we can assume certain demographic concepts and techniques which would apply only to males or only to females in a population with a different age-structure.

We shall assume that:

1. the sexes are exactly equal in all respects;

2. the same number of boys and girls are born in any interval;

3. the death-rates for males and females are identical;

4. at the birth of any child the ages of its parents coincide, or at least that the average age of the parents is equal.

In the analysis of any actual population, these assumptions might lead to several errors, because:

1. the number of boys born is usually a little larger than the number of girls;

2. in societies without modern medical facilities the death rate of women at all ages tends to be rather higher than for men;

3. the marriage age for men tends to be rather higher than for women by some two to five years.

The combined effects of all our assumptions is however emphatically not likely to effect the validity of our model to any marked degree; in particular, the distribution of the extent to which children survive their parents will not vary by more than one or two percentage points in any age-group.

b. Mathematics. In our life-table as constructed so far, the 100 children of 10 years of age expect to live, altogether, for 1,810 man-years. For a stable population, this is the same as saying that if there are 100 persons reaching ten years, the total model population of ten years and over is 1,810 persons.

On the assumption given above, these 1,810 persons will be 905 male and 905 female; and the number of persons under ten years of age in such a population is given an upper limit by the age-structure of this population of 905 females.

The years between ages 15 and 49 are usually taken as the conventional period for child-bearing, so that we need a quinquennial age-structure of our 1,810 persons. For convenience, let us round the

124

total to 1,820 persons; and then the quinquennial age-structure may be represented by interpolation thus:

Quinquennial Age	Number of Persons	
10–14	465 ⎫	
15–19	390 ⎭	855
20–24	315 ⎫	
25–29	245 ⎭	560
30–34	180 ⎫	
35–39	120 ⎭	300
40–44	70 ⎫	
45–49	30 ⎭	100
50 and over	5	

On this distribution there are 675 women of child-bearing age in this stable population at any one time. Our problem is to make some guess about the number of children they are likely to bear in any given year, and we approach this by a series of successively smaller maxima.

The *mathematically maximum fertility* of 675 women is 675 births on the day or in the year under consideration. But the *demographically maximum fertility* is smaller than this, because fertility is not evenly distributed throughout the range of 15 to 49 years: it rises, reaches a peak about age 27, and then declines. Empirical formulae have been derived to measure this variation in several aspects, and from one of these formulae;

$$\frac{\text{fertility at age N}}{\substack{\text{fertility at age of} \\ \text{maximum fertility} \\ \text{(taken here as 27 years)}}} = \left(\frac{N-15}{12}\right) \left(\frac{50-N}{23}\right)^{\frac{23}{12}}$$

it is possible to calculate that the demographically maximum fertility is approximately two-thirds of the number of births given by mathematically maximum fertility. But, once more, the *biologically maximum fertility* is less than this, because suckling and other consequences of birth mean that a woman's fertility is limited to (at most) about one birth in two years. There may also be social limits on fertility,

125

but leaving these aside, the upper limit for the number of births in our model population is of the order of $(675 \times \frac{2}{3} \times \frac{1}{2})$ per annum, that is, 225 births a year.

If we round this down to 200 per annum we shall still have a very high figure, but one that does not pass the bounds of credibility. When placed in the series with the rest of our model numbers, it gives us of course a death rate of 50 percent in the first ten years of life, which seems broadly compatible with the other figures, on the assumptions we have been using.

v. The life-table. We can now construct several complete series of figures for our hypothetical population in terms of 1,000 children born. Interpolation for five-year age-groups presents no difficulty and calls for no special comment, except to note that we assume that childhood mortality is concentrated in the earliest years. The quantitative series are given in Table X below, and illustrated in Figure i.

TABLE X

QUANTITIES OF THE MODEL POPULATION

Age	Number of Survivors at age	Total Population in each Quinquennium		Expectation of Life at Age (in Years)*
0	1000	4,125	7,000	16.1
5	650	2,875		18.4
10	500	2,313	4,250	18.1
15	425	1,937		15.9
20	350	1,575	2,800	13.8
25	280	1,225		11.6
30	210	900	1,488	9.6
35	150	588		7.5
40	85	350	512	6.3
45	55	162		3.4
50	10	25		2.5

*It may be noted that the expectation of life under ancient Greek conditions has been examined by J. L. Angel ('The Length of Life in Ancient Greece' in *Journal of Gerontology* 2 (1947) 18 ff.) using the evidence from skeletal material (384 skulls covering the period 3500 B.C. to A.D.1300). His approximate estimates are of the order of: 17–21 years at birth; 19–24 years at age 10; then steadily declining to about 10 at age 30, about 6 at age 40. These figures refer to *males* only. The close correspondence between his estimates and those indicated here suggest that the model used in this study is by no means inconsistent with archeological evidence.

On these figures of a stable population, the birth-rate is 1,000/16,075 or 62.2 per mille, and, in a stable population this is of course also the death-rate overall. The figure is high without being fantastic: the typical birth-rate today in advanced countries is of the order of 20 per thousand; at the beginning of this century it was of the order of 40 per thousand, and – if we may speak without at all overlooking the deficiencies of census figures in such circumstances – a birth rate of around 60 per thousand has often been estimated for illiterate rural populations.

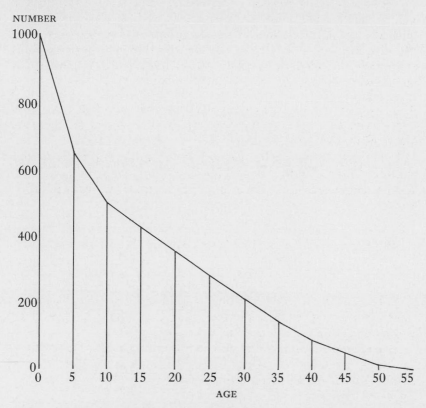

Figure 1: Age-distribution of the Model Population.

Table X is therefore our Ancient Model. It is constructed entirely from biological (mainly skeletal) and demographic evidence, and is quite independent of any written records (which will prevent any circularity of argument later). It contains, as a demographic assump-

127

tion, a reproduction period of 27 years within a population most of whose members were dead by the age of 40, and nearly all by the age of 50 years. Yet, so far as the evidence goes, it appears that populations of this age and fertility structure represent by far the majority of the human race, past and present. We may therefore usefully spend some time in preparing a device that will enable us to see how a population governed by these quantities would work out in practice.

vi. Derivation of a random experimental card-index. We need a device which would present us with pictures of a number of families, such that in sum the life-spans and reproductive ages would make up the quantities of our Ancient Model. The simplest device for this purpose is a Random experimental card-Index, which is constructed as follows:

1. It is given by the Ancient Model that out of 1,000 boys born 425 survive to age 15; of these, 75 die in the interval 15–20 years, 70 in the interval 20–25, and so on.

Take 425 cards, number them 1 to 425 in the top right corner. Assume 15 die in 16th year, 15 die in 17th year, and so on. Put in top left corner a number corresponding to year in which each dies, thus:

16	1

2. It is given by the Ancient Model that these 425 males will produce 1,000 sons, born over the reproductive span of the group: 169 in the age-range 16th year to 20th year, and so on.

Divide these quinquennial numbers into single years, say 25 born to fathers in their 16th years. Select 25 cards at random (e.g. by shuffling pack and selecting each 15th card); and write on the cards selected '16' below top left corner, thus:

43	362
16	

128

This means that the 362nd card represents a person who dies in his 43rd year and has a son born in his 16th year.

3. Now discard all cards with 16 at top left; re-shuffle, select appropriate number for births to parents in 17th years; and thus work through the whole pack.

A typical card at the end of this process will be as follows:

```
┌─────────────────────────┐
│  36          283        │
│                         │
│  19                     │
│                         │
│  21                     │
│                         │
│  31                     │
│                         │
│  33                     │
└─────────────────────────┘
```

The 283rd card: person born in year 0 dies in year 36; his sons born in the years 19, 21, 31, and 33.

We have now recorded the births of 1,000 sons who form the second generation; and must next record their deaths.

4. It is given by the Ancient Model that out of 1,000 sons born, 350 die before reaching the age of 5 years. We may assume the life-table to run:

Year   Number of Persons Alive

0	1000		125 died in first year.
1	875		75	second
2	800	which equals	50	third
3	750		50	fourth
4	700		50	fifth
5	650			

Assume further that of the 125 children dying before their first birth-

129

day, 75 die in the same calendar year and 50 in the following calendar year, and so on, then:

born in year N: 1000
died in year N: 75
died in year (N+1)   50+40
                 (N+2)   35+25
                 (N+3)   25+25

and so on.

Select at random from the shuffled pack (excluding those cards which show no children born) 75 cards (extracted one by one and returned after marking) and on each write against one child's birth date 'O' thus:

```
36              283

19
21  0
31
33
```

Here there are four children to choose from; a convenient way of determining which one to mark is by the use of dice.

The card as now marked means that the child born in year 21 died in the same year.

5. If we proceed in this way until a death-date is assigned to every child, the final appearance of the card will be:

```
36              283

19  27
21   0
31  41
33  11
```

130

Every such card is a two-generation male genealogy; our example would be rendered as in the genealogical table below.

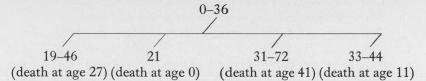

| 19–46 | 21 | 31–72 | 33–44 |
| (death at age 27) | (death at age 0) | (death at age 41) | (death at age 11) |

That is, one son dies in infancy and three survive their father, of whom one dies a child; and two reach maturity.

Every set of cards made up with a Random Index in this way will of course differ in detail, but each set will illustrate an operation of the model quantities for two generations of one of the sexes. In the following discussions we shall be using one set throughout; the reader who has prepared his own set or sets may usefully repeat these discussions.

vii. Non-quantitative evidence. In all the ancient and many of the modern communities to which the Ancient Model or approximations to it may usefully apply, there is to be found non-quantitative information on the existence and treatment of some of its component and implied problems. Much of this information is vague, and the laws and customs concerned could exist in almost any population structure (apart from that of the most advanced modern communities); other information is more specific, and the laws and customs concerned seem to be much illuminated by consideration of the matters with which they deal, with the aid of the Ancient Model. For these purposes, the quantities of the Ancient Model need not be taken as directly applying to the community in question; it is sufficient if we suppose that the quantities are those towards which the community was always tending to fall in times of natural disaster (famine and plague) or historical eclipse (loss of empire).

For classical Athens, we have some information on legal and customary ages in the life of the male of citizen status. The first registration of his existence was not at birth, but at the age of three or four years; and the registering body was not the state or local government unit, but his father's phratry, a 'kinship' organization. The registration involved acceptance or rejection of the father's oath that the child was his, and legitimate: this was a religious as well as a civil ceremony. The age at which it was customarily conducted is illu-

131

minated by the high death-rate for the infantile quinquennium in the Ancient Model—we may suppose that parental optimism made the age as low as possible in face of the experience of the incidence of infantile mortality, and the cost of the customary sacrifice.

The legal age of puberty was 16 years for the male citizen; he came of age, entered his two years of military training, and could marry at 18 years; he could vote at 20 years and hold political office at 30 years. The late age of puberty, though a legal and not a physiological quantity, could possibly be ascribed to a recognition of fact (and then would perhaps be related to a far from modern level of nutrition), but is at least as likely to be due to a desire not to put adult burdens on young shoulders, and the feeling that the provisions for guardianship were adequate.

Although a citizen could vote at the age of 20, he was not eligible for office until he was 30. Full political rights and responsibilities therefore were exercised, even in the 'extreme democracy' of Athens, only by those men who survived to the age of considerable discretion (though the Assembly of all voters could be stampeded). The Ancient Model gives 1,012 men of 30 and over out of a total population of 16,075, or 6.3 percent; and however much we increase this proportion for the days of Athenian prosperity, it is clear that, generally, actual responsibility for public affairs fell on a small portion of the citizen population, among whom 'extreme democracy' avoided, no doubt, much friction.

The quantities of the Ancient Model also seem to illuminate the concept of the *oikos* or 'house' which, so far as can be made out, was clearly but not rigidly understood by the Athenians. 'The oikos of X' seems to have consisted of X as a mature man and leader, in economic activity and social relations, of a number of kinsfolk and dependents; and on the figures of the Ancient Model this number would average 15—aged parents, widowed pregnant sisters-in-law, younger brothers and sisters, widowed or divorced elder sisters, orphaned nephews and nieces and cousins, as well as X's own wife and children. Again, however much we modify this figure for imperial Athens, it is clear that the *oikos* was this kind of institution.[2]

There is also a group of laws which gives us much less vague in-

---

[2] Xenophon's story (*Mem. Soc.* 2.7.2.) of the household of fifteen unemployed in the days of Athenian disaster illustrates our figures very neatly.

formation on family and kindred organization, and which are correspondingly illuminated by the quantities of the Ancient Model (taken, as above, as quantities to which the population tended to fall). These laws are those concerned with the protection and redistribution of surviving children, and the quantities which can be relevantly abstracted from the Random Index are given in Table XI.

TABLE XI

TYPES OF PATERNITY ACHIEVED BY MEN OF 16 OR MORE YEARS IN THE MODEL POPULATION

Father's Age at Death	Number of Cases in Which					
	0 Sons Born	All sons minors and pre-decease father	All survivors die before 16	All 16+ sons pre-decease	All 16+ sons mature after father's death	At least one son 16+ at father's death
16–19	54	0	3	0	3	0
20–24	40	12	14	0	6	0
25–29	12	14	15	0	27	0
30–34	2	16	15	0	29	0
35–39	1	13	12	0	23	15
40–44	0	10	6	0	11	12
45–49	1	7	1	1	8	23
50+	0	9	0	1	3	6
TOTAL	110	81	66	2	110	56

(1) Athenian law distinguished modes of inheritance primarily into those which required a legal process and those which did not. The latter class comprised only those cases where a man died with a son or sons of mature age (18 years or more): in such cases the heirs entered upon their patrimony (all sons sharing equally) without reference to the courts. In all other types of succesion the courts were in one way or another concerned.

The relevant quantities of the Ancient Model and Random Index on this point are the 13 percent (56/425) of men who are succeeded

133

by mature sons, and the 87 percent of men who are not. However much more favorable the Athenian balance between the two classes of heirs, the quantities of the Model serve to illuminate the fundamental legal distinction.

(2) Inheritances which required a legal process were of three principal kinds: (a) minority successions, (b) collateral inheritances, and (c) adoptions.

(a) Minority inheritances required the appointment of guardians or trustees under the supervision of the titular head of state (the archon eponymos) and the courts. The relevant quantity in the Ancient Model is the combination of the 66 cases where minors survive their fathers but die before reaching 16 years, and the 110 cases where minor surviving sons attain maturity after the father's death: 176/425 or nearly 42 percent of inheritances. Even if we reduce the proportion for historical athens to a third, a quarter, or a fifth of all inheritances, the quantities of the Ancient Model still illuminate the size of the problem met by the laws for the protection of minors.

(b) Collateral inheritances included in Athens a special sub-class in which the heir male was required to marry or dower the heiress of line. This special sub-class does not appear in the quantities of our Ancient Model. Other collateral inheritances required either (i) proof before the courts that the claiment was within five (bilateral) degrees of kinship to the decedent; or (ii) decision by the courts between such claimants; or (iii) proof that no such persons existed, when the inheritance went to the nearest agnate of any degree. In the Ancient Model the relevant quantities are the 110 men who have no sons, the 81 men who have no surviving sons, and (ultimately) the 66 men whose surviving sons die during their minority: 257/425 or nearly 61 percent of all inheritances. Again however much we reduce this proportion for Athens, it is clear that the courts exercised their discretion over a substantial proportion of the inheritances in each generation.

(c) As a counterforce to this public decision of the destination of inheritances there existed the device of adoption, of which three modes were present: adoption during the lifetime, adoption by will, and posthumous affiliation by the kindred of one of their members as son to the deceased kinsman. Since all sons succeeded equally, adoption was frequently a means of redistributing children among the lineages of a kindred, maintaining the existing divisions of prop-ery rather than creating new ones, and reducing the proportion of legally collateral inheritances: 'keeping the number of *oikoi* constant'.

This proliferation of modes of adoption is remarkable, and is partly explained as due to the desire to avoid determination of the destination of property by the courts. But this of course implies that the proportion of men who were not succeeded by sons of their body was considerable.

In the light of these family laws as compared with the Ancient-Model quantities, we can more clearly appreciate the importance of the kindred. In Athens this consisted of all persons of five degrees or less of kinship; among the Dorian Greeks it seems to have extended to seven degrees. This kindred or cousinhood had corporate res-ponsibilities in matters of homicide, and may supposed to have of-ten acted corporately in questions of marriage and adoption; in some respects it was regarded as a body of interrelated *oikoi*. The age-struc-ture of the Ancient Model and its particular results in types of pater-nity (once more, however much we modify them for Athens) suggest that *oikoi* and linages required the support of the kindreds for the pro-tection of orphans and the provision of substitute children through adoption, and that they could scarcely have continued to exist as identifiable social entities without that support. In the Model, out of the 166 cases where sons (immediately or ultimately) succeed their fathers, 110 cases (67 percent) show a period of orphanage. However much we reduce this figure for Athens, it seems probable that there were few men of, say, over thirty years of age who had not at some time been either wards or guardians, and many must have had ex-perience of both states.

These non-quantitative pieces of evidence suggest that even imperial Athens had a population structure not unlike that of our Ancient Model, and that her family laws were in part designed to provide for situations implicit in such a structure. Non-imperial Greek states, or less favoured sections of imperial populations, pre-sumably approximated more closely to the Ancient Model than did the Athenian citizenry.

B. DEMOGRAPHY AND HISTORICAL TIME. All encoun-ters between demography and history involve historical time, which is not among the foundations of demographic models of stable populations, but indispensable to all histories. Taken strictly, this

135

difference between the two disciplines means that demography is equally interested in all the classes, sections, and groups of the population so far as measurement of their lives is concerned, while history is to a high degree especially interested in children who survive their parents and replace them in the institutional pattern which they maintain or modify. A quantitative question of common interest to both disciplines is therefore that of the proportion of children who survive their parents, and the proportion of parents survived by at least one child.

The maintenance or modification of institutional patterns is a subject which can only be sensibly discussed on the basis of a knowledge of the opportunities (open to the people concerned) to do either; and one of the opportunities is the time available. One question which history can ask of demography therefore is that of how long surviving children survive their parent.

The relationships between individual accident and the maintenance or modification of institutions is one of the ways in which the subject-matter of history could be described; and wherever the membership of an institution has been hereditary (in whole or in part) demography can assist history by determining certain quantities and ensuring that history, unaided, does not infer false quantities. We have in this field a group of interrelated quantities:

(1) The reproductive period, or demographers' 'generation': how long, in the circumstances of the given population, it takes a man to produce a man to succeed him in the population. This is a non-institutional quantity, except in so far as the 'population' may be institutionally defined, for instance, as the members of some state.

(2) The survival period in a direct line, that is, ignoring collateral ancestors of the last known member of a descent. This average is obtained by adding together the years of survival by each son of his father in the direct line, and dividing by the number of cases of such survival; it is not the same quantity as the next and is non-institutional except in so far as the 'population' may be institutionally defined.

(3) The foregoing direct-line or ithagenic quantities of the average reproductive and average survival periods are demographic rather than historical in that they are, in a certain sense, non-institutional. Another quantity is the ithagenic dividend, or the result obtained

136

when the total years of a dynasty (or some other hereditary institution) is divided by the number of persons in the direct ancestry of the last member. This is institutional in that the total number of years is institutionally determined: in the case of a dynasty, the years of its founder before the foundation are not counted, and the years (if any) of the last member after its fall are not counted; it is demographic in that where a son predeceased his father, and that son's son continues the direct line, the predecessor is counted as one of the persons in the divisor. Thus a grandfather ruling for 20 years succeeded by a grandson (son of a predeceased son) who rules for 40 years, together rule for 60 years: the divisor comprises three persons and the ithagenic dividend is 20 years. The ithagenic dividend is the length of time, on the average and in the circumstances of the given institution, that it takes a hereditary member to produce a hereditary member to replace him. This is the historians' 'generation' and by its nature it is always an empirical fact, unique and applicable to its own population only, not part of a demographic model.

Since it is not, and cannot be, part of a demographic model, demographic inferences from it are impermissible. For example, if an ithagenic dividend is 20 years, it cannot simply be assumed that either the reproductive period or the survival period of that population was 20 years.

What is permissible is comparison of the average survival period with the ithagenic dividend, and examination of possible or evidenced reasons for their identity or divergence. But where they are identical, no inference is permissible about the value of the reproductive period: there are too many possibilities. Without very much more information it is impossible to choose between the following cases:

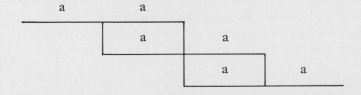

(i) a situation where, on the average, a grandfather is dying not only at the time his son is succeeding, but also at the time his grandson is being born;

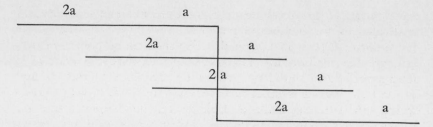

(ii) a situation where, on the average, a great-grandfather dies at the time his great-grandson is born;

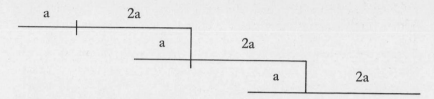

(iii) a situation where, on the average, sons who succeed are born after their fathers succeed;
or any particular mixture of these possibilities.

Comparison of the various quantities given by the dated genealogies of historical successions is chiefly useful in relation to some such measure as the Ancient Model. Points of divergence and identity within the quantities for any succession suggest questions, and more and wider questions are suggested by comparison of the empirical quantities with such a demographic construct. In this part of our enquiry therefore we shall be concerned with five quantities in the Ancient Model and some historical material. The quantities are:

(1) the proportion of children born who survive their parent;

(2) the average period of survival, and distribution of survival periods;

(3) the average ithagenic survival period, and distribution of these periods;

(4) the average reproductive periods;

(5) the ithagenic dividend.

The historical material chosen for this experiment consists of two kinds. From the ancient world there is now available the dated genealogical record of the last seventy kings of Assyria who (in two dynasties) ruled for a thousand years.[3]

As historical samples go, this is sizeable, though of course by demographic standards it is minute. From the medieval world (and in some cases continuing later) we have five well-documented Moslem dynasties of various types and circumstances: the Abbasid Caliphs; the imperial Ottomans and Moguls; the Nasrids of Granada and the Khans of the Crimea in western and northern frontier provinces.[4]

These can be compared with one another and, as a body, with the Assyrians in the historical material; and with the Ancient Model and a modern model in the demographic material.

For a special enquiry under the head of the ithagenic reproductive period, there is also the historical material of the Kings of Judah.[5]

i. The proportion of children born who survive their parent in the Ancient Model. To discover this quantity, the first step is to determine the distribution of births to the parents' age-groups, remembering that the age-structure of our Model is such that figures are interchangeable between the sexes. With a total population of 2,000 at the Model death-rates, we should have the age-distribution:

Age (years)	Number of Persons of Both Sexes
0–4	512
5–9	358
10–14	288
15–19	242
20–24	196
25–29	152
30–34	112
35–39	74
40–44	44
45–49	18
50 and over	4

[3] A. Poebel 'The Asyrian King-List from Khorsabad' in *Journal of Near Eastern Studies* 1 (1942) 247ff, 460 ff. and 2 (1943) 56 ff., Albright *American Journal of Archaeology* 47 (1943) 491 ff.
[4] S. Lane-Poole *The Mohammedan Dynasties* (London 1894).
[5] E. R. Thiele 'Chronology of the Kings of Judah and Israel' in *Journal of Near Eastern Studies* 3 (1944) 137 ff.

Therefore the 418 women from 15 to 49 years of age will have a total of 124 children annually.[6]

These will be distributed to the mothers' age-groups in accordance with the rise and decline of fertility as follows:

Age of Mothers (years)	Number of Children
15–19	21
20–24	38
25–29	34
30–34	22
35–39	7
40–44	2
45–49	0

On the basis of these figures we can now calculate the children who survive their parent.

If we take the group of children born in one year as 124 in a total population of 2,000, the number of them who will die in the first five years, the next five years, and so forth is determinable from the Model death-rates: age $0 = 124$ survivors; age $5 = 124 \times 0.650 = 81$ survivors; age $10 = 124 \times 0.500 = 63$ survivors, and so forth.

We can calculate the number of the batch of 124 mothers who will die in the first, second, and succeeding quinquennia. Out of the group of 242 persons aged 15–19 years, 196 will survive to form the group aged 20–24 years five years later; so 46 will die in the next five years; therefore out of the group of 21 parents aged 15–19, the number that will die in the next five years is $21 \times \dfrac{46}{242} = 3$, and so on.

These two calculations give the following figures.

Quinquennia	Number of Survivors	
	Children	Parents
at given date	124	124
1. after 5 years	81	91
2. after 10 years	63	62
3. after 15 years	53	38

[6] $418 \times \frac{2}{3} \times \frac{1}{2} \times$ (for rounding down) $\frac{8}{9}$; see above p.126.

4. after 20 years	43	20
5. after 25 years	35	8
6. after 30 years	26	2
7. after 35 years	19	0
8. after 40 years	11	
9. after 45 years	7	
10. after 50 years	1	
11. after 55 years	0	

The next step is to translate these figures into probabilities of death in the five-year periods. If there are 124 persons at a given date, and 81 of them are still alive five years later, the probability of any random individual dying in the five-year period is $43/124 = 0.347$, and so on. We can thus construct a list in which the probability of a parent's death in a period is $P(n)$, and the probability of a child's death is $C(n)$:

n	C(n)	P(n)
As 1 above	0.347	0.266
2	0.145	0.234
3	0.081	0.194
4	0.081	0.145
5	0.065	0.097
6	0.073	0.048
7	0.056	0.016
8	0.065	
9	0.032	
10	0.048	
11	0.008	

The probability of a child dying in the same quinquennium as its parent will then be $\Sigma P(n).C(n)$ for all values of n from 1 to 7, that is $(0.266 \times 0.347) + (0.234 \times 0.145) + (0.194 \times 0.081) + (0.097 \times 0.065) + (0.048 \times 0.073) + (0.016 \times 0.056)$, which equals > 0.164. That is to say, the chances that a child will die in the same quinquennium as its parent are about one in six.

The chances that a child will die in an earlier quinquennium than its parents will be $\Sigma P(n).C(n)$ where n is greater than m; and the corresponding probability for a child dying in a period later than its parent will be the same expression, but with m greater than n. The

141

numerical values are: for a child dying earlier; 0.370, and for a child dying later; 0.466.

If we assume that when parent and child die in the same quinquennium it is equally likely which of them dies first, then for our model population $0.370+0.082=0.452$ or 45 percent of children die before their parent, and $0.466+0.082=0.548$ or 55 percent survive their parent.

ii. Historical material. From the quantities of the Ancient Model therefore we derive the information that in such a population 55 percent of the children born survive their parents. From the Random Index of the same population we are informed (in Table XI above) that 55 percent of persons attaining maturity are survived by children, 26 percent are childless, and 19 per cent are predeceased by their children.

When we turn to our historical material, we must of course first note the great selectiveness of the records. In the Assyrian case for example, the genealogies of the two dynasties include only three men who did not reign. This means that all the sons of a polygamous dynasty have passed through a political sieve before reaching the records, and the great majority therefore are unknown. What we have in such records is an institutionally determined sample of a population; and *a priori* we have no reason to believe in any single case that the institutional effect would reinforce or diverge from the unknown demographic quantities of this population.

The records give the following figures as listed below:

Dynasty	Percentage of Men Survived by Son(s)	
Assyrians	64	
Abbasids	62	
Nasrids	61	
Ottomans	65	59%
Moguls	54	
Crimeans	47	

In some of these cases we know, and in others may reasonably suspect, that there was a higher level of attention to continuation of the lines than we may take for granted in the general population. Even the strict and curious customs of the Ottomans however fail to raise the

142

sample figure more than 10 percent above the 55 percent of the Random Index, and among the anarchic Crimeans the figure falls towards the 42.5 percent of children born who reach maturity in our Ancient Model.

Comparison of the institutionally determined samples with the figures of the Ancient Model therefore suggests that there is very little distortion due to the selectivity of the records; and that divergence of these royal populations from the Model figures is due to the institutional efforts made to secure continuation of lines. The relative slightness of the effect of elaborate and expensive institutional effect is noteworthy.

An important inference follows from this comparison. If between one-half and two-thirds of persons are on the average survived by children, then in a royal genealogy we should expect on the average something like three reigns in two generations: two kings of one line, and a collateral kinsman (elder brother dying childless or the like). Long runs of father-to-son inheritance, uninterrupted by collaterals, are therefore to be suspected, and the number beyond which suspicion is to become active is suggested by the following documented long runs of this kind:

Crimeans: none
Nasrids: last three inheritances
Abbasids: last six inheritances
Assyrians: seven inheritances (kings 72–79)[7]
Moguls: first eight inheritances
Ottomans: nine inheritances (Nos.7–16)
Assyrians: ten inheritances (kings 95–105)[7]

It is thus a guiding rule that any alleged run of more than ten inheritances without collaterals is either an ithagenic abstract from the complete genealogy, or a fiction, or both. A case in point is the Herodotean 22 successive Lydian inheritances παῖς παρὰ πατρός this is either an ithagenic abstract from a genealogy containing collaterals or a fiction. (Herodotus' Spartan lists are not open to this objection, for they claim to be ithagenic lists.)

---

[7] This demographic analysis suggests that, if the 'high Assyrian chronology' is correct, the errors or omissions of the king list are most likely to have occurred in these parts.

iii. Survival periods: distributions and averages. We can now calculate, for our Model population, the extent of survival of those who survive their parent. Taking the whole group of survivors (55 percent of all the children) as 100 percent, the calculation gives the distribution indicated below.

Extent of Survival in Years*	Percentage of Survivors
0–4	23 ⎫ 38 ⎫
5–9	15 ⎭ ⎬ 63
10–14	13 ⎫ ⎭
15–19	12 ⎭ 25
20–24	11 ⎫ 20 ⎫
25–29	9 ⎭ ⎬ 37
30–34	7 ⎫ ⎭
35–39	5 ⎭ 12
40–44	3 ⎫ 5
45–	2 ⎭

*The overall average survival period is about 15 years.

iv. Historical material. The two Assyrian dynasties correspond very roughly to the Bronze and Iron Age periods of Assyrian history, and the 61 known pairs of dated father and son (31 in the senior and 30 in the junior dynasty) show the distribution of survival periods as given below.

144

Extent of survival in Years	Percentage of survivors		
	Senior	Junior	Overall
0–9	23 ⎱ 72	26.7 ⎱ 53.4	25 ⎱ 59
10–19	49 ⎰	26.7 ⎰	34 ⎰
20–29	3 ⎱	26.7 ⎱	16 ⎱
30–39	16 ⎸ 28	10 ⎸ 46.6	15 ⎸ 41
40–49	6 ⎸	3.3 ⎸	5 ⎸
50+	3 ⎰	6.6 ⎰	5 ⎰

*The overall average survival period is about 20 years.

Comparison of the two Assyrian dynasties with one another shows a considerable difference in the distributions, and this of course raises the question of whether the samples are large enough for such differences to be significant and whether the differences in these figures are supported by the difference in other figures still to

Extent of Survival in Years	Percentage of Survivors					
	Abbasids	Nasrids	Ottomans	Moguls	Crimeans	Overall
0–9	28 ⎱ 53	28 ⎱ 42	15 ⎱ 33	57 ⎱ 57	17 ⎱ 36	26 ⎱ 43
10–19	25 ⎰	14 ⎰	18 ⎰	0 ⎰	19 ⎰	17 ⎰
20–29	12.5 ⎱	42 ⎱	15 ⎱	13 ⎱	14 ⎱	17 ⎱
30–39	22 ⎸ 47	8 ⎸ 58	25 ⎸ 67	13 ⎸ 43	25 ⎸ 64	20 ⎸ 57
40–49	9.5 ⎸	0 ⎸	15 ⎸	17 ⎸	6 ⎸	10 ⎸
50+	3 ⎰	8 ⎰	12 ⎰	0 ⎰	19 ⎰	10 ⎰

be examined; if so, whether the differences are apparent only, due to some change in succession law or practice, or to a real increase in longevity. Comparison of the Assyrians with the Ancient Model shows, among other matters, that the first decade of survival among the Assyrians is not the most populous as it is in the Ancient Model, and we may be right here in suspecting an institutional effect—the choice of the most robust among the available candidates.

The Moslem dynasties show the distributions as given on p. 145.

The overall average survival period is 25.5 years, and for the separate dynasties this period is: Abbasids, 22.3 years, Nasrids, 22.5 years, Ottomans, 28.6 years, Moguls, 17.3 years, Crimeans, 31.6 years. The Abbasids and Nasrids resemble the Ancient Model in that the first decade of survival is more populous than the second, but differ from it in that there is not a steady decline thereafter; the Ottomans and Crimeans may show the institutional effect of choice of robust candidates; the Moguls seem to show to a high degree an institutional effect of a period of dynastic dissension early in the eighteenth century. As we shall see, the ithagenic survival period distribution gives a rather different picture.

To the historian, survival periods and their distribution are gen-

Extent of Survival in Years	Percentage of Survivors			
	Ancient Model	Assyrian dynasties	Moslem dynasties	Modern model
0–9	38 ⎱63	25 ⎱59	26 ⎱43	8 ⎱21
10–19	25 ⎰	34 ⎰	17 ⎰	13 ⎰
20–29	20	16	17	19
30–39	12 ⎱37	15 ⎱41	20 ⎱57	22 ⎱79
40–49	5	5	10	19
50+	0	5	10	19
Average survival period (years):	15	20	25.5	34

146

erally interesting in that they delimit one kind of opportunity—the time available—for the maintenance or modification of institutions. In the above distribution tables, in addition to the distribution by decade of survival, each column is also divided into percentages of survival of less and more than 20 years, on a convention or assumption that a man may learn enough to continue his father's acts in less than 20 years, and have after 20 years enough experience both to continue and to innovate accumulably. From this point of view, the empirical figures show a steady historical trend towards enlargement of opportunity (See p. 146.).

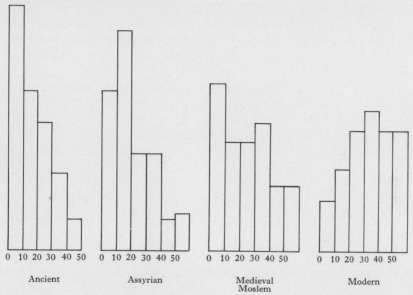

Figure 2. Distribution of Survival Periods.

In the Ancient and modern models the populations concerned are large and cover practitioners of all arts, not only those of war and government: the difference in the opportunity for accumulation of knowledge and experience from the increase of longevity alone (quite apart from literacy and similar matters) is obviously great. A number of the Moslem dynasties are said to have been weak and debauched; and the Greeks said the same about the Assyrians (whose own records give a different account): one of the values of these quantitative studies is that they suggest that such qualitative statements may require re-examination.

147

v. Ithagenic survival periods: distributions and averages. Our historical material enables us to abstract from each dynastic record the direct line of descent (from the founder) of the last member. There is no such information in our Ancient Model, but we may, for comparative purposes, elicit some information which is to some degree comparable: the distribution of extents of survival by the 394 persons who, in the Random Index, both survive their sixteenth birthdays and survive their fathers. This distribution is given below.

Extent of Survival in Years	Percentage of Survivors
0–9	17 ⎫
	⎬ 48
10–19	31 ⎭
20–29	25 ⎫
30–39	20 ⎪
	⎬ 52
40–49	7 ⎪
50+	0 ⎭

Survival here is almost equally divided between less and more than 20 years; the peak decade, nevertheless, is the second.

vi. Historical material. In the direct line of descent, the two Assyrian dynasties show the distribution of survival periods given below.

Extent of Survival in Years	Percentage of Survivors		
	Senior	Junior	Overall
0–9	11 ⎫	15 ⎫	13 ⎫
	⎬ 58	⎬ 35	⎬ 46
10–19	47 ⎭	20 ⎭	33 ⎭
20–29	5 ⎫	35 ⎫	20 ⎫
30–39	26 ⎪	15 ⎪	21 ⎪
	⎬ 42	⎬ 65	⎬ 54
40–49	11 ⎪	5 ⎪	8 ⎪
50+	0 ⎭	10 ⎭	5 ⎭

The overall distribution is very similar to that of the roughly comparable figures from the Ancient Model, and the figures of the senior dynasty provide a rather extreme example of this kind of distribution. In the junior dynasty however another type of distribution appears, in which the peak decade is the third, and the population of the first two decades is little more than half of that of the rest. This shift in the distribution may be due to (1) mere accident, or an apparently coincidental effect of a number of minor causes (improvements in diet, in selection of mothers of the heirs, better sanitation and water supply in the palaces, and so forth); (2) a change in the succession rules (such as a new preference for a son of a wife, even if a minor, over sons of concubines, even though mature); (3) an increase in real longevity in a privileged population.

To these dubieties in general it is in turn doubtful whether one should add the historical evidence of some unwontedness in the succession of one of the longest survivors, Tiglath Pileser III, who lived for 56 years after his father died. It was for long believed that he had no genealogical connection with his immediate predecessors, whose monuments were defaced; and it remains difficult to believe that none of his three elder brothers had sons.

Extent of Survival in Years	Percentage of Survivors					
	Abbasid	Nasrid	Ottoman	Mogul	Crimean	Overall
0–9	6 ⎤	25 ⎤	16 ⎤	18 ⎤	25 ⎤	16 ⎤
	⎬ 46	⎬ 25	⎬ 32	⎬ 18	⎬ 25	⎬ 32
10–19	40 ⎦	0 ⎦	16 ⎦	0 ⎦	0 ⎦	16 ⎦
20–29	14 ⎤	50 ⎤	16 ⎤	27 ⎤	25 ⎤	21 ⎤
30–39	20 ⎪	25 ⎪	32 ⎪	18 ⎪	25 ⎪	24 ⎪
	⎬ 54	⎬ 75	⎬ 68	⎬ 82	⎬ 75	⎬ 68
40–49	14 ⎪	0 ⎪	10 ⎪	37 ⎪	12.5 ⎪	15 ⎪
50+	6 ⎦	0 ⎦	10 ⎦	0 ⎦	12.5 ⎦	7 ⎦
Average ithagenic survival period (years)	28	23	28	30	31	28.5

149

The average ithagenic survival period for the senior dynasty is 23.95 years; that for the junior dynasty is 25.55 years unless we exclude the 56 years of Tiglath Pileser, in which case the average for the junior dynasty is the same as that for the senior, in spite of the shift in the distribution figures.

Comparison between the distributions, and of the distributions with the averages, raises here a number of problems, the chief of which is whether institutional effects have in fact occurred.

In the direct lines of descent, the Moslem dynasties show quantities as given on p. 149.

There are some curious relationships between these figures. The Nasrid ithagenic average is about the same as the Assyrian but could be neglected because of the smallness of the sample (four generations of direct descent) if it were not for the fact that the Abbasid average is somewhat misleading, since that ithageny contains two sons who predeceased their fathers; had they survived for a short time, the average Abbasid survival period would be very near the Nasrid.

On the quantities alone therefore, the Moslem dynasties would seem to fall into two groups, the Arabic and the Turkic, but it is known that very different institutions, at least in some respects, existed within the Turkic group. The strict and careful preservation of Ottoman sons contrasts with the rapid Mogul fractricides, and both with the wide Crimean cousinhood from which Khans were chosen, often several times between depositions. It is thus completely doubtful, within the Turkic dynasties, whether these institutional differences nevertheless converged in quantitative effect, and (if so) whether the apparent increase in longevity over the Arabic dynasties is due to these institutions; or whether the real or apparent superior longevity of the Turks was due to some other cause, institutional or otherwise.

vii. Reproductive periods (demographic generations). The ithagenic reproductive period is from birth to birth in a direct line of descent, neglecting all collaterals. The Random Index of the Ancient Model provides us with corresponding data, for we can abstract from it the average age of the parent at the births of all children, eldest children, or any other type of offspring it contains.

The average reproductive period for all children is 27.8 years – a wholly predictable figure in the middle of the most fertile quinquennium, and of course already built into our Model by the for-

150

mula of fertility distribution. Similarly, the average period for only children is 26 years.

The average reproductive period for eldest children is 23.8 years, and for youngest 30.8 years, but the spread (on average) naturally varies with the size of the family.

Parent of	Age of parent at birth of children (in years)					
	1st child	2nd child	3rd child	4th child	5th child	6th child
two children	24	31				
three children	23	27	32			
four children	22	26	31	35		
five children	21	25	30	33	36	
six children	21	25	29	32	35	38

viii. Historical material. The only surviving document which yields the ages of fathers at the birth of their heirs in the ancient world is part of the list of the Kings of Judah, which gives the ages of the kings at death, from which the reproductive age may be calculated.

Name and Sequence of King	Length of Reign in Years	Age at Accession in Years	Age at Death in Years	Age at Birth of Heirs in Years
4. Jehoshaphat	22	37	59	22
5. Jehoram	7	37	44	22
6. Ahaziah	0	22	22	21
(+Athaliah	6)			
7. Joash	39	7	46	21
8. Amaziah	29	25	54	15
9. Azariah	27	39	66	31
10. Jotham	4	35	39	20
11. Ahaz	20	19	39	14
12. Hezekiah	29	25	54	33
13. Manasseh	45	21	66	44
14. Amon	2	22	24	16
15. Josiah	32	8	40	17
Averages:	22	24	46	23

151

The surviving fragments of the *Acts of the Kings of Tyre* show that once similar figures were given in these chronicles, and there may in fact have been very considerable information available in the ancient world from local chronicles of Semitic dynasts. The relevant figures for Judah are given on p. 151.

The average ithagenic reproductive period of 23 years in this dynasty corresponds to the Model period for eldest sons. But some of the figures above show that we are not to infer a rule of strict primogeniture from this correspondence. We observe that there is no case of direct succession by a grandson and that there is the series given below.

Name and Sequence of King	Age at Death in Years	Age at Birth of Heir in Years
13. Manasseh	66	44
9. Azariah	66	31
4. Jehoshaphat	59	22
12. Hezekiah	54	33
7. Joash	46	21
5. Jehoram	44	22
15. Josiah	40	17
10. Jotham	39	20
11. Ahaz	39	14
14. Amon	24	16
6. Ahaziah	22	21

It is incredible for a polygamous dynasty that Manasseh had no sons before he was 44, Azariah no sons before he was 31, or Hezekiah no sons before he was 33; we must infer from this series that 'the eldest son' means one of the eldest sons surviving at the time of the king's death. Josiah is succeeded by three sons, born when he was 17, 25, and 30 respectively, so that in this case at least it was not the eldest son absolutely who was the first choice. The rule of succession was therefore apparently that one of a small group of eldest surviving sons was preferred to all grandsons, and the other circumstances (average longevity, etc.) of this dynasty were such that the resulting average reproductive period coincides with our Model period for eldest sons.

Thus, even where we have full biographical data we cannot say more than that in the circumstances there was a coincidence between the empirical averages and a Model figure.

ix. Experimental material. Since the fertility distribution built into our Ancient Model is *ex hypothesi* constant for all populations,[8] we should be able to use the 23-, 27- and 30-year averages historically wherever the material is sufficient for us to decide which is to be selected.

'The most authentic of all ancient Greek pedigrees' is inscribed on the gravestone of Heropythes of Chios, who died about ?475 B.C.[9] This 'barren list of empty names' contains a surprising amount of information.

Greek descents usually show repetition of names in two-generation cycles; Heropythes' ancestors show none of these, but some rather similar repetitions.

(a) The name of Hekaos is echoed in that of his grandson's grandson Hekaides. The -*ides* form of the name suggests that Heropythes called himself a Hekaid, or that this ithageny (and others) constituted a body of kindred called the Hekaidai, all claiming descent from Hekaos. It would be reasonable therefore to suggest that Hekaos, son of Eldios of Cyprus, was the founder, the first member of this kindred to settle in Chios.

(b) The name of Hippotion is borne by Hekaos' son, and by his grandson's grandson; instead of Hippotion, the grandson has the name of Hipposthenes. Repetition of the grandfather's name was often, perhaps generally, the privilege of the eldest of a family of grandsons. Younger brothers often bore similar names, as Hipposthenes stands to Hippotion. It is quite likely therefore that Hipposthenes is a younger son, but since the name Hippotion recurs later, there was probably some intermarriage which brought it back. (The kind of relationship we might expect would be that Hipposthenes

---

[8] Except of course that in populations of much greater longevity the average age of parents at the birth of youngest children will be more than 30 years (and therefore the average of 27 years for all children will tend to rise if 23 years for eldest children is not reduced).

[9] A. Wade-Grey *The Poet of the Iliad* (Cambridge 1952) p.8 f., L. H. Jeffery: *The Local Scripts of Archaic Greece* (Oxford 1963) p.414, no.47. It reads: Ηροπυθο | το Φιλαιο | το Μικκυλο | το Μανδροκεος | το Αυτοσθενεος | το Μανδραγορεω | το Ερασιο | το Ιπποτιωνος | το Εκαιδεω | το Ιπποσθενος | το Ορσικλεος | το Ιπποτιωνος | το Εκαο | το Ελδιο | το Κυπριο

153

had an elder brother Hippotion who had no sons, but a daughter who married Hekaides.)

(c) Similarly the name of Mandragores is echoed but not repeated in that of Mandrokles, which again suggests a younger brother.

(d) Heropythos himself apparently had a son Mikkylos II whose name suggests either that he was a younger son (his elder brother having pre-empted the name Philaios), or that there had been some intermarriage.

In general, therefore, it does not look at all as though Heropythos was descended from Hekaos through a series of eldest surviving sons, so that application of the 23-year reproductive period seems definitely to be excluded. On the other hand, we should not assume without evidence that the descent happened to be regularly through younger sons. This means that we are left with the 27-year reproductive period.

The reproductive period runs from birth to birth, so we have to postulate a birth-date for Heropythos. The inscription is dated ?c.475: perhaps this means 460±15 at least. We have no notion of Heropythos' age at death, but if we can perhaps take it as 50±10, so that his birth date is 510±25. We then have:

Average Date of Birth	Name	Adult AKME (Age Thirty Years)
888 (±25)	Kyprios?	858
861 (±25)	Eldios (of Cyprus)	831
834 (±25)	Hekaos	804 (±25)
807	Hippotion I	787
780	Orsikles	750
753	Hipposthenes	723 (±25)
726	Hekaides	696
699	Hippotion II	669
672	Erasies	642
645	Mandragores	615
618	Autosthenes	588
591	Mandrokles	561
564	Mikkylos	534
537	Philaios	507
510 (±25)	Heropythos	480 (±25)

This dating implies that Hekaos settled in Chios somewhere around

154

800 B.C. The archaeological evidence from Chios so far shows no post-Mycenean settlement until the harbour site at Phanai was occupied in 'perhaps the late ninth century'.[10]

Chios was supposed to be a Euboian colony, and about 800 B.C. Euboians were also settling at Al Mina in Syria. This seems to be the right context for the settlement of Hekaos, son of Eldios of Cyprus, among the Euboians of Chios.

The traditional history of Chios said that the great-grandson of the founding king was named Hektor, and that he brought Chios into the Ionian League. He should therefore be roughly something like contemporary with Hipposthenes, and it may be that the pride of Chios in his time is shown in another aspect in the name of Hekaides, which transmutes the simple name of Hekaos into one of nobility and pride of descent.

Another possible association of the Chian Hektor has been discussed, in common with the name of Agamemnon of Kyme, whose daughter married Midas of Phrygia. Kyme, like Chios, claimed Euboian origin; 'Midas' stands for the Phrygian empire between the fall of Urartu at the battle of Musasir in 743 B.C. and the defeat of Phrygia by the Kimmerians in 696 or 676. Agamemnon and Hektor are therefore likely to have been contemporaries at least approximately; and their names may bear some relation, either of borrowing or lending, to the composition of the *Iliad*, which on other grounds is now often dated around the middle of the eighth century.

Our experimental material thus seems to fit, and help illuminate, a context of eight century Euboian settlements and system of communications from Kyme through Chios to Al Mina. Such a context in turn provides a rational background for the emergence of Homeric epic and its derivative, through Euboia to Boiotia, in Hesiod. Thus in so far as our experiment can be checked, either by archaeological or historical evidence, it seems to stand.

x. The ithagenic dividend. In our historical material so far, in default of information on reproductive periods (except for the kings of Judah), we have examined survival periods for all known sons, and ithagenic survival averages. We can of course add the survival averages for the collaterals and obtain the following table.

---

[10] J. Boardman, *The Greeks Overseas* (Penguin 1964) p.51.

	Assyrians	Abbasids	Nasrids	Ottomans	Moguls	Crimeans	all Moslem
Average survival	20	22.3	22.5	28.6	17.3	31.6	25.5
Ithagenic survival	c.24	28	23	28	30	31	28.5
Collateral survival	10.5	17	22	30	5.6	32	23.4

The dynasties, on these quantities, fall into two groups: those where ithagenic and collateral survival averages diverge widely, and those where they do not: the Assyrians, Abbasids and Moguls against the Nasrids, Ottomans and Crimeans. The divergences are sometimes readily explicable (as by the series of rapid Mogul fratricides), and sometimes are partly misleading, as among the Abbasids; among the Assyrians the reason is unknown.

The Mogul figures exemplify the very high effect which special events may have. The high effect of course raises the question of the importance of such special events: were the Mogul difficulties entirely due to misplaced ambition in unruly characters, or was there some more general and important breakdown of dynastic or more widely political organization? Was there, as a byproduct of a successful empire, a small privileged population of marked longevity whose energies found full employment only in 'misplaced ambition'? Such questions could be asked of the quantities shown for every dynasty; but historians have also attempted to proceed to more general problems.

A period of continuity, such as that represented by a dynasty, is or may be also a period of accumulating knowledge, experience, skill, and art. When a period of continuity ends, one question is plainly why this accumulation was not sufficient to meet the problems; and often there is the possibility that the accumulation itself, or the means it employed, or its unforeseen byproducts, were also the problems it failed to meet. The quantities of the continuity may help to provide methods of approaching such problems; and at this general level it would be most convenient if a single kind of quantity could have special reference to continuity, and at the same time be related to less general quantities such as survival periods.

The historical 'generation' is an attempt to provide such a quantifiable continuity. Usually it is vague or wrongly quantified because it is not used in association with demographic evidence; as soon as the two bodies of thought are brought together, the historical generation is seen to be an ithagenic dividend, for the total period of continuity is divided by the number of generations, or the number of generations is multiplied by some constant figure to give the total period of continuity.

We may usefully distinguish between crude and refined ithagenic dividends. The crude form for, let us say, the Moguls is: Babar became emperor in 1526, and Bahadur II was deposed and exiled in 1857; in this period of 331 years there were twelve generations in the direct line from Babar to Bahadur, both included. The crude ithagenic dividend is thus 27.59 years, as against an average survival period for this dynasty of 30 years.

Clearly, the ithagenic dividend would be more generally useful if it were less arbitrarily related to the average survival period. The difference between the two figures in the Mogul case is due merely to the fact that Babar's conquest occurred only four years before his death at the age of 48; his military career had in fact begun 23 years earlier, so that the crude ithagenic dividend is based on an arbitrary selection, and is somewhat misleading.

A more refined ithagenic dividend is more closely related to the average survival period. This is obtained by neglecting, in every case, the reign of the founder of the dynasty—the point at which arbitrary selection can have a misleadingly large effect. The calculation for the Moguls now becomes: Humayun succeeded Babar in 1530, and Bahadur II was deposed in 1857. In these 327 years there were eleven generations in the direct line; Bahadur II died in 1862,

Dynasty	Ithagenic Dividend in Years	Average Ithagenic Survival in Years
Assyrians	24 and 25	about 24
Abbasids	25	28
Nasrids	24	23
Ottomans	29	28
Moguls	30	30
Crimeans	31.6	31
all Moslem	28.5	28

157

so that we can, if we wish, add five years to the total period to bring history closer to biography and demography; then there are eleven generations in 332 years. In either case, the dividend is almost 30 years, which corresponds to the average ithagenic survival period.

Similar refined ithagenic dividends for the other dynasties are given in the table on p. 157.

The remaining divergence is that of the Abbasids, and this is not a misleading figure; the ithagenic dividend takes account of two sons who predeceased their fathers, and who therefore do not appear in the survival figures. We have, that is to say, a proper reflection, in the quantities, of some real circumstances.

Dividend of 24 Years   Life-Length and Succession

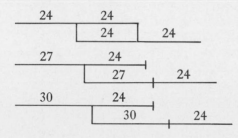

48-year lives
succession by an elder son

51-year lives
succession by an elder son

54-year lives
succession by an elder son

Dividend of 27 years

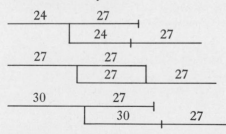

51-year lives
succession by any son

54-year lives
succession by any son

57-year lives
succession by any son

Dividend of 30 years

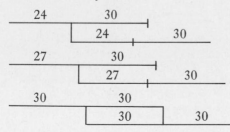

54-year lives
succession by a younger son

57-year lives
succession by a younger son

60-year lives
succession by a younger son

158

The refined form of the ithagenic dividend now expresses continuity in quantitative accordance with the ithagenic survival period (which is not concerned with continuity). The question now is whether some similarly rational relationship to the ithagenic reproduction period can be found.

No immediate inference is either possible or methodically permissible, since we should need at least one other figure (age at accession or age at death), and these are available (at least in the secondary sources we are using) for none of our dynasties. We can however devise a geometric representation, under certain simplified conditions, of the relationships concerned.

From the Random Index we have derived the values of 23.8, 27.8, and 30 (+) years for various reproductive periods; and our dynasties show ithagenic dividends of 24–25, 29–30, and 32 years. Let us simplify these values to 24, 27, and 30 years for both sets of periods, and combine the two sets in all the ways which make lifetimes: 24+24, 27+24, 30+24, and so forth. Then we may construct the table on the opposite page.

With the aid of this geometric simplification, we can see some of the kinds of evidence a historian must look for before making any inference from the ithagenic dividend to the reproductive period. For instance, 54-year lives are compatible with any of the three dividends under different succession rules; if minorities were permitted, the whole relationship between the dividend and lifetimes would be changed;[11] if early fertility was an object of special dynastic

---

[11] In the dynasty of Judah, minorities were permitted, so that together with a dividend of 22 years and an average lifetime of 46 years, we have the distribution of survival periods:

Years	% of Survivors	Total %
0–9	33 ⎫	
10–19	0 ⎬	33
20–29	42 ⎫	
30–39	17 ⎪	
40–49	8 ⎬	67
50+	0 ⎭	

This distribution shows two-thirds of the survivors survived more than 20 years, and the peak decade is the third—a pattern quite unlike that of the Ancient Model and Assyrians, but paralleled in the Moslem dynasties (where a greater average longevity may be the cause). The divergence of these Judahic figures from those of other ancient material may be due entirely to the institutional effect of the permissibility of minorities.

159

concern (as some of the reproductive dates of Judah may suggest), then other numerical values would apply, and so forth. The use of this geometric model is to supply questions, not answers, and only two general rules can be directly elicited: that (if minorities are not permitted) a short dividend implies short lifetimes and therefore a preference for elder sons as heirs, and a long dividend implies long lifetimes and the passing of the ithagenic line through younger sons. For the ancient world, longer *average* ithagenic lives than 54 years are unreasonable, and so (in the absence of minorities) 30-year dividends or 'generations' would imply ithagenic continuity consistently through younger sons. This is not likely to have been frequent, and unless there is some countervailing evidence in any particular case, the longest dividend attributed to ancient ithagenies should be 27 years or so. This was the reproductive value we used for the Chiot ithageny in the last section; had we been using the ithagenic dividend, our calculation would have been in 27-year intervals back from the death of Heropythes in *c*.475? to the death of Hekaos in *c*.799?— a simpler but not less approximate calculation.

xi. General method. The encounter of demographic procedures and conventions with historical time and the kind of information usually available for populations of the ancient world have led us to derive from the Ancient Model and genealogical records the average survival period, the average ithagenic survival period, the average reproduction period, and the refined ithagenic dividend. The relationships between these quantities have also been examined for the sources of divergencies, and for the construction of a geometric model which defines the questions to be asked about the relationship between the average reproduction period and the ithagenic dividend, as these relations operate through the average of lifetimes.

When we wish to apply date-values to an undated ithageny, we must do so in accordance with this general method, and not arbitrarily choose some figure like 'three generations to a century', because any figure has demographic implications (about lifetimes and reproductive periods), and some of these are, on the demographic evidence, either very improbable or impossible. The main question is always what kind of generations—whether there were succession rules (and if so what), whether minorities were permitted, whether early fertility was institutionally encouraged, and so forth. In the

Greek material especially there is always the question of whether the filiation is by nature or by adoption.

C. THE CHRONOGRAPHIC GENERATION-LENGTHS.

We come now to a study of the Greek 'generations' of 23, 27, 36, and 39 years used by the chronographers: and one main purpose is to discover why these lengths were adopted, and how they were applied.

These generation-lengths fall into two groups. Those of 23 and 27 years are paralleled in the demographic work done in the previous sections, and here the question is of the nature of the parallel – is it accidental or not? The 36- and 39-year generations are not so paralleled, and the question here is how the chronographers obtained and applied them.

i. The 23-year generation. Ancient chronography and historiography overlap to a small degree with the historical material used in the previous sections in that they showed, especially in Hellenistic and Roman times, considerable (if rather romantic) interest in Assyrian history. The main notions were always Greek, centered in the tales of Semiramis and Sardanapalos, and attempts to correct these tales were always faced with the difficulties of language and of access to records. The second of these was the more serious, since the destruction of Assyria meant that the records available were those of Babylon, which on Assyrian history were not always perspicuous. We do not know which version of the Babylonian narratives was published by Berosos, and only tantalizing fragments remain of the world historians who (presumably) used his work: Alexander Polyhistor (273 F 81) knew of the two Assyrian dynasties, and Kephalion (93 F1) reports that, after Semiramis and her son, there was a millenium of Assyrian kings in the direct line, none of whom reigned for less than 20 years. This figure looks very like a misunderstanding of some arithmetical statement from the period of learning, but it is useless to guess what the original may have been, except that it probably claimed to be an ithagenic abstract.

The material which establishes the use of the 23-year generation is Herodotus' account of the dynasties of Lydia. He reports (1) a remote and undated dynasty: (2) the Herakleid ithageny of 22 kings in $505 = (23 \times 22) - 1$ years; (3) the Mermnad ithageny of 4 kings in $156 = (39 \times 4)$ years; and (4) Croesus, who ruled for 14 years down to 547/6 B.C.: he was 35 years of age at his accession, and his reign included three extra years granted him by Apollo; at his fall therefore he was $49 = (23 \times 2) +$ the extra 3 years of age.

This is the most complete surviving account of Lydian history. The 156 years of the early Mermnads were not accepted by later writers, who preferred shorter calculations than the Herodotean 39×4, but apparently the best later authorities agreed with Herodotus that Croesus' 14 years were historical, and to be kept outside the chronography. The 'three extra years' apparently come from Delphic tradition,[12] and are the period by which Croesus survived the Persian conquest of Media: they seem to be the starting point of the argument that Croesus' kingdom should have ended when he was 46, and therefore that he was 35 years of age when he acceded.

The proper Lydian generation for Herodotus was thus of 23 years; special circumstances affected Croesus; other special circumstances presumably affected the four preceding Mermnads; and the missing year in the Herakleid total is presumably a minor adjustment.

The preceding sections of our enquiry show that the belief that the Lydian generation should be of 23 years does not seem to be open to criticism: it agrees with the Assyrian and Judahic evidence for ancient polygamous dynasties. Indeed, Assyrian references to Gyges, the first Mermnad, which place his death in 648 or later, show that a calculation of $23 \times 4 = 92$ years before Croesus' accession in 561/0 would have been much nearer to the historical truth than the calculation of 39×4 years, and probably this false calculation was due to some synchronisms with Greek history in the Mermnad period (see below).

The question is therefore how the Greek historians arrived at the conclusion that a 23-year generation was the correct value for oriental polygamous dynasties.

We can probably safely assume that the question of the possibility of attributing some value would naturally arise in any learned world of which Pythagorean mathematics was a part;[13] and we may concentrate entirely on the technical question of the 23 years. In principle, the necessary investigation may have taken one of the two following forms.

(1) Although the Assyrian records, as we know them, were probably never available, it is possible that the chronicles of Jerusalem and

---

[12] *Klio* 41 (1963) 72.
[13] *Klio* 46 (1966) 1 ff.

Tyre are typical of those of minor Semitic dynasts, and that there were therefore a relatively large number of such records in existence. The language difficulty would not be insuperable to a scholar with friends in Cyprus (living side by side with Phoenicians) or in the Persian administration where the official language was Aramaic. But there seems to be no trace of any work of collecting and studying of such minor dynastic records, at least, as early as the fifth century.

(2) It is possible that more was known about the Lydian dynasties than Herodotus records—for example, a succession rule or practice favoring elder sons. This could have been the starting-point for an enquiry in a contemporary population about the average age of fathers at the birth of eldest surviving sons.

Of these two possible procedures, the first would correspond to our historical enquiries into the Assyrian and Judahic records; the second would correspond to the construction of our demographic Ancient Model, only based on biographical instead of skeletal data. The balance of probability seems to be in favor of the supposition that the second method was used to establish the figure.

The scholar who performed such an enquiry must have been a historian of substantial learning and achievements, and the only— and completely satisfactory—candidate is Hellanikos, the great chronicler. His interest in oriental affairs is shown by his books on Cyprus, Lydia, and Persia, and it is possible that these contained some enquiries into the historical material either to establish or to confirm the 23-year value. It also seems likely that, in Herodotus' statement that there were 22 Herakleid kings of Lydia who succeeded παῖς παρὰ πατρός, we have a shadow of another necessary part of Hellanikos' method—the abstraction of an ithageny to which the value could properly be applied. The form of Herodotus' statement, as though reporting a historical fact, is perhaps not entirely due to Herodotus' misunderstanding of method: we must also remember that scientific prose is an exacting art with which Herodotus was not concerned.

The existence of the 23-year value in Greek chronography, and its coincidence with the Ancient Model value for the eldest son reproductive period, and with the Assyrian and Judahic figures, has considerable implications—for ancient learning, for ancient reality, and for our Ancient Model. It means that ancient learning, in the person of Hellanikos, was capable of arriving at demographic values which can scarcely be bettered in accuracy today; it means that

163

ancient reality (either historical or biographical) was given at least one statistical measurement in the fifth century; and it means that the fertility distribution built into our Ancient Model is to some degree confirmed by unexpected evidence. These implications may be used to test and be tested by our examination of the other chronographic generation-lengths.

ii. The 27-year generation. Although the 27-year generation was apparently not introduced to Sicilian chronography until Philistos used it, it was very widely employed in Greek chronography generally and probably also goes back to the work of Hellanikos. It coincides with the value given by our Ancient Model for the average reproductive period for all children, and the hypothesis is therefore that Hellanikos found it by enquiries among a contemporary population, and applied it for the purpose of dating ithagenic records. A test of this hypothesis would be the identification of an ithageny as treated by Hellanikos.

In 443/2 B.C., Athens expelled the ancient ruling kindred of the Neleidai from Miletos and imposed or supported a new democratic government.[14] There had been dissension in Miletos for some time, and only shortly before Athens had supported the Neleidai against their rivals. In fact, support of the Neleidai was the traditional Athenian policy, because this kindred was descended from a brother of Medon who in the post-heroic period founded the Athenian ruling kindred of the Medontidai. Medon's son Akastos was the first Athenian archon and the historical archontic oath of office still contained his name; the hereditary archonship continued in his lineage for twelve more generations, only being opened to other candidates (according to all our sources) in 713/2 B.C. This is $270 = (27 \times 10)$ years before the expulsion of the Neleidai from Miletos.

The Medontids therefore were held to have lost their monopoly of rule in Athens ten generations before the Neleids were expelled from Miletos. Such a comparison would of course be of some academic interest at any time, but equally clearly it would be most relevant as a statement made just at the time of the change in Athenian policy. To justify the change, not only on grounds of present policies, but also because a Neleid government was ten generations out of date,

[14] J. P. Barron 'Milesian Politics and Athenian Propaganda' JHS 82 (1962) 1 ff.

would have an obvious democratic appeal in the assembly of 443/2.

It appears therefore that in 443/2 the Athenians believed that their Medontidai had not ruled for ten generations; and that Hellanikos gave the ithagenic value of 27 years to these generations. This identification of an ithageny dated by Hellanikos is probable, but not firm enough to provide a test of the hypothesis. It is however confirmed to some degree by other considerations.

We have a list of names of successive Medontids down to 713/2 B.C., and we can apply the 27-year value to these names and examine the chief traditions attached to them in relation to some archaeological evidence. The dated list reads:

1253	Periklymenos of Pylos, killed in the sack of the city by Herakles
1226	Penthilos
1199	Boros
1172	Andropompos married Henioche of Thessaly
1145	Melanthos became king of Athens and founded the festival of the Apatouria – that is, introduced the phratric organization
1118	Kodros, the last king of Athens, killed in the Dorian Invasion of Attika
1091	Medon, founder and eponym of the phratry of the Medontidai, (brother of Neleus ancestor of the Neleidai of Miletos)
1064	Akastos, remembered in the archons' oath of office
1037	Archippos
1010	Thersippos
983	Phorbas
956	Megakles
929	Diognetos
902	Pherekles
875	Ariphon
848	Thespieus
821	Agamestor
794	Aischylos; Alkmeon
767	Charops and Aisimides sons of Aischylos
740	Kleidikos, son of Aisimides, Hippomenes
713	Eupatrid archons begin
686	
659	
632	

165

605 (Phorbas oecist of Elaeus may have been a Medontid)
578
551
524
497 (Melanthios, commander of the Athenian forces in Ionia, probably a Medontid)
470
443 Expulsion of the Neleids of Miletos

These values give the following dates to be compared with archaeological evidence.

(i) The sack of Pylos by Herakles is placed at 1226; the archaeological date for the sack of the palace is before 1200.

(ii) The arrival of Melanthos, son of a Thessalian, is placed at 1145: cist-graves of northern type are found on the akropolis c.1150.[15]

(iii) The 'Dorian Invasion' of Attika and the end of the kingship is placed at 1092; an attack on the akropolis, and the end of habitation there so that the akropolis became a cult-center, is archaeologically dated about 1100 B.C., when wells on the akropolis cease.

(iv) The introduction of the phratric organization and archontic government is complete by 1037; the early Proto-Geometric revival in Athens, and the introduction of iron and cremation, is archaeologically well under way about the middle of the eleventh century.

These correlations are exact; and if accepted inform us that the list of Medontid names forms an ithagenic descent which was in the fifth century known to continue for another ten generations: since the name of Kleidikos recurs in Athenian prosopography, these ten generations were presumably his descendants.

There has in the past been much destructive criticism of this list of Medontid names, but the criticism has in the main rested on assumptions now known to be either false or unproveable. It was long believed that the Medontidai were a *genos*, an 'artificial' kinship group: it is now known that they were a phratry, and that some phratries at least were organized around an *oikos*, a 'real' lineage. The sociological

15 E. L. Smithson 'Dorians on the Akropolis' in AJA 69 (1965) 176. I should like to take this opportunity of thanking Mrs. Smithson for much archaeological advice, generous and invaluable.

evidence now therefore is in favor of the recognition of the list of Medontid names as that of an ithagenic line of descent. We do not in consequence, of course, need to suppose that there were never any collaterals—Nestor the brother of Periklymenos, Neleus the brother of Medon, Charops the brother of Aisimides, Alkmeon, and Hippomenes are collaterals mentioned in our sources, and no doubt if we possessed any of the Atthides we should hear of more.

The other kind of argument directed against the Medontid list is founded on the fact that some of the names are, in the historical centuries, found in other lineages: Megakles and Alkmeon among the Alkmeonids, Agamestor among the Philaids, and Ariphron among the Bouzygai. This has been held to show that the Medontid list was made up in the sixth century, to give the Alkmeonids and others a royal past. This really assumes that 'the Medontidai' is a sociological fiction. Now that we know that the phratry existed in historical times, the argument loses most of its force, and the residue is removed by the reflection that we have no evidence at all that names such as Megakles *originated* in the other lineages concerned—they may equally well have been introduced through Medontid marriages.

The complete hypothesis is therefore that the phratry of the Medontidai was organized around an *oikos* of which the ithagenic record is preserved; that this record became politically topical in 443/2 B.C., that about that time Hellanikos applied to it the 27-year value for a generation; and that the archaeological evidence demonstrates he was correct in doing so. The various lines of evidence and argument converge and cohere with one another. It appears therefore that the 23- and 27-year generation values were obtained by Hellanikos from 'demographic' enquiries and at least in some cases correctly applied: the 23-year eldest son average to the Lydian dynasties (not wholly consistently), and the 27-year general average to the Medontid ithageny.

iii. The 36- and 39-year generations. In the light of the preceding arguments, it is clearly probable that these chronographic generation-lengths are also of 'demographic' origin; but they are not paralleled either in our Ancient Model or in the historical material we have used. The probability that they are serious calculations is however much increased by evidence that some dates derived from these high values were approximately correct. For example, we have seen that the dates for the foundation of Syracuse in 736/5 and 758/7 were calculated as seven high-value generations before Gelon. The archaeologists, after much discussion, hold that the date of 736/5 is about correct, and the margin of error that they are prepared to allow seems to be equivalent to a value of 35 ± 1 for the average of the seven generations concerned.

Similarly, Herodotus reports that the twelve-year war between Miletos and Lydia began six years before the accession of Alyattes, and preceded Alyattes' six-year war with the Medes which ended with the 'eclipse battle' of May 25, 585 B.C. Therefore (if the sequence is right) the latest possible date for the beginning of the Milesian War is 17 years before 586/5, that is, 603/2 B.C. We now examine the ancient absolute dates to find the number of generations.[16]

(i) Herodotus' date for the accession of Alyattes places the commencement of the Milesian War in 623/2, this is $180 = 36 \times 5$ years before the expulsion of the Neleids from Miletos in 443/2 B.C.

(ii) The Parian Marble reports a date for the accession of Alyattes which places the beginning of the Milesian War in 611/0: this is $168 = 36 \times 4\frac{2}{3}$ years before 443/2.

(iii) Kastor's date[17] for Alyattes places the start of the Milesian War in 616/5, which is $69 = (23 \times 3)$ years before the fall of Sardis in 547/6 B.C. This is the numerate form of the statement that Sadyattes, who began the Milesian War, was the father of Alyattes, the father of Croesus whose reign ended in 547/6.

Thus Kastor's date is calculated on the Lydian genealogy; the dates given by Herodotus and the Parian are calculated from a Milesian base-year, and no doubt on the Neleid genealogy. They inform us that the fifth generation before 443/2 was beginning, or had begun, at the latest in 603/2 B.C. The Herodotean version, that the fifth generation was then beginning, yields an average of 32 years; the Parian version, that the fifth generation had begun, yields 34.3 years, and this is within the 35 ± 1 years evidenced from Syracuse.

It thus seems clear that Greek institutions were in reality capable of producing a 'generation' of well over thirty years.

Over a substantial part of chronographic time, many Greek

---

[16] These identifications are much simpler than, and therefore much preferable to, the suggestions in 'Herodotus as Chronographer' *Klio* 46 (1966) 1 ff.

[17] *Klio* 41 (1963) 67.

communities did not possess dynasties: they were ruled by oligarchies which were groups of interrelated, intermarrying, and interadopting lineages or *oikoi*. Leadership of these institutions was (at least sometimes) identified with priestly office, and incumbency passed from brother to younger brother and cousin, exhausting the surviving membership of one generation before passing to the members of the next. This process must have generally avoided minorities and produced men of some maturity as leaders; the demand (of which we hear occasionally) that candidates for office should be fathers of living sons, fits very well into the life of such institutions. There were, however, limits upon the extent of kinship for these purposes: among the Ionian Greeks a man could be succeeded by his first cousin's son, while the Dorians admitted the second cousin's son: among the Ionians second cousins, among the Dorians third cousins, could not succeed.[18]

Thus it would often follow that the representative of an *oikos* or lineage was thenceforth excluded since a second or third cousin could not be succeeded; and the lineages thus excluded would often be those of elder sons, so that over the generations the limited cousinhood would tend to favor the junior lineages.

We have also seen, in discussing non-quantitative evidence above, that the population structure was probably such that lineages could hardly have survived without the support of the cousinhoods and kindreds, which provided spouses for many of their members, guardians for orphans, and substitute sons for the childless. The detailed genealogy of a kindred must often have been extremely complex; if a man's parents were third cousins, if his wife were also his niece, if his widowed daughter-in-law were also a second cousin's daughter, and if he adopted his brother-in-law as his son and heir, since each of these persons had recognized duties to and rights in the well-being of every one of their kin to the fifth or seventh degree bilaterally reckoned (including equal shares in patrimonies and recognized customary proportions for dowries), then only a committee of learned grandmothers is likely to have been in command of all the details of the situation. Certainly for purposes of public legal records and determination of priestly or official incumbencies and property inheritance, there must have been conventions of simplification, reducing the details, for example, about a nephew and brother-in-law who was

---

[18] See Broadbent, *Studies in Greek Genealogy* (Leiden 1968) 39 ff.

also an adoptive son to the statement that he was a son. In brief, the public legal record of a cousinhood would have a very similar appearance to that of an ithageny.

But there is of course no *a priori* reason to believe that the ancient historians were deceived by this similarity; they knew their society and in collecting legal records for historiographic purposes would usually know whether the list of generations referred to an ithageny or a cousinhood. Nor is there any *a priori* reason to suppose that when the historians practised chronography they would omit consideration of the question whether ithagenic and cousinly generations should be assigned the same quantities.

There are two approaches to the determination of quantities for cousinly generations. First, we have seen that in the Ancient Model and the historical dynasties the proportion of fathers with surviving sons means that on the average there were approximately three reigns to two generations. Thus generation-lengths designed to include cousinly collaterals would be $23 \times \frac{3}{2}$ and $27 \times \frac{3}{2}$, which yield about 35 and 40 years respectively. Second, we have seen that in the Ancient Model the average reproductive periods for eldest and youngest sons are 23 and 30 (+) years. We can thus ascertain the average period to all equally possible first heirs in the next generation, as follows.

Let us suppose that a senior incumbent assumes office in year 69, and that (after his brothers and cousins have succeeded and died) the first heir of the next generation is the oldest survivor, up to the limit of second cousin's sons. The whole range of these equally possible heirs may be shown schematically in the form of genealogical table (below) of persons descending by 23 and 30 (+) year generations, represented in the table by their possible 'accession' dates according to these generations:

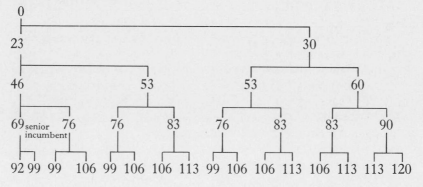

The average of all these schematic periods is 36.6 or nearly 37 years. On the other hand, if we add the possibility that a man might adopt an orphan grandson, whose 'accession' date would be 46 or 60 years later than his own, then the average for possible heirs rises to 38.4 years. We thus have 35 and 37 years, and 38 and 40 years, as possible values by different lines of calculation. The chronographers' figures were 36 and 39, and we conclude that they were found by some such computation.

It is obvious that no one, whether ancient or modern, could regard these calculations as very satisfactory or exact, but from the historians' point of view they are better (both in method and result) than the alternative of applying ithagenic values to cousinly generations. It could follow that the ancient chronographers used their high values where the genealogical records were not those of polygamous dynasties, nor of ithagenies, but of cousinhoods.

a. Attribution of a 36-year generation to the Neleids of Miletos. The story of the 'Ionian Migration' led by Neleus son of Kodros from Athens has two aspects. One is that Neleus established a new government in Miletos, and the sanctuary of Poseidon Helikonios on Mykale; his son Aipytos founded the city of Priene which Androklos of Ephesos, Neleus' brother, died defending. This story is about a new government in Miletos, and a new sanctuary and a new town nearby: there is no archaeological evidence as yet which would serve to check the story or date the events. The second aspect of the story is that brothers and other kinsmen of Neleus settle in the other Ionian towns, where residence of Neleids was sometimes a condition of admission to the Ionian League. This wide cousinhood is part of the Neleid tradition as far back as it can be traced in literature.

The absolute dates for the 'Ionian Migration' given in our sources are:

1077/6 ('814 years since', in Medon's reign) by the Parian Marble. Medon's name occupies the twenty-fourth generation before 443/2 in the Medontid list, but the thirteenth and fourteenth generations consist of two decennial archons in each case, and so require altogether 40 years instead of 54. The calculation is thus $(24 \times 27) - 14 = 634$ years before 443/2, and this is derived from the Medontid ithageny, not from the Neleid cousinhood.

1044/3 Eratosthenes. This $546 = 39 \times 14$ years before the outbreak of the Ionian Revolt in 498/7, and is probably calculated on the

171

pedigree of Hekataios. If so, the date informs us of Eratosthenes' belief that Hekataios' ancestral generations were cousinly.

1037/6 Eusebius. This is $594 = 36 \times 16\frac{1}{2}$ years before 443/2, and no doubt places the 'Ionian Migration' halfway between Neleus and his son Aipytos. This count of $16\frac{1}{2}$ generations will therefore come from the Neleid genealogies.

Until more archaeological evidence is forthcoming, these calculations cannot be checked, except in the case of the Lydian war of Miletos, a little less than five generations before 443/2. If we apply the same value of 35 ± 1 years to Hekataios' and the Neleids' generation-counts, they give 988 ± 14 and $1021 \pm 16\frac{1}{2}$ respectively, and these meet just before 1000 B.C. We should therefore take this date as that provided by the literary evidence for the arrival of Neleus in Miletos, to be checked when the archaeological evidence becomes available.[19]

The long Herodotean generations of the first four Mermnad kings were presumably in part derived from the high Milesian value: the synchronism available for the Milesian War fixed the date of the accession of Alyattes. Other Ionian records probably provided other synchronisms – for example, the genealogy of the collateral descendants of Archilochos (the contemporary of Gyges) in Thasos and Paros. In the Neleid case, so far as we can tell, Hellanikos was correct in assigning a high value to cousinly generations, but he did not take into account enough purely historical evidence as, apparently, did the Parian's source when he found reason to place the outbreak of the Milesian War some time after the beginning of its generation. But of course this only means that Hellanikos' dates were a first approximation, to be revised by local historians in the light of local detail.

b. Attribution of a 39-year generation to the Spartan kings. Our surviving sources on the Spartan Kings always present the records of the twin dynasties in an ithagenic form, but Herodotus' date for Herakles[20] shows that the 39-year value was already applied. This should mean that for Hellanikos (and all his successors) the apparent Spartan ithagenies were in fact simplified cousinly records, and that, if we had a full list of kings, there would have been two or more rulers of each line in many of the generations.

---

[19] With Medon in 1091 and Neleus in 1000, their 'brotherhood' must have been that of members of the same phratry.

[20] *Klio* 46 (1966) 1 ff.

In historical times (that is, from the late sixth century onwards) inheritance passed in both lines from father to son, often with long minorities and regencies. For this period, Herodotus reports a succession rule (7:3): that sons born after the king's accession were preferred, and the operation of such a rule would of course have these effects. A geometric model of such a situation would be something of the kind below.

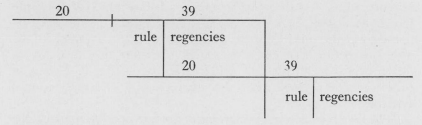

Here the 'regencies' simply replace one legal form of the cousinly generation by another—which however retains the main claimants or candidates in one direct line instead of permitting the possibility that this direct line would be excluded.

Evidence for the earlier and chronographic period is confused. Herodotus gives a pedigree of the Eurypontid Leotychides, Pausanias a pedigree of his predecessor Demaratos, and neither authority seems to know the other pedigree—Herodotus presumably had not collected that of Demaratos, and Pausanias apparently was using a mere handbook source which followed the one-name-to-a-generation convention without explanation. The two accounts also seem to be inconsistent:

Pausanias	*Herodotus*
	Theopompos
Theopompos	Anaxandrides
Archedamos	Archedamos
(predeceased his father)	
Zeuxidamos	Anaxilaos
Anaxidamos	Leotychides
Archedamos	Hippokratides
Agesikles (also Hdt. 1.65	Agesilaos (Agis) was not king
without pedigree)	
Ariston (also Hdt. 6.62)	Menares was not king
Demaratos, deposed and replaced by Leotychides about 490 B.C.	

173

With the information from the chronographers that they believed the Spartan generations were cousinly, modern study does not have to emend the text of Herodotus, or believe that one or another of these accounts must be wrong *in toto*; the task is only to criticize both from the point of view of cousinly inheritance, and from this point of view the inconsistency is easily resolved as in the genealogical table below.

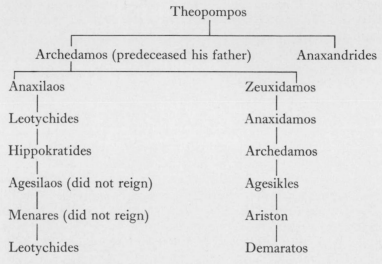

This combination of the evidence of our two sources carries the following implications.

(1) When the generation of Hippokratides and Archedamos was exhausted, Agesikles was the senior survivor of the next generation; but his third cousin's line was excluded by the fact of Agesikles' accession, and was in fact only restored, in the person of Leotychides, in the belief that Ariston had no son and that, therefore, his line was extinct.

(2) Herodotus or his informant, in abstracting a list giving one name to a generation, made a slip by saying that Archedamos was son to Anaxandrides. As the common ancestor of Leotychides and Demaratos, Archedamos was an important person though he never reigned; the king of that generation was Anaxandrides and therefore his name also could not be omitted. The attempt to operate the convention of one name to a generation has led to the error.

(3) Another pressure on the material which will have assisted the error will have been the desire to give the same number of Eurypontid

174

as of Agiad generations from Herakles to the kings of the Persian Wars. Herodotus' version succeeds in this, and he makes Agis and Eurypon the sons of the twin sons of Aristodemos. But with Archedamos and Anaxandrides in one generation (that is, with Anaxandrides omitted, as in Pausanias) there is one empty generation in the upper part of the list, and this is filled by putting the name of Soos as the father of Eurypon. Soos' name was apparently remembered solely as that of a notable warrior of early times; there may have been a number of such anecdotal kings whose precise place in history was long forgotten. This correction of Herodutus' Eurypontid list was presumably not long after his publication, and may have been due to, or brought into general knowledge by, Ephoros.

If, however, the Spartan dynasties down to the time of Agesikles were organized as cousinhoods, we should be able to make out the time when the rule changed to the historical form. This seems to have been in the reigns of Ariston and Anaxandrides, both of whom make extraordinary efforts to secure sons to succeed them: Ariston married three successive wives (Hdt. 6.62), and Anaxandrides, yielding to apparently protracted pressure from the ephors, two at once (5.39 ff.). These stories seem to make it certain that the succession rule was changed early in these reigns.

A new succession law giving the posterity of two particular kings the monopoly of royal office is clearly most likely to have won acceptance and enactment when two young kings were associated with a successful new policy. Anaxandrides and Ariston are associated with the story of the Bones of Orestes, which is taken to mean the formation of the Peloponnesian League, and often dated to the ephorate of Chilon, placed in our sources in 556/5. This is very likely to be a historical date; and the new succession law should therefore have been enacted within a year or two of 550 B.C. Since sons of Anaxandrides and Ariston were active field commanders in 480/79, they will have been born not earlier (and probably not later) than the 530's, so that anxiety about the consequences of the new succession law will have become effective some fifteen to twenty years after it came into force.[21]

So far as we can see therefore the Spartan dynasties were organised as cousinhoods down to about 550 B.C. when a new mode of succession was introduced. Hellanikos' use of high values for dating

---

[21] This suggests that elder sons by the earlier marriages had died.

these Herakleids illuminates the surviving genealogical records, and these in turn seem to justify his high values in principle. But this problem remains: why he used 39 years for Sparta instead of the 36 years used for cousinly generations in Miletos.

The decision was probably dependent upon some traditional synchronisms with Athenians whom Hellanikos had already dated. Aristodemos was a leader of the Dorian Invasion of the Peloponnese which drove Melanthos from Pylos; his twin sons were allies of Aletes of Corinth whose Dorian Invasion of Attika resulted in the death of Kodros. By dead reckoning of the ithagenic average, Melanthos is placed 638–612 years, and Kodros 611–585 years, before 480/79; and Aristodemos is seventeen generations, his twin sons sixteen generations, before the same date. By using the 39-year value, Aristodemos is placed 663–625 years before 480/79 (by dead reckoning) and so has time to expel Melanthos before the latter becomes king of Athens; the twins similarly are dated 624–585 years before 480/79 and die at about the same time as Kodros. The use of a 36-year value for the Spartan generations would not achieve these results, but puts the beginning of Aristodemos in 1092/1 B.C., too late for the synchronism with Melanthos.

Apart from these traditional synchronisms, there is no reason to believe that the Spartan cousinly generations were longer than those elsewhere, and while we can understand Hellanikos' acceptance of the traditions, modern study has no reason to follow him. The Dorian Invasion, like the Trojan War or the voyage of the Argonauts, was one of the events used in Greek historiography, and before that in poetry, to bind together the pasts of the many Greek communities. Aristodemos and his twin sons were a subject of non-Spartan poetry known to Herodotus; it is unlikely that reliable historical tradition in Sparta (as distinct from romance or epic about the conquest) went back beyond the generation of the eponyms, if as far. If we apply the 35 ± 1 value to the lists of names from the eponyms downwards, we have:

	Agis (eponym of the Agiadai)	
976($\pm$12)	Echestratos	Eurypon (eponym of the Eurypontidai)
941	Leobotes	Prytanis
906	Doryssos	Polydektes
871	Agesilaos	Eunomos

176

836	Archelaos	Charilaos	
801	Teleklos	Nikandros	
766(±6)	Alkamenes	Theopompos	
731	Polydoros	(Archedamos)	Anaxandrides
696	Eurykrates	Zeuxidamos	Anaxilaos
661	Anaxandros	Anaxidamos	Leotychides
626	Eurykratides	Archedamos	Hippokratides
591	Leon	Agesikles	(Agesilaos)
556	Anaxandrides	Ariston	(Menares)

Archaeological checks on these dates are not easy to find. The Spartan colony at Taras may be 'a little earlier' than the last decade of the eighth century,[22] and is not dated to a Spartan reign in the surviving literature (this may mean that it occurred under kings not named in these selective lists). It was however unanimously agreed that the colony followed the conquest of Messenia achieved under Theopompos (assisted at first by Alkamenes, then by Polydoros). The conquest is not itself archaeologically datable, but it is connected with the story of the displaced Asinaioi. These supported Nikandros in his attack on Argos so that their city was, in revenge, destroyed by the Argives; the survivors joined the Spartan forces in Messenia and were given land there at the settlement after the conquest. The destruction of Asine is archaeologically dated to the Late Geometric period (from 735 onwards), and the narrative does not require that the destruction occurred in Nikandros' time, only that it preceded the end of the Messenian War. Thus, if Taras is to be dated (say) 715 ±5 and followed the end of the war, Asine was destroyed (say) 725 ±5, during the war (when Argos was, perhaps, free of the fear of Spartan reprisal).[23] This archaeological evidence does not give a very exact check, but it is sufficient for us to decide between cousinly and ithagenic averages for the Spartan generations. The 35-year value places Theopompos' long reign correctly relative to the date of Taras, while the 27-year value places the beginning of Theo-

[22] Boardman, p. 194.

[23] The destruction of Asine is dated c.725 by the last Proto Corinthian there: BCH 82 (1958) 590; but the latest Argive pottery gives a date c.710: *Bibliothèque des Ecoles françaises d'Athènes et de Rome* 208 (1966); Paul Courbin: *La Céramique Géometrique de l'Angolide* p.565. Apart from the absolute dating, it is perhaps a question of whether the 'destruction' of the literary sources is to be equated with the cessation of imports, or the end of habitation.

pompos' time in 718 which is the approximate date of the foundation of Taras, and therefore too late.

We have thus been able, to some degree, to check Hellanikos' use of eldest son, ithagenic, and cousinly values for generations in Lydia, Athens, and Miletos and Sparta. So far as we can see, he was in principle right in all these cases, although his dates are of course in the nature of first approximations. His accuracy in dating was, so far as we can make out, due to the excellence of his 'demography' in fixing upon the 23- and 27-year values, and the strictness of his sociology in observing institutional effects; in both fields the information he gives us is still valid and valuable for historical purposes.

D. THE MEETING OF HERODOTUS AND HELLANIKOS

(*4 T1*). Suidas is our source for the story that Hellanikos and Herodotus spent some time together at the court of Amyntas of Macedon. Since the Athenian and Milesian datings rest upon the expulsion of the Neleids in 443/2 and Herodotus' chronographic dates give the year 440/39 as the base-year of his reports in ἐς ἐμέ terms[24] (and no one will suspect that Herodotus made his constructions unaided), this meeting will have occurred between these years— after Herodotus achieved fame in Athens and before he went to Thourioi. At this date, Amyntas of Macedon will not have been a king (as Suidas calls him), but the brother of Perdikkas of Macedon.

To this conference, Herodotus brought a great fund of knowledge, reports from the λόγιοι all over Greece and the Near East. Hellanikos had probably already published his great systematic genealogical work, the Deukalioneia in which he was still ignorant of Lykourgos, of whom Herodotus had been informed in Sparta. Vast knowledge thus encountered a passion for system in what must have been one of the most fruitful conferences in the history of science: historiography was created by an electric union of epic with mathematics.

---

[24] *Klio* 46 (1966) 1 ff.

PART SIX

THE ORIGINAL INFORMATION AND THE HISTORIANS' INFERENCES

THE PROBLEM IN THE FOLLOWING DISCUSSION is to distinguish (so far as our knowledge permits) the information received by the historians, from their inferences and constructions. We have seen that, for example, oracular verse has, in general for Sicily, little claim to be regarded as either authentic or more ancient than the late sixth century, but some of it was certainly among the primary sources of prose historiography: a case in point is the Astylos oracle which provided the synchronism of Syracuse and Kroton until its authority was overthrown by criticism. Here, the primary source was probably false to historical fact, and the criticism which arose from 'inference and construction' probably true; in many cases however we should expect that the primary sources will be truer than 'inference and construction', and sometimes (where the progress of learned argument can be traced) this can even be demonstrated, as in the change from 36- to 39-year cousinly generations at Syracuse. But the fragmentary state of most of our literary sources means that, in general, we must place a heavy reliance on archaeological information not only to assess the truth of statements, but also for assistance in tracing out the development of the learned tradition itself, by giving it a firm starting-point.

A. THE CHALKIDIAN AND MEGARIAN CITIES. These cities fall into several groups:
(1) Naxos, Leontinoi, and Katane on the Laistrygonian plain: Naxos was the oldest *polis* in Sicily. Naxos and Katane were depopulated in 476/5, their inhabitants being sent to Leontinoi, and Aitne being founded on the site of Katane.

(2) Trotilon, Leontinoi, Thapsos, and Megara Hyblaia are the early sites of the Megarians: they quickly abandoned Trotilon and Thapsos, and were expelled from Leontinoi. Megara Hyblaia was itself de-

179

populated about 484/3. Selinous, founded from Megara, was captured by the Carthaginians in 409/8.

(3) Zankle and Rhegion in the straits, of which Zankle was founded from Cumae. Chersonesos-Mylai (if this identification is correct) and Himera were founded from Zankle. Zankle claimed to be the oldest of this group and was said to have been originally a pirate's nest; after her own constitution as a *polis* she assisted the establishment of Rhegion. Soon after the defeat of the Ionian Revolt in 493/2, Zankle was repopulated by Samians, and again, soon afterwards, by Messenians sent from Rhegion who changed the name to Messene; another resettlement occurred in 461/0. This was the city which possessed a probably genuine Delphic oracle of the fifth century forbidding the names of the oecists to be used in ritual. Mylai was the granary of Zankle; Himera's founders included the Myletid exiles from Syracuse: the town gave its name to the great battle of 481/0 or 480/79. It was partly repopulated (after its defeat by Theron) in 466/5, again in 461/0, and destroyed by Carthage in 409/8.

Among these foundations, those where a continuous population had the opportunity of forming a continuous tradition down to the time of Antiochos (424/3) were Leontinoi, Chersonesos-Mylai, Rhegion, Selinous, and, partially, Himera. The effects of the depopulations elsewhere may have been various: the Naxian and Katanaian groups in the population of Leontinoi after 476/5, the Megarian group in Syracuse after 484/3, may have maintained their identity and confirmed it by preservation of their traditions; or they and other groups may have been demoralised and either abandoned their history or elaborated it propagandistically; these are questions to be discussed in each case.

The archaeological evidence provides as yet nothing for the foundation period in the cases of Katane, Himera, Rhegion, and Trotilon. There is some eighth-century material from Naxos, Leontinoi, Zankle, Thapsos, and Megara, and from Mylai where the oldest material is comparable with the earliest from Syracuse. More complete publication of the Selinous material places that foundation earlier than the beginning of the Ripe Corinthian period, and in terms of the absolute dates given to the rate of stylistic development, this means that the foundation of Selinous occurred about 650 B.C.

Direct evidence for genealogical data is limited to the report that Anaxilas of Rhegion (like the contemporary Deinomenid and Emmenid tyrants) had a genealogy.

180

The geography of these settlements makes it certain that the Euboians of Cumae were mainly interested in metal; those at Mylai, Naxos, Leontinoi, and Katane in agriculture; those in Zankle and Rhegion in shipping, transport and communications. By the end of the eighth century therefore there was an important Euboian enclave in the west, self-sufficient in food-supplies overall, and feeding metal into the world market over and above the defence and industrial requirements of the Euboian settlements themselves. Given this enclave, with Zankle able to call on the agricultural surplus of Naxos and her daughters as well as on Mylai, the function of Zankle and Rhegion is clear; to assist and expedite cargoes moving to and from Cumae, and to admit competitors only when they operated in Cumaean interests. This amounts to 'piracy': the forcible exaction of imposts or control of movement within waters unilaterally decided to be territorial: and this designation of piracy seem to be the only surviving historiographic reflection of the geographical facts of the foundation period.

i. Naxos and Trotilon.   We have seen above that Hellanikos dated Naxos and at least one other city (Leontinoi, or Trotilon or Megara); and that Antiochos accepted or re-worked this date as 737/6 for Naxos and Trotilon.

The year 737/6 is $36 \times 7\frac{1}{4}$ years before the depopulation of Naxos in 476/5, and it seems probable that this was Antiochos' calculation, given a *terminus ante* by the priority of Naxos over Syracuse. Given, therefore, a date for Syracuse and the historical date of the depopulation of Naxos, Antiochos could devise the date of 737/6 for Naxos without requiring local Naxian genealogical evidence – though it seems plain from the summary of the foundation narrative in Thucydides, and references to it in our other sources, that the Naxians were able to preserve something of their traditions, probably in connection with the hero-cult of Theokles.

The narrative (though not the date) seems also to have been accepted by Ephoros, probably on the authority of Philistos. Ephoros dated Naxos together with Megara, but in the tenth generation from Troy, that is before 760 B.C. (It seems likely that Ephoros took the $7\frac{1}{4}$ generations of Antiochos, reworked them as $39 \times 7\frac{1}{3}$ years, and so added 286 years to the depopulation date of 476/5 to arrive at the year 762/1.)

The Eusebian source however seems to have separated Trotilon

181

from Naxos. Naxos in 741/0 is $225=27\times8\frac{1}{3}=36\times6\frac{1}{4}$ years before the Naxian thalassocracy which began in 516/5: local Sikeliote historiography is here replaced by local island historiography, and this date will ultimately have come from Aglaosthenes or one of the other local historians of Naxos. The Eusebian year of 758/7 for Megara (i.e. Trotilon), takes the Antiochine date as 36×7 years before Gelon came to Syracuse in 485/4 and re-works it as $39\times7=273$ years. But of course with the Megarians dated to 758/7 and Naxos to 741/0, the narrative of the Megarians in Theokles' convoy must have been abandoned and replaced by some other story, no doubt provided by local historians of old Megara.

In these datings therefore there is a considerable difference between the earlier and later chronographers: the earlier rest upon the Sikeliote narrative of Theokles' convoy and the Sikeliote statement that Naxos was the earliest *polis* to be founded. The later, as represented for us by Eusebius, derive from the local histories of the metropolitan Megara and Naxos, and in the dating of Naxos we observe that the work came to Eusebius through the 'sea-power historian'. In no case need we suppose the existence or use of genealogical data.

ii. Katane and Leontinoi. Antiochos placed Katane later than Leontinoi, but Thucydides does not report the year, and the only surviving date is Eusebian. This is 736/5, which is $260=39\times6\frac{2}{3}$ years before the depopulation in 476/5, and $26=39\times\frac{2}{3}$ years later than the Ephoran Naxos. It seems likely therefore that the Eusebian date comes ultimately from Ephoros-Philistos, and that it was not in origin intended to synchronise with Syracuse: probably the synchronism (taken as definitely establishing or illustrating the seniority of Naxos to Syracuse) was due to some such compilatory chronographer as Apollodoros. Once more, the foundation narrative which makes Katane the younger daughter of Naxos, is sufficient to account for the date; we do not need to suppose the use or existence of genealogical data.

For Leontinoi, the elder sister of Katane, we have two foundation-dates. Antiochos' year of 731/0 is $65=39\times1\frac{2}{3}$ years before his Akrai, $130=39\times3\frac{1}{3}$ years before his Kamarina, and $247=39\times6\frac{1}{3}$ years before his base-date in 484/3: that is, his Leontine history is tied in with his Syracusan-Megarian dates. This suggests the existence of a narrative of Syracusan-Leontine disputes and agreements on their common frontiers in the Heraian hills, but once more we do not need to look for a Leontine genealogical source: a foundation after Naxos but within the lifetime of Theokles leaves very little room for choice within the possible model dates.

This is perhaps why the alternative date for Leontinoi is only a year earlier, in 732/1, which is $234 = 39 \times 6$ years before the accession in Gela in 498/7 of Hippokrates, who ended Leontine independence. This historiography however seems to have emphasized the connection of Leontinoi with Megara Hyblaia rather than with Syracuse, for it is presumably from the same source that Eusebius derives his date of 615/4 for Panaitios of Leontinoi, the first of the Sicilian tyrants, who came to power as the result of a war with Megara: his year is $143 = 39 \times 3\frac{2}{3}$ years after Trotilon in 758/7; $117 = 39 \times 3$ years after Leontinoi in 732/1 and $117 = 39 \times 3$ years before Hippokrates in Gela in 498/7. The basis for these calculations is unknown to us, but looks to be of the latest kind, while the assertion that Panaitios was the first of the Sicilian tyrants is polemical. We should not therefore suppose that any local Leontine genealogy is involved.

No date for the constitutionalist and law-giver Charondas of Katane survives, though there were probably several given in the ancient literature.

iii. Megara Hyblaia, and Selinous. Antiochos' date of 737/6 for Naxos, together with the foundation narrative, carried with it the date of 737/6 for the settlement of the accompanying Megarians at Trotilon; and similarly the settlement at Leontinoi in 731/0 gave the date for the cooperation of the Megarians in that settlement. Apparently he placed the Megarians at Thapsos in 730/29, and the final settlement at Megara Hyblaia in 729/8; Selinous in 629/8 is $108 = 36 \times 3$ years after the arrival at Trotilon.

Ephoros similarly by accepting the story that the Megarians travelled in Theokles' convoy gave the same date to Trotilon as to Naxos (762/1?).

Eusebius' source however dates Trotilon to 758/7 and Naxos to 741/0, so he clearly believed that the Megarians came to Sicily independently of Theokles' convoy. The mention of Megara with the foundation of Leontinoi in 732/1 however guarantees for this source also the cooperation of the Megarians in that foundation: presumably Thapsos and the death of Lamis were dated to 731/0, which is $81 = 27 \times 3$ years before the foundation of Selinous in 650/49. This dating

183

therefore continues to maintain Selinous at 108 years after Trotilon, but adds the reckoning of 81 years from the death of Lamis. This probably means that Lamis' successor as leader of the Megarians was a junior foundation-member of the colonizing force, and that Selinous was founded at the beginning of his great-grandson's generation: Antiochos counted 108 years from Trotilon to Selinous, the Eusebian source counted $81 = 27 \times 3$ years from the succession in Thapsos to the foundation of Selinous. The earlier date for Selinous is presumably due to Philistos, who seems in this case to have used more detail from the foundation narratives than is given to us by Thucydides.

iv. Zankle and her colonies. Since Eusebius synchronizes Trotilon with Zankle, presumably his source brought the Megarians to Sicily in a Chalkidian convoy, but not that of Theokles of Naxos. The problems of the dates of Zankle and her colonies are however considerable.

The only certain surviving date for Zankle is the Eusebian 758/7 contemporary with Trotilon. At this placing, Zankle is an alternative for Naxos as the companion of the Megarians, and is therefore probably no more than a necessary part of the Megarian doctrine: we need not look for genealogical or other evidence.

As we have seen, Philistos' era year of 756/5 is probably his date for the foundation of Zankle, for the surviving dates of two Zanklaian colonies are chronographically connected with it. Chersonesos-Mylai is dated by Eusebius to 717/6, which is 39×1 years later than 756/5, but seems to be connected with no other dates; it is also too late for the archaeological evidence which places Mylai as coeval with Syracuse. We do not, therefore, know why a 39-year generation was in this case chosen: the choice was wrong.

Himera in 648/7 is $108 = 36 \times 3$ years after Zankle in 756/5, and $168 = 36 \times 4\frac{2}{3}$ years before the Battle of Himera dated to 480/79 (contemporary with Salamis). There is not yet archaeological evidence available from Himera, but it is obviously possible that the generations are too long. The year 648/7 is also important for the history of Syracuse: the Myletidai who joined in the foundation of Himera were exiles from Syracuse (though we do not know why); and the year is also that of the first known Syracusan victory at Olympia, won by Lygdamis, the Sicilian Herakles. It is therefore quite as likely that the generation-count came from Syracusan material as from Himeraian, or the Myletidai may have had a genealogy. The date of 756/5 for Zankle seems to continue this generation-count upwards, but on what evidence is quite obscure.

Zankle began as a pirate settlement and achieved an independent and regular constitution later; in Thucydides' list the name appears after that of Gela, which suggests that the regular constitution was dated after 691/0. After this achievement, she founded Rhegion with help from Chalkis and some Messenians: this seems to be supported by Diodorus (VIII 21), whose fragments place the foundation of Rhegion between that of Gela (691/0 in probably all authorities) and the legislation of Zaleukos at Lokroi (663/2 in Eusebius).

The foundation of Rhegion was the subject of a considerable narrative, of which we seem to have fragments of several versions. Strabo (VI 1.6) apparently quoting Antiochos (555 F 9) says that the Chalkidians were preparing to send their colonists to Rhegion when they were joined by some Messenians lingering in Makistos, whither they had been expelled for wishing to repair the sacrilege at the sanctuary of Artemis at Limnai. This sacrilege is placed by Pausanias among the preliminaries to the first Messenian war, fought by Theopompos of Sparta, but if Thucydides rightly represents Antiochos on the regular constitution of Zankle after 691/0, and the foundation of Rhegion still later, then Antiochos cannot have agreed with Pausanias that the sacrilege occurred before the Theopompos war and about 745 B.C.

Pausanias (IV 23.6 ff.) is also our authority for the statements that Alkidamidas the Messenian went to Rhegion at the end of the Theopompos war, and that he was great-grandfather of the tyrant Anaxilas of Rhegion (494/3–476/5), who brought the Messenians Gorgos and Mantiklos to Rhegion and Zankle-Messene in 664/3, at the end of the second Messenian war. This is plainly one of Pausanias' muddles, but in view of the Thucydidean and Strabonian evidence on Antiochos' narrative, it may be suspected that Pausanias was only increasing an already existing difficulty. It is in fact unlikely that, in Antiochos' time, mainland historiography knew (or had constructed) much of the relations between Sparta and Messenia other than the bare fact of a conquest, and the notion that revolts were frequent. It is consequently probable that Antiochos derived his date for Rhegion (and so, possibly, his date for the regular constitution of Zankle) from Rhegine material on the period of Messenian dominance in that city, using at least the genealogy of Anaxilas. It seems likely that there also existed a genealogy of the descendants of Mantiklos, for a priest of Herakles

185

Mantiklos (most probably a descendant) appears in the stories of the restoration of Messenia (Paus. IV 26.3).

v. Chalkidian and Megarian tradition in general: the 'Euboian lacuna'. In this group of cities, our search for original information has divided into two pursuits, one for genealogical and the other for narrative material. So far as can be seen, in only one case was there any substantial change from the Antiochine narratives known to us from Thucydides: the Eusebian source, dating Trotilon in 758/7 and Naxos in 741/0 must have made Lamis' expedition independent of Theokles' convoy.

The noteworthy fact about the inferred genealogical material is that it is all apparently Dorian. The dates for Rhegion seem to depend on the Messenians; those for Zankle and Chersonesos-Mylai are of unknown or Megarian origin; Himera is probably dated from the Myletidai of Syracusan extraction. Naxos, Leontinoi, and Katane are derived from the dates given to Syracuse and the narratives; the dates of Selinous are Megarian and Dorian. This characteristic of the inferred genealogical material may reflect a characteristic of the historians, for both Antiochos and Philistos are themselves Dorian, but at least in Antiochos' case this does not seem wholly probable. It is possible therefore that, in Greek history in general, we may have to reckon with a Euboian lacuna in the material most suited to chronographic treatment, an absence of lineage-records as a characteristic of Euboian culture and tradition.

B. THE RHODIAN AND KNIDIAN CITIES. These cities are:
(1) Gela, its colony Akragas, and the associated settlement at Lipara. We have already discussed the Akragantine controversy in several aspects, and seen that in the first instance at least the high dating by Philistos did not necessarily involve a reconstruction of the Emmenid genealogy.

(2) Ebesos in the Balearics, occupied by the Carthaginians at the expense of the Rhodians. This event, dated to 654/3, seems in Philistos' historiography to be the starting-point for the series of foundations in the mid-seventh century: Selinous, Akragas, Himera, and Lipara.

(3) Much more vaguely, Pandosia and Makalla in Italy: Pandosia if

it is the town near Siris and represents the Rhodian settlement before the Kolophonians there; and Makalla if the Eusebian entry is rightly read, and is a variant tradition about the Rhodian settlement after the Trojan war.

The archaeological evidence provides as yet nothing for Pandosia and Makalla: Makalla indeed has not yet been identified, unless it is Petelia. Pandosia may be part of the later Siris, which has not been dug, but which according to Antiochos was founded by Kolophonians after their defeat by Gyges. Gyges died in or after 648, so the Kolophonian settlement was probably not long before—say 655 ± 5, and the Rhodian should then be earlier. In the Balearics, the Carthaginian occupation is to be dated about 575, though whether before or after the expedition of Pentathlos which resulted in the colonisation of Lipara it is impossible to say. The archaeological evidence from Gela, Akragas, and Lipara supports the Antiochine dates and rules out Philistos' seventh-century foundations.

Direct evidence for genealogies is found in that of the Deinomenids in Gela (which possibly went back to the foundation), that of the Emmenids in Akragas (which went back to the death of Phalaris if not before), and in the statement that Pentathlos of Lipara was descended from Hippotes, presumably the Herakleid father of the Corinthian Aletes.

i. Gela. Only one date is known, in 691/0, and it may have been universally accepted. It may be Hellanikan in origin, and have in the first place meant five cousinly generations before the expedition of Dorieus in 511/0, for his Carthaginian war was inherited by the Deinomenids. For Antiochos and the Eusebian source the date meant also $45 = 36 \times 1\frac{1}{4}$ years after Syracuse: for Philistos $65 = 39 \times 1\frac{2}{3}$ years after Zankle; for Timaios it would mean $91 = 39 \times 2\frac{1}{3}$ years before Massalia, as well as, in all cases, five cousinly generations before Dorieus. All the chronographic systems therefore accommodate the date, and it is probably one of their main determinants. If so, it is the genealogy and historiography of the Deinomenids which is a constant in Sikeliote dating, and this document (whether existing then in a written form or not) was already in being when Herodotus abstracted from it – and indeed it is not likely to have been first composed after 466/5 B.C.

We have seen in previous chapters that this Deinomenid document, as it came to the historians, can scarcely have itself included a year-date for the foundation either of Gela or of Akragas; while it is presumably the same document which is the source for the very exact dating of the successive tyrants. That is to say, its original information provided historical year-dates only, to which the chronographers later added their computations: these historical year-dates begin after the foundation of Akragas about 575, and before Gelon's seizure of power in Gela in 491/0. It now appears that we should raise this historical horizon by at least twenty years, and say that the historical dates begin at latest with the expedition of Dorieus in 511/0. Since this was used as the base-date for reckoning the foundation-date of Gela, it was also probably the earliest historical date given in this document. This perhaps implies that from 511/0 onwards the document became in part a historical narrative proper, laying out (in however tendentious a fashion) a sequence of events linked by cause and effect, and centering in the story of the struggle with Carthage.

From the point of view of a Sikeliote historiography of which the Deinomenid record was the foundation document, we should probably see Philistos' elaboration of the struggle with Carthage as one kind of derivative, and the Eusebian source's attempt to date early events from the accession of Hippokrates another kind—an endeavour to carry exact annals back before 491/0. But because these calculations are made from Hippokrates' first year, and do not in fact (so far as we can see) provide annals for his reign, we should infer that from 511/0 to 491/0 the original document was not in fact annalistic, but gave only time elapsed and lengths of reigns, while from 491/0 onwards it was so detailed that it was possible (for Philistos, probably) to translate its figures very precisely into Olympic years.

Since Thucydides says that the foundation of Gela in 691/0 was a 'reinforcement', presumably the document mentioned Rhodian and Cretan visits to the area of Gela before the definitive colonisation. It is however unlikely that the document included either the Hellanikan account of the mythical eponym, or the synchronisation of Gela with Phaselis, both of which seem to be poetic in origin. What we should like to know, and do not, is whether the document gave any information, or hints, on the relationship between the foundation of Gela and the Assyrian victories over Greeks in the Levant in 696 and preceding years—the only statement which is preserved and might be relevant is that which derives the Deinomenid priesthood from Cyprus. No doubt in time the archaeological evidence will be able to provide more exact information on the precise time-sequence between the events of 696 B.C. and the foundation of Gela.

ii. Akragas. The *traditio* of this foundation begins in pre-chronographic times with Pindar's date of *c*.575: undoubtedly this date comes from, or was compatible with, an Emmenid document analogous to that of the Deinomenids in Gela, but not preserved like theirs. The chronographic renderings of this information provide the years 583/2 and 580/79: the first of these is Antiochine, and places the foundation two cousinly generations before Dorieus in 511/0. This is probably a slight adjustment for tidiness' sake, and may be criticized by the authority who preferred 580/79 reckoned directly from Theron's Olympic victory in 476/5.

These dates in the period 580 ± 4 are supported by the archaeological evidence and derived from local tradition: only Antiochos' version gives a wider context, by numerical relations with Geloan and Syracusan dates, and there is no evidence that even he supported his numbers with any extensive narrative. But when Philistos raised the date to 652/1, it seems certain that he did so because he placed Akragas in a general historiographic context, the opening of a new period of relations between the Sikeliotes and Carthage: we shall return to this below. The effect on local tradition was, as we have seen, ultimately very confusing, but Philistos himself did not need to tamper with the genealogy at all, and little with the narrative—merely changing the fall of Phalaris from an event in the old age of Telemachos to an event in his youth.

One of the more obscure statements in the Akragantine controversy is that attributed to Aristophanes of Byzantium: the Emmenidai were a *phatria*. In the context of Sikeliote historiography, it is difficult to dissociate this genealogical statement from the attribution of cousinly values to some generations (including, apparently, those of the Emmenids). If by a *phatria* Aristophanes meant a genealogical record to which historians agreed in attributing cousinly chronographies, then he need not have had any special information or theory about the Emmenidai: and Aristarchos' denial that the Emmenid name came from the phatria organization is then at least in part a refusal to admit the propriety of drawing chronographic and genealogical inferences from poetic language—a refusal no doubt based on encounter with innumerable 'historical' inferences from Homer.

189

iii. Ebesos. The archaeological evidence available here shows that Greeks began to visit the Balearics about 600, and were expelled by Carthage about 575. Timaios, almost certainly drawing on Philistos, dates the Carthaginian occupation to 654/3, while Strabo includes Rhodian Ebesos among the settlements resulting from voyages made 'a good many years before the first Olympiad'. For these authors, the Carthaginian occupation presumably drove out the Rhodians, and Timaios at least must have somehow explained the relationship between this event, and the Samian and Phokaian interest in Tartessos, usually dated from about 640 onwards.[1]

Carthaginian Ebesos in 654/3 is the first of a series of mid-seventh-century foundations which are all probably due to Philistos and are part of one of his principal historiographic theses: Ebesos in 654/3 provokes a Greek response expressed in the foundations of Akragas in 652/1, Selinous in 650/49, Himera in 648/7, and Lipara in 630/29. Among these dates, archaeology supports that of Selinous, is silent on Himera, and contradicts those of Ebesos, Akragas, and Lipara, but places the last three at about the same date, *c.*575. We may therefore infer that Philistos started from the approximate contemporaneity of Ebesos, Akragas, and Lipara as set out in some narrative, and from the achievement of a more accurate date for Selinous than had been given by Antiochos: the problem is how he combined these data into a false thesis.

One of his reasons may be geographical: Selinous is further west than Akragas, and the choice of this site may imply that Akragantine territory was already recognised as pre-empted by Gela. This argument may have been reinforced by narratives about Geloan visits to, and settlement in, Akragas at an earlier time than the 570's, for there is archaeological evidence for both by the late seventh century. With the date of Selinous fixed to 650/49 therefore, the problem was to find somewhat earlier dates for Ebesos and Akragas. For Akragas a generation after the foundation of Gela was compatible with the Emmenid genealogy and with the narrative of Telemachos slightly adjusted: and this would be sufficient. For Ebesos however as the starting-point of the series of foundations and the historiographic view, more substantial evidence would surely be required.

Ebesos in 654/3 is $247 = 39 \times 6\frac{1}{3}$ years before the next recorded

---

[1] The problems thus raised for the dating of Kyrene probably account for the Eusebian date of 762/1 for the first ('Theban') foundation: this is $108 = 36 \times 3 = 27 \times 4$ years before the Carthaginian occupation of Ebesos.

Carthaginian foundation, that of Therma in Sicily in 407/6 (Diod. Sic. XIII 79). It we take the same number of generations, but use the ithagenic value of 27 years, we obtain the period of 171 years and therefore the date of 578/7 for Carthaginian Ebesos, which agrees with the archaeological evidence. The inference is therefore that Philistos used, and misvalued, a lineage record to fix the date of Carthaginian Ebesos.

iv. Lipara. Timaios reports that Pentathlos was descended from Hippotes, presumably the father of Aletes of Corinth: and from Corinth in 1152/1 to Lipara in 580/79 is $572 = 39 \times 14\frac{2}{3}$ years. We do not know Philistos' date for Dorian Corinth, but his date for Lipara in 630/29 is $18 = 36 \times \frac{1}{2}$ years after the expulsion of the Myletidai from Syracuse in 648/7, and also $522 = 36 \times 14\frac{1}{2}$ years after 1152/1. It may be therefore that Philistos shared Timaios' date for Corinth and the genealogy of Pentathlos, but gave the generations a different value.

v. Pandosia and Makalla. Eusebius pairs Pandosia with Metapontion, probably in 771/0, and Makalla with Kaulonia? in 757/6: Pandosia probably stands for the Rhodian phase in the development of Siris, and Metapontion (according to Antiochos) was organized by Sybaris as an outpost against the Spartan Taras; Kaulonia was a settlement by Achaian Aigion, but organized by Kroton. The Eusebian dates therefore seem to present a thesis: that Metapontion and Kaulonia existed before Sybaria and Kroton, and that at this early date their Pandosian and Makallan partners were Rhodian.

These very late and tendentious datings are only of interest in so far as we can discern through them a tradition resting on older material. The year 771/0 is 39×7 years before 498/7, and 757/6 is $378 = 36 \times 10\frac{1}{2}$ years before the destruction of Kaulonia in 389/8. If we apply ithagenic values, we obtain 687 for Pandosia and Metapontion, 674 for Makalla and Kaulonia, and these dates agree with the available archaeological evidence: at Metapontion, votive figurines from the temple of Apollo Lykeios perhaps go back to 700, and at Kaulonia fragments of early seventh century pottery have been found.

It is noteworthy that in these cases the ithagenic values are supported by the archaeological evidence; in Sicily on the other hand cousinly generations are correct for Syracuse, Gela, and Akragas; in Ebesos, Philistos interprets as cousinly a generation count which the archaeology shows should have been ithagenically valued. The variety,

191

if not the number, of the original sources available to the historians was obviously great, and in the absence of really detailed and wide-ranging accurate narratives, giving true synchronisms—that is, of a regional view of the history even in the oral period—errors of inter-pretation could scarcely have been avoided.

C. THE CORINTHIAN CITIES. These form two groups:

(1) Syracuse and her colonies, Akrai, Kasmenai, and Kamarina;

(2) other foundations synchronized with Syracuse by various historians: Achaian Kroton and Corinthian Corcyra. The synchron-ism with Kroton depends on the Astylos oracle, and is abandoned after criticism.

The archaeological evidence from Corcyra is not yet clear; that from Syracuse upholds the Antiochine 736/5 against the earlier date, and Kamarina around 600 is also acceptable. At Akrai however none of the pottery seems as early as 650, and if Monte Casale is Kasmenai the earliest pottery is of the late seventh century.

There is no record of any genealogies from these cities: Archias of Syracuse is said to have had daughters only[2] which should mean that by the time of the source of this statement he had no known lineage in Syracuse. But the Gamoroi (and the Myletidai) will certain-ly have included some lineages who knew their genealogies.

i. Syracuse. The seven generations of the Gamoroi provide both of the known dates, in 736/5 and 758/7. We must assume that the figure was well established in general report long before our historical sources were published.

ii. Corcyra. There is very wide divergence in the dates for Corcyra: synchronized with the Ephoran Syracuse, the foundation is dated to 758/7; while Timaios dates it in 708/7 and Eusebius in 706/5. Antiochos' date is unfortunately unknown.

Corcyra had no local historians, and probably no genealogical material survived the various civil wars: for all historians therefore her foundation-date would be inferential.

From the tyranny onwards, the Corinthian community seems to have consisted of the metropolis Corinth herself, and a group of outposts inhabited by Corinthian citizens at Molykreion, Chalkis,

---

[2] Plt. *Am. Narr.* 2 ad fin.

Sollion, in Leukas, at Anaktorion and in Ambrakia. Corcyra and her colonies at Epidamnos and Apollonia stand outside this compact Corinthian community as a constant threat, temptation, and anachronism. In this situation we may properly suppose that a high date for Corcyra represents the thesis that her freedom was as ancient as that of Syracuse, while a low date expresses the Corinthian view that her seniority was not great enough to exempt her from Corinthian control. Timaios' low date is connected with a narrative that makes her founder Chersikrates expelled from Corinth with dishonour, which suggests that Corinthian propaganda added insult to injury: yet the relative seniority of Corcyra to the colonies of the tyranny could not be disputed—the controversy was whether the seniority was great enough to command exemption from Corinthian control.

The Eusebian date of 706/5 for Corcyra seems to be connected with the story of an earlier Eretrian settlement, for 706/5 is 216 = 27 × 8 = 36 × 6 years before the destruction of Eretria in 490/89; and with a narrative that synchronized Corinthian Corcyra and Spartan Taras in a joint political venture in the west, 195 = 39 × 5 years before the expedition of Dorieus.

The earlier date seems to be no less constructive. Strabo (VI 2.6) is probably drawing on Ephoros for his picture of a Corinthian στρατία led by Archias and Chersikrates—an undertaking even more firmly organized than Theokles' convoy. The generation-count of 'tenth from Temenos' and therefore ninth from Aletes (given by the Parian Marble, also from Ephoros) places Archias and Chersikrates in the same generation as king Telestes: and Jerome at Telestes' third year has the entry *Trieres prima nauigauit in Corintho*. It appears therefore that Ephoros equipped Archias and Chersikrates with triremes.

One of Thucydides' sources however placed the invention of the trireme later, and reported that the Corinthian Ameinokles built ships for Samos in or about 704/3, which is around the time of the lower date for Corinthian Corcyra. It is possible therefore that Timaios and Eusebius have reworked a date for Corcyra and the trireme given by Antiochos on Corinthian information, while Ephoros dated them both in deference to Corcyrean opinion.

There is some reason to believe that in this as in other cases Ephoros was inspired by Philistos. Philistos' account of the foundation of Carthage was shared with his contemporary Eudoxos of Knidos, which is a fairly curious point of agreement; and Knidos was the metropolis not only of Lipara, but also of the Black Corcyra in the

Adriatic; it was the Knidians too who persuaded the Samians to let the Corcyrean boys go free. It may well be therefore that the Corcyrean case was presented to Philistos through Knidian sources, together with other information which Philistos shared with Eudoxos.

iii. Kamarina. Antiochos dates this foundation to 601/0, which is $3\frac{1}{4}$ cousinly generations before 484/3, when the Kamarinaioi became Syracusan citizens. Timaios' date in 612/1 is $36 \times 1\frac{2}{3}$ years before the first Syracusan conquest of Kamarina in 552/1, and the anonymous (Ephoran?) date of 597/6 is $27 \times 1\frac{2}{3}$ years before the same conquest. This ithagenically valued reckoning, like Antiochos' differently based computation, agrees with the archaeological evidence. The date of 552/1 may be historical, or approximately so.

iv. Akrai and Kasmenai. These foundations are dated, to our knowledge, only by Antiochos, to 666/5 and 646/5, and these years do not agree with the archaeological evidence. Akrai is $65 = 39 \times 1\frac{2}{3}$ years, Kasmenai $45 = 36 \times 1\frac{1}{4}$ years, before Kamarina: Thucydides records no oecist for either foundation, although Kamarina has two, from Syracuse and Corinth. This absence of oecists has sometimes led to the supposition that there was some difference or disagreement in Antiochos' view between Corinth and Syracuse at this time. We should add that the 39-year computation for Akrai is unusual among Antiochos' Sicilian datings, and that in any case cousinly generations for such short periods seem out of place.

The inference is that Antiochos was moved by some external consideration to place the dates of Akrai and Kasmenai as early as was compatible with Syracusan tradition, and that this consideration arose from Corinthian history. We shall examine this question below.

The dates for the colonies of Syracuse imply either genealogical material, or its equivalent in fairly detailed narratives.

D. CONCLUSIONS. It is clear from the foregoing that the most important kind of original information in almost all cases was a narrative about the foundation. We do not know how these narratives were preserved, but we may guess that the annual herocult of the oecists normally included hymnography, in which the exploits and achievements of the hero were glorified. Whether the history to which these hymns referred was formally taught as part of the music lesson of the choirs, or recapitulated in some form as is found in the traditional *Seder*, or regarded as part of the natural equipment of every respectable family, is not clear: probably all three means were used, in varying balance in the different communities.

Oracular poetry probably for the most part developed from these hymns, and became independent with the growth of learning, since as 'Delphic' it was pan-Hellenic and would not weary the reader with tiresome local detail. Two oracles have been noted as of special importance: that of Zankle because it is genuine; that of Astylos because it was accepted as giving a synchronism between Syracuse and Kroton.

Historiographic theory, as an independent source of statements, is of importance in the case of Philistos' series from Ebesos to Lipara. We have not yet examined the effects of historiographic correlation between the colonies and their metropoleis, though in the very various stories about the Messenians of Rhegion its effects are obvious.

Ideological tendentiousness, as an independent source of statements, is again of importance in the case of Corcyra, where the motivation is transparent.

In general therefore, although hero-hymns would naturally be subject to at least a slow process of revision and renewal, and although oracular, historiographic and ideological elements would enter into these revisions and more strongly into the supporting oral commentaries, still it appears that by the time of Antiochos most of the statements that could be abstracted from these sources were reasonably sound.

In the Ionian communities, so far as we can see, genealogies and lineage-records were either not part of local learning or were not of any precise and historically usable form. Among the Dorians they were apparently frequent and precise, and the historians relied upon this Dorian habit to find exact year-dates by chronographic methods. There were, apparently, both cousinly and ithagenic records, and the historians sometimes mistook one kind for another—we have seen how the abbreviated legal form of a cousinhood record would approximate in appearance to a lineage. In some cases (as at Gela) the genealogy mainly used by the chronographers is known to us from prose, independently of the arithmetical evidence; in some cases (the Mantiklids of Rhegion and Zankle-Messene) prose references help us to identify possible sources of the arithmetic; in other cases (pre-eminently Ebesos) the arithmetical is the only surviving evidence.

195

The genealogies identified or inferred as the basis of chronographic arithmetic are:

1. the Deinomenidal at Gela

2. a general report agreed upon by the Herakleids among the Gamoroi at Syracuse;

3. the Emmenidai at Akragas

4. the ancestry of Anaxilas, and probably the descendants of Mantiklos, at Rhegion and Zankle;

5. the Myletidai at Himera;

6. an unknown source at Selinous, probably the ancestry of Pamillos' fellow-oecist from Megara Hyblaia;

7. an unknown source used by Philistos to fix the date of Carthaginian Ebesos;

8. either genealogies or detailed narratives were used to fix the dates of Akrai, Kasmenai, and Kamarina.

It is now possible to draw up a table of dates for these colony foundations, derived from the literary and mathematical evidence, in the light of archaeological knowledge presently available. The most useful interpretation of genealogical values is probably that of the refined dividend, ignoring the first generation of an institution because that is unpredictably variable. But in these particular cases it is precisely this unpredictably variable foundation date that we seek, and therefore the final column in the table gives the crude dividend dates, the *terminus ante quem non*, in each case where genealogical calculation can be supposed.

The final and much hoped-for release of the archaeological time-scale from dependence on the literary evidence could be achieved by a partnership with demography. There are now enough materials for a figure to be obtained—say from fifth-century Athenian pottery—for the average working lifetime of potters and painters. Once obtained, this figure could be applied to pottery of earlier style and the inter-mediate transitional periods thus built up.[3] Once this is done for Proto-Corinthian and Corinthian, we shall have an independent measure for the average lengths of the ithagenic and cousinly generations of the original material, and can then judge more precisely the accuracy of the ancient chronographers.

---

[3] Compare, for other but similar contentions, C. M. Robertson, 'Attic Red Figure Vase-painters' in JHS 85 (1965) pp.90 ff.

TABLE XII

FINAL MODEL DATES

Best (or only) chronographic date	FOUNDATION	Archaeological date	Ancient Base-date and calculation or derivation	Crude dividend date (*terminus ante quem non*)
758/7	1. ZANKLE pirates	C 8	derived from Megara or from Himera	—
737/6	2. NAXOS	C 8	derived from Syracuse	—
	3. TROTILON	—	derived from Naxos	—
736/5	4. SYRACUSE	C 8	7 cousinly generations of Gamoroi before 484/3	729±7
731/0	5. LEONTINOI	C 8	in the lifetimes of Theokles and Lamis	—
736/5	6. KATANE	—	derived from Naxos	—
729/8	7. MEGARA	C 8	derived from Leontinoi	—
717/6	8. CHERSONESOS-MYLAI	coeval with Syracuse	a cousinly generation after 756/5	—
691/0	9. GELA polis	confirms	five cousinly generations before 511/0	686±5
	10. ZANKLE polis			
666/5	11. AKRAI	after 650	1½ cousinly generations before Kamarina	642
664/3?	12. RHEGION polis	—		
650/49	13. SELINOUS	confirms	three ithagenic generations after Megara	
648/7	14. HIMERA	—	4⅔ cousinly generations before 480/79	643±4 if generations rightly taken as cousinly
646/5	15. KASMENAI	later	over a generation before Kamarina	597?
597/6	16. KAMARINA	confirms	1⅔ generations before 552/1	c.575
580/79	17. AKRAGAS	confirms	Pindar's century	c.575
580/79	18. LIPARA	confirms		c.575

197

PART SEVEN

RELATIONS OF MAINLAND AND COLONIAL HISTORIOGRAPHY

So much of our surviving material for mainland history comes from sources notably later than the classical Sikeliote historians that we are faced with a number of quite open questions: what history of Corinth was assumed, or worked from, by Antiochos and Philistos; what effects did their work have on the Corinthian portions of the universal histories of Ephoros and Timaios? what was the history of the Messenian wars according to the Mantiklids of Rhegion and Zankle-Messene, and what effect did these traditions have on Messenian history after 369/8 B.C.? The questions could be multiplied, but in this discussion, *exempli gratia*, we shall confine ourselves to the Corinthian and Messenian departments of universal history.

A. THE CORINTHIAN CONNECTIONS. The literary tradition of Corinthian history recognizes four periods: that of the kings, that of the Bacchiad oligarchy, that of the tyranny, and that of the historical republic. Our information is all from the universal historians and chroniclers: we have no Corinthian source, and there was none of note except the work called the 'prose Eumelos'.

The alternative source for tracing out the steps in Corinthian development is the archaeological evidence which, for Dorian Corinth, begins with a period of relative depopulation and poverty. The Geometric period however sees an increasing prosperity, with considerable trade landwards, north and south of the Isthmus, and western sea-borne interests developing early as far as Ithaka. Eastern sea-borne trade is beginning to develop, through Thera to Crete, Rhodes and Cyprus, before 725, but a substantial volume of east-west trade through the isthmus only appears about 700. From that time onwards, Proto-Corinthian pottery is the most widely exported of fine wares. After 650, the style changes, and becomes the Ripe Corinthian style: this continues to be exported until it gives way to Athenian pottery in the period 575–525.

The literary and archaeological histories of Corinth thus seem to cover in general the same period, down to the end of the tyranny on the one hand, and to the falling away of pottery exports on the other. The literary tradition is of course primarily concerned with the events and persons who made the historical republic of Corinth what it was; archaeology also has other preoccupations.

Looking at the evidence as a whole, the turning-point in Corinthian history comes with the foundation of Molykreion, Chalkis, Sollion, Leukas, Anaktorion, Ambrakia, Herakleia, and Potidaia, under the tyranny. Before this time Corinth appears as a single city, exporting men to Syracuse and Corcyra, and goods to all available markets; afterwards, the community of 'the Corinthians' consists of the metropolis and the six or more settlements under her direct control in the Corinthian Gulf, the Adriatic approaches, and Potidaia. To this community of 'the Corinthians' Syracuse was, at least in material culture, a loyal outlier down to about 530 B.C.; Corcyra, with her own colonies at Epidamnos and Apollonia, was a much nearer neighbour and danger, felt no doubt by successive Corinthian régimes to be an anachronism, and by her own citizens (or some of them) a heroic custodian of ancient freedoms.

The turning point within the archaeological evidence itself seems to come with the transition from the Proto-Corinthian to the Ripe Corinthian style. These styles differ, it would seem, in addition to technical matters, in their notion of what art can do. Proto-Corinthian, according to the experts, is miniaturist and concerned with the decoration of a curved surface in fine workmanship—that is, with the visual art as such, giving pleasure to the eyes of observers whose minds, it is assumed, are not its concern. Ripe Corinthian art on the other hand is narrative and composes as though for flat surfaces: it is concerned with visual sequences which create thought-patterns in, or communicate them to, the observer. The differences in finish and workmanship between the two styles correspond to the two different artistic aims.

Obviously the question arises of how the narrative style of painting was related, if at all, to other spheres of Corinthian life: primarily literature, but also the other areas in which sequences of action are or may be important. The narrative painting becomes an established style in the years 650–625, and some fifty years later produced a

199

famous analogue in the 'chest of Kypselos' dedicated at Olympia. The great narrative poet of ancient Corinth was the Bacchiad Eumelos, who is certainly older than the tyranny and is said by our sources to have survived the foundation of Syracuse. But his fragments are full of eastern references—to Sinope, Kolchis, Borysthenes, Lydia, Phrygia, Thrace: and the Pontine names at least should mean that the poet was writing after 675, when Greek acquaintance with the Euxine seems to begin. Pausanias believed (V 19.9) that he could detect something Eumelan in the inscriptions of the 'chest of Kypselos', and this probably means that he recognized some kinship of narrative style between visual Corinthian art and Corinthian epic verse.

We have no means of judging Corinthian narrative prose, except through such intermediaries as Herodotus. It is plain that the Corinthians possessed narratives of their history, and equally plain that they were not much in the habit of writing them down. The overall impression of the thought, if we may speak loosely and generally, is one of orderliness, comprehensive but not generous and therefore not problematic: four generations of Herakleid kings, four of Bacchiads, an oligarchy internally rigid and externally arbitrary; the kindly and able Kypselos, the forceful and active Periandros—all characterizations simple and invariant, comprehensive and quite provoking.

The Corinthian ideal is summed up, apparently very truthfully, by Pindar: Eunomia, Dike, and Eirene, daughters of Themis. The same divinities were honored by the Corinthians of Ambrakia, where they were introduced by Apollo;[1] at Corinth itself the temple of Apollo was founded in the 540's, after the tyranny. The Corinthian ideal, thus made articulate in cult and poetry, seems to derive from the development traceable back to Eumelos and the seventh century.

The political forms taken by this ideal in the tyrannical period seem to include the organization of Corinthian settlements overseas. So far as can be made out, these were founded as parts of the Corinthian state and Kypselid domain, and after the tyranny fell, the membership of the Corinthian state either remained, or was restored.

A state whose ideals were expressed in the cult of Apollo support-ed by Eunomia, Dike and Eirene is not likely to have been a com-

---

[1] Athenadas of Ambrakia, Jac. 303 F 1.

munity of merchant adventurers, hardy explorers, and audacious traders. The Corinthian metropolis and its outposts commanded one sizeable plain in Ambrakia, and the large island of Leukas; dispersal of the population in some half dozen centers must have meant, at worst, that shortage of grain would not arise in all areas at once. This dispersed population was also presumably well supplied with fish, the Greek protein; some believe also that the series of outposts up to Ambrakia controlled a silver route from Illyria, while a slave trade was no doubt very possible in the Adriatic. But a dispersed and naturally diversified economy of this kind must also have meant very customary and well-established channels of exchange, easily institutionalized; while the dispersed population cannot have found political innovation easy to organize. The tumultuous and dramatic events recorded from before the settlement of Syracuse to the fall of the tyranny thus seem to have resulted in a composed and wealthy community, and we are now to see whether its history, as it survives in our sources, is due entirely to metropolitan tradition, or whether Sikeliote sources made some contribution; or whether on the other hand Sikeliote history was written against the background of a settled and changeless version of Corinthian history.

i. The orthodox chronography: a. Ephoros. In discussing Ephoros' dates for the foundation of Syracuse in 758/7, and for Naxos and 'Megara' in ⟨762/1⟩, we have identified also some of his Corinthian dates: the beginning of Aletes' rule in 1070/69 (which is $312 = 39 \times 8$ years before 758/7); the statement that Archias was 'tenth from Temenos' and therefore ninth from Aletes, and so of the same generation as Telestes, the last king of Corinth. The statement that triremes were first sailed at Corinth in the third year of Telestes has been connected with Ephoros' story of the στρατία of Archias and Chersikrates in 758/7.

The Telestes date for the triremes comes from Eusebius, who places it at a much earlier absolute year: his source for this entry was therefore not the same as his colony source, but came from an authority on the Corinthian king-list. His immediate authority can be identified as Africanus; for another derivative of Africanus, the Barbarian, reports a Corinthian king-list which exactly fits the terminal dates we identify as Ephoran, and consequently we infer that Africanus copied Ephoros' Corinthian king-list, and with it the trireme annal. We therefore attribute to Ephoros:

201

1070/69 Aletes reigned 35 years ⎫ 105 years
1035/4 ⟨Anaxion[2]⟩ 37 ⎬ =
998/7 Agelas I 33 ⎭ $(39 \times 2\frac{2}{3}) - 1$

965/4 Prymnis 35 ⎫ 104 years
930/29 Bacchis 35 ⎬ =
895/4 Agelas II 34 ⎭ $39 \times 2\frac{1}{3}$

861/0 Eudemos 25 ⎫
836/5 Aristomedes 35 ⎮
801/0 Agemon, his brother, reigned 16 years ⎮ 103 years
785/4 Alexandros, a usurper 25 ⎬ =
760/59 Telestes, son of Aristomedes ⎮ $(39 \times 2\frac{1}{3}) - 1$
758/7 3rd year: Syracuse, Corcyra, the trireme ⎭
751/0 Automenes reigned 4 years
747/6 the Bacchiad oligarchy begins

We can to some extent follow out modifications of this Ephoran chronography in later sources. Timaios' Corcyra in ⟨708/7⟩ is 39 years later than the beginning of the oligarchy in 747/6, as well as $36 \times 12\frac{1}{3}$ years after his Aletes in 1152/1. Aletes at this date is $36 \times 11\frac{1}{4}$ years before the oligarchy, which shows that Timaios counted reigns rather than generations as 36-year units. We do not know Timaios' date for Syracuse, but if he reverted to Antiochos' date of 736/5, this is $39 \times 10\frac{2}{3}$ years after Aletes in 1152/1, which again shows a count of reigns rather than of generations.

b. Apollodoros. Apollodoros seems to have dated Aletes in Corinth 30 years later[3] than the Return of the Herakleidai in 1104/3: for these chronographers who followed him therefore Aletes in 1074/3 is $338 = 39 \times 8\frac{2}{3}$ years before Syracuse in 736/5: this is nearer to Ephoros than to Timaios, but retains Timaios' view that Syracuse was founded early in the oligarchy, rather than Ephoros' synchronism with the reign of Telestes.

Eusebius omits these thirty years, and so carries back all the dates of the kings, and makes the oligarchy begin in 777/6.

The Corinthian king-list of Apollodoros, provided by Eusebius'

─────────────────

[2] This name appears in the Eusebian derivatives as Ixion, and the occurrence of the heroic name has always been somewhat puzzling in this Dorian king-list. The new fragment of Satyros (Pap. Oxy. 2465) now gives us what is undoubtedly the correct form.

[3] Didymos ap. Σ Pind. *Ol.* 13.17: accepted as Apollodoran, or rejected, by various moderns: see E. Will *Korinthiaka* (Paris 1955) pp.259 ff.

quotation of Diodorus' report (VII 9), should therefore be given absolute dates as follows:

1074/3	Aletes reigned	38 years	$\Big\}$ 76 years $=(39 \times 2)-2$
1036/5	Anaxion	38	
998/7	Agelas I	37	
961/0	Prymnis	35	$\Big\}$ 107 years $=(39 \times 2\frac{2}{3})+3$
926/5	Bacchis	35	
891/0	Agelas II	30	
861/0	Eudemos	25	$\Big\}$ 90 years $=(39 \times 2\frac{1}{3})-1$
836/5	Aristomedes	35	
801/0	Agemon	16	
785/5	Alexandros	25	
760/59	Telestes	12	
748/7	Automenes	1	65 years $=39 \times 1\frac{2}{3}$
747/6	the oligarchy first 11 years		
736/5	Syracuse		

This differs very little from the Ephoran list, though there are changes of detail in the earlier reigns, the reasons for which escape us. From 861/0 however the dates are the same except for the distribution of years between Telestes and Automenes. Automenes here has only one year, like the oligarchic prytaneis who succeeded the kings: it appears therefore that Apollodoros is here compromising between the view that Automenes was a king, and that according to which Telestes was the last king: Pausanias (II 4.3 f.) represents this view when he reports that Telestes was murdered by Arieus and Perantas, and that there were no more kings.

The Bacchiad oligarchy continued to rule Corinth until it was overthrown by Kypselos. Apollodoros (244 F 331) dated Kypselos' usurpation 447 years after the Return, that is, in 657/6: the oligarchy therefore lasted 90 years. Eusebius places the beginning of the oligarchy in 777/6 and Kypselos in 660/59, so the oligarchy lasts 117 years: $90=27 \times 3\frac{1}{3}$ while $117=36 \times 3\frac{1}{4}$ years. The durations for the oligarchy are consequently alternative variations of the same generation-count and we have no evidence in this case whether the 117 years is peculiar to the late chronicler, or whether it was taken by him from some pre-Apollodoran source.

The Apollodoran detail of the tyranny is contained only in a damaged passage of Diogenes Laertius (I 95 = 244 F 332), who reports that Periandros died aged 80 years, Σωσικράτης δέ φησι πρότερον Κροίσου τελευτῆσαι αὐτὸν ἔτεσι τετταράκοντα ? καὶ ἑνί ? πρὸ τῆς τεσσαρακοστῆς ἐνάτης ὀλυμπιάδος . . . ἤκμαζε δὲ περὶ τὴν τριανοστὴν ὀγδόην ὀλυμπιάδα. Καὶ ἐτυράννευσεν ἔτη τετταράνοντα.

This tells us that Periandros' *akme* fell in the years 628/7–625/4, and his death forty or more years before Croesus (died), presumably at the fall of Sardis in 547/6; the 40-years' reign of Periandros means therefore that he was dated either to 627/6–588/7 or to 626/5–587/6. The former date would mean that Apollodoros gave Kypselos 30 years in agreement with Herodotus. In that case, Periandros died in the first year of Ol.48, and it is not immediately obvious what event or person Sosikrates may have dated 'before Ol.49'.

Eusebius dates the accession of Kypselos to 660/59 and says that he tyrannized for 28 years; he nevertheless places Periandros' accession in 628/7 and enters the fall of the tyranny in 588/7. This seems to be a confusion of two sources, one of which is Apollodoros-Sosikrates.

The Apollodoran dating of the tyranny seems therefore to have included the placing of Kypselos in the years 657/6–628/7 and of Periandros in the years 627/6–588/7. If this was the orthodox chronography of the tyranny, the Eusebian evidence shows that it may not have been older than Apollodoros, and that it was not the only dating to survive to the late chroniclers.

Little light is thrown on these matters by the statement of Strabo (VIII 6.2) that the Bacchiads ruled Corinth for 200 years before Kypselos. Strabo is probably misrepresenting Diodorus here: οἱ δ' ἀπὸ Ἡρακλέους Βακχίδαι, πλείους ὄντες διακοσίων, κατέσχον τὴν ἀρχὴν καὶ κοινῇ μὲν προεϊστήκειααν τῆς πόλεως ἅπαντες, ἐξ αὐτῶν δὲ ἕνα κατ' ἐνιαυτὸν ᾑροῦντο πρύτανιν, εἰς τὴν τοῦ βασιλέως εἶχε τάξιν . . . Diodorus goes on to give the figure of 90 years, but Strabo perhaps did not read far enough, and assumed that the 200 Bacchiadai exercised an annual prytany for 200 years.[4]

We have seen reason to believe that Antiochos dated Akrai and Kasmenai as early as chronographically possible (in 666/5 and 646/5) because of some consideration arising from Corinthian history, which did not also operate to affect the date of Kamarina (in 601/0). This last year was, by any reckoning of which there is the slightest evidence, well within the period of the tyranny: consequently, on this argument, we are to hold that Syracuse (according to Antiochos) in 601/0 was prepared to co-operate with the Kypselids and summon an

---

[4] So also other moderns: E. Will, *Korinthiaka* p.279.

204

oecist from Corinth, while she was not prepared to co-operate with the Bacchiads over Akrai and Kasmenai—and (on this argument) this means that, for Antiochos, Kypselos seized power after 646/5. If Antiochos' sequence and narrative was true, moreover, the modern archaeological evidence from these foundations would lower the date of Kypselos' usurpation considerably further.

Beloch argued that the true historical date of the Kypselid tyranny was about 610–540, and that these were the dates implied by the early historians, especially Herodotus. E. Will has recently[5] re-worked the material in detail, rejected some of the older arguments, but come substantially to the same conclusion, ending in favour of the dates 620–550. In re-treading this ground once again, we may perhaps plead first that we are now armed with some knowledge of chronography in general and Herodotus' use of it in particular; second, that the Antiochine evidence has not previously been brought to bear; and third, that we must discriminate carefully between the historical truth, and the historiography of our earliest sources of both direct and indirect evidence, until they are proved to coincide. These earliest sources are Herodotus, Antiochos, the Athenian archon list, Hippias' Register of Olympic Victors, and Philistos, all of whom wrote before Ephoros dated the oligarchy to 747/6.

ii. The pre-Ephoran datings: a. Herodotus on the tyranny. One of Herodotus' sources for the Corinthian tyranny was Athenian. He reports[6] that Peisistratos captured Sigeion from the Mitylenians and placed aegesistratos, his son by Timonassa of Argos, there as tyrant. This statement is followed by the comment that Hegesistratos did not hold Sigeion without fighting; and this situation is explained: there was a long war (ἐπολέμεον γὰρ . . . ἐπὶ χρόνον συχνόν) in which the Mitylenians held Achilleion and the Athenians Sigeion . . . the quarrel war finally submitted to the arbitration of Periandros, who judged that each side should own what it held: in this way Sigeion became Athenian.

The account is ambiguous. It could mean that Peisistratos captured Sigeion and gave it to Hegesistratos, who continued the war ἐπὶ χρόνον συχνόν and was finally given title to his conquest by Periandros. Or it could mean that Peisistratos or Hegesistratos was legally justified in his Mitylenian war because the Athenian title to Sigeion

---

[5] *Korinthiaka* Paris 1955.
[6] V 94 f.

205

had *previously* been established by Periandros. Is this ambiguity due to Herodotus or to his Athenian source?

I have tried to show elsewhere[7] that all our chronological information on the Athenian tyranny comes from a single oral Common Source, which (whether true or not) was never in any doubt that Peisistratos ruled from 560/59 to 555/4, when he was exiled; that he ruled again from 549/8 to 543/2, when he was exiled; that he returned for the last time, fought the 'battle' of Pallene, and established his administration, in 533/2. Herodotus misunderstood the figures he was given from this source, imagining that the 36 years of rule were continuous and applied to Peisistratos' sons; but the Athenian source was never under any misapprehension on these dates. The Ath Pol[8] however notes that there was one event which was chronologically controversial (and which therefore the Common Source did not date): it was disputed whether Peisistratos married Hegesistratos' mother in his first reign or during his first exile. Herodotus' informant knew that Hegesistratos was Timonassa's son, so there may have been room for ambiguity in his account at this point. But if so, and if Periandros arbitrated for Hegesistratos, then Periandros is brought down to a very low date indeed: Hegesistratos cannot have been born before 559/8 even if we take the earliest possible of the dates in dispute; it is not reasonable to suppose that he was less than say twenty years of age when he was put in command at Sigeion—at earliest therefore in 539/8; if it was his war that continued and was followed by the arbitration, we are approaching at least the later 530's. There is no evidence of any kind which would support our attributing such a chronology of Periandros either to Herodotus or to his Athenian source.

If we reject this extremely late chronology, we are faced with a choice between two other alternatives in interpreting this passage: either both the Athenian source and Herodotus meant that Peisistratos was legally justified in his Mytilenian war because of a previous arbitration by Periandros which is not dated in any way; or Herodotus believed here as in other passages that Hegesistratos, like his brothers, was old enough to rule by 546/5, and that Peisistratos was already in his third tyranny[9] by 549/8: the arbitration is then dated (as Beloch

---

[7] *Klio* 37 (1959) pp.42 ff.
[8] 17.4.
[9] *Klio* 41 (1963) p.77.

held) for Herodotus, in the late 540's. But since the Athenian Common Source on the tyranny never shared Herodotus misunderstanding, we must suppose, in this second case, that Herodotus' belief is peculiar to himself, and is not evidence for either a generally believed or a historically true date for Periandros. If we reject the dating of the arbitration to the late 540's, we must hold that Herodotus' informant placed it at some unknown earlier date, and was concerned with the legality of Peisistratos' action.

Herodotus' own belief is perhaps illuminated by another famous passage[10] on Periandros and the Corcyrean boys, drawn this time from Samian and Corinthian sources. The boys were despatched by Periandros to Alyattes: on Herodotus' dates, Alyattes died in 561/0.[11] The boys sought and received asylum in Samos, and while their escort was seeking instructions, Periandros died. The Samians then sent the boys home to Corcyra, and 'a generation' later the memory of this insult was still green in Corinth, so she joined the Spartans, who had other matters to avenge, particularly the theft of a winebowl being sent to Croesus in 547/6 'at the same time' as the insult to Corinth.

It is difficult to see what is meant by saying that an event in or before 561/0 occurred 'at the same time' as an event of 547/6. We must either suppose that 'at the same time' is a mistaken gloss which has entered the text; or it is a note by Herodotus himself attempting to make this Corinthian information consistent with what he believed his Athenian source had told him – that Periandros was alive in the 540's. If the latter is the case, then it is clear that Herodotus knew his sources needed to be made consistent, because they were not so in origin.

The Spartan and Corinthian attack on Samos followed an appeal by Samian mutineers who left Polykrates' service at the time of Cambyses' invasion of Egypt. Herodotus believed that this invasion occurred in Cambyses' first year,[12] 530/29; so he will have supposed that the attack on Polykrates belonged to 529/8 or 528/7. The Samians freed the Corcyrean boys 'a generation' before, and this must mean a date before the death of Alyattes in 561/0. For Herodotus, acquainted with the new chronographic techniques of Hellanikos,[13] 'a generation'

---

[10] III 48.
[11] *Klio* 41 (1963) pp.63 f.
[12] *Klio* 37 (1959) p.36.
[13] *Klio* 46 (1965) pp.109 ff. and above, Part V.

is not a vague term: he means either 39 or 36 years before 529/8 or a
year later as the date for the freeing of the Corcyrean boys: one of the
years from 568/7 to 564/3. The freeing of the boys followed soon after
Periandros' death: that is to say, from his Corinthian and Samian
sources Herodotus obtained a date for Periandros' death hardly
earlier than 569/8, nor later than 564/3.

Herodotus has yet a third, and Milesian, source for Periandros:[14]
he was ruling by the time of the last year of the Milesian war with
Lydia. On Herodotus' dating of the Lydian kings, this war ended in
612/1: so this is the latest possible Herodotean date for the accession
of Periandros.

The problem of Herodotus' meaning in his various passages on
Periandros is thus a problem of his combination of different sources –
Athenian, Samian, and Milesian, and of the degree of his awareness
of discrepancy (if any) between them. In this connection it is noticeable that when he is summarizing a Corinthian source on the tyranny
in general[15] he gives as a Corinthian figure the duration of 30 years
for Kypselos' reign, but none for Periandros. There must have been
such a Corinthian figure available, and consistent with the details
that Periandros' sons were 18 and 17 years old when their disagree-
ments with their father began, and that Lykophron was still a νεανίας
and νεανίσκος when he was murdered in Corcyra. Herodotus' omission of the figure must then be taken as deliberate: that is, he was
aware of some discrepancy between his Corinthian and his other
information.

We may at this point derive some illumination from a comparison
of some of Herodotus' statements on the Corinthian tyranny with
Aristotle's summary of its history. Herodotus (V 92) reports that
Kypselos ruled for 30 years; that (I 20) Periandros was reigning in
612/1 and (III 48) died in or after 569/8, that is, that he reigned at
least 43 years; that (V 92) Delphi supported Kypselos' usurpation,
but foretold that his grandsons would not rule; and that (III 53)
Periandros planned to retire to Corcyra while his son succeeded in
Corinth. Aristotle[16] reports, according to his manuscripts, that
Kypselos ruled 30 years, Periandros 44 years, and Psammetichos his
nephew 3 years, which gave a dynastic total of 73 years 6 months.

Both authorities agree on Kypselos' 30 years; and they agree

---

[14] I 20.
[15] V 92.
[16] *Politics* V 12.

approximately on Periandros' 44 years; the great discrepancies are within Aristotle's figures, and between the Delphic oracle and the existence of Psammetichos' reign. These two discrepancies however, in the light of Periandros' plan reported by Herodotus, may be one and the same: we should infer that Psammetichos reigned in Corinth while Periandros ruled in Corcyra, and that Psammetichos did not survive his uncle, but was assassinated as soon as the news of Periandros' death arrived in Corinth. Then:

Kypselos ruled 30 years;
Periandros ruled 40½ years in Corinth
Periandros in Corcyra
Psammetichos in Corinth } rule 3 years

a total of 73½ years, on which Herodotus and Aristotle seem to agree. Thus, since, for Herodotus, Periandros was ruling in 612/1 and died in or after 569/8, his absolute dates (in Olympic terms) for the Corinthian tyranny are:

Kypselos ruled 30 years, acceding in 642/1 or 642/*1*;
Periandros, first 40 years begin in 612/1 or 612/*1*;

last 3 years are: 572/*1* to 569/*8*, or 571/0 to 568/7.
The freeing of the Corcyrean boys is thus dated to 568/7 or 568/7, which is one 39-year generation before 529/8.

These Herodotean figures are derived from his Samian, Corinthian, and Milesian sources, and leave the problem of his Athenian source on one side, unless in fact the note 'at the same time as the theft of the wine-bowl' is Herodotus' own.[17] Herodotus' silence on the Corinthian figure for Periandros' reign would however be quite sufficiently explained by a discrepancy between his Corinthian and Milesian sources. And that such a discrepancy existed is almost certain, for the Corinthian duration of Periandros' reign was probably historical, while the Herodotean date for the Milesian war with Lydia is certainly chronographic.[18]

---

[17] It seems to be much more readily explicable as a later interpolation. When Periandros' death was dated to the 580's and Cambyses' conquest of Egypt to 526/5, they could not of course be connected by any length of 'a generation', and this term then required an explanation. The interpolation is apparently attempting to explain the 'generation' as one of 23 years, from the seizure of the wine-bowl in 547/6 to the expedition against Samos dated to 524/3.
[18] See Part V above Ciii (a).

209

Consequently we should probably conclude that in comparing and combining his three main sources on Periandros, Herodotus was very confident of the Milesian synchronism, and relied upon the chronographic date; that although he rejected the Corinthian tradition for the duration of Periandros' reign, he accepted the Samian date for his death, and the Corinthian tradition for Kypselos' duration; and that his Athenian information on the arbitration of Sigeion was in fact legal and undated, but that either Herodotus himself or another may have thought it implied Periandros' survival to the 540's and consequently added 'at the same time as the seizure of the wine-bowl' to the account of the Corcyrean boys.

We are now faced with the question whether Aristotle's agreement with the Herodotean durations, and addition to them of the three years of Kypselos-Psammetichos, means that he shared Herodotus' absolute dates—that is, that Herodotus on the Corinthian tyranny represent also Hellanikos' dates for the Kypselids in the Priestesses, and that this remained the orthodox chronography down to Aristotle's time.

b. Hellanikos on the Kypselids of Athens. Nothing survives of Hellanikos' dating of the Corinthian Kypselids, and the best we can do is to consider his datings of the Athenian Philaids, who intermarried with the Kypselids.

The lineage record of Miltiades was first published by Pherekydes (3 F 2), and again by Hellanikos in his Asopis (4 F 22): from Didymos it came to Marcellinus' *Life of Thucydides*, where the text is damaged and deficient. Didymos presumably quoted Pherekydes because his was the first publication; he probably quoted Hellanikos because that chronographer added dates.

The fragment begins with Philaios, the eponym and first member of the lineage to live in Athens, and gives the names of his descendants down to Agamestor, τοῦ δὲ Τίσανδρος ἐφ' οὗ †ἄρχοντος† ἐν 'Αθήναις, τοῦ δὲ Μιλτιάδης, τοῦ δὲ ⟨   ⟩ 'Ιπποκλείδης, ἐφ' οὗ ἄρχοντος Παναθήναια ἐτέθη, † τοῦτ δὲ Μιλτιάδης, ὅς ᾤκισε Χερρόνησον.

Herodotus' information enables us to correct this account:[19] Hippokleides was the son of a Tisandros and related by descent to the Kypselidai in Corinth; Miltiades the oecist was the son of a Kypselos; his maternal half-brother was Kimon the son of Stesagoras, father of another Stesagoras and Miltiades the victor of Marathon. The text of

---

[19] VI 128.2; VI 34.1; VI 38.1, 103.2, 39.1.

210

Hellanikos' fragment thus omits the names of the fathers of the last two members of the line whom it names, and makes them father and son: we should read ... Μιλτιάδης τοῦ δὲ ⟨Τίσανδρός τε καὶ Κύψελος, ἐκείνου δὲ⟩ Ἱπποκλείδης, ἐφ' οὗ ἄρχοντος Παναθήναια ἐτέθη, τού ⟨του⟩ δὲ Μιλτιάδης ...

We also possess a large number of reported dates in the lives of this group of kinsmen. Kypselos of Athens is recognized as a grandson of Kypselos of Corinth, and now appears on a fragment of the archon-list[20] as archon in 597/6. His son went to the Chersonese with the blessing alike of Delphi, Peisistratos, and Croesus: this must mean in 549/8.[21] Hippokleides is a wooer of Agariste while the Kypselidai are still 'in Corinth': if they were overthrown in 569/8 and the wooing followed an Olympiad, this means at latest that Hippokleides was in Sikyon in 572/1 and 571/0; but if the Kypselidai fell during 568/7, then this will also be the year of Kleisthenes' Olympiad and of the wooing of Agariste. The date of Hippokleides' archonship in 566/5 is derived from Eusebius' entry on the Panathenaia in that year.[21a] Kimon Koalemos was three times Olympic victor, certainly in 532 and 528, and also either in 536 or 524: his son Miltiades was archon in 524/3 and died in 489/8, leaving Kimon as his heir.

Thus the generation of Hippokleides, Miltiades, and Kimon Koalemos is active in public life from 566/5 onwards; Miltiades represents his generation either from 524/3 (his archonship) or 527/6 (if his father was killed in 528/7); and Kimon represents the family from 488/7 onwards. This gives an average generation of 39 years, and we may set out the genealogy as follows:

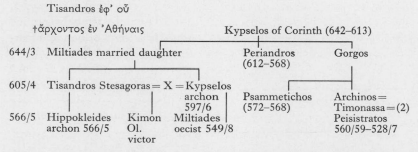

The hypothesis is, clearly, that Hellanikos (following Pherekydes)

---

[20] D. W. Bradeen 'The Fifth-century Archon List' in *Hesperia* XXXII (1963) 187 ff.
[21] *Klio* 41 (1963) 79 f.
[21a] See also J. A. Davison, *From Archilochos to Pindar* (1968) 28 ff.

211

made a special study of this group of kinsfolk in Athens; that from him or Pherekydes Herodotus abstracted various details which he recorded; and that Hellanikos included his results systematically in his monograph, the *Asopis*.

The note attached to the name of the elder Tisandros is generally secluded as some kind of repetition of the note to Hippokleides' name. But when we extrapolate the 39-year generation dating, we find that Tisandros' generation begins in 683/2. It is probable therefore that we should recognize in the date the first year of the annual archons, and read in the text ἐφ' οὗ ἄρχοντ⟨ε⟩ς ἐν 'Αθήναις, supposing that some tradition about Tisandros provided the synchronism, such as that he was the first annual polemarch.

In view of the close connection between this genealogy and the Athenian archon-list, we should probably add Miltiades the archon of 659/8, who is $135 = 27 \times 5 = 36 \times 3\frac{3}{4}$ years before Miltiades' archonship in 524/3. This early archon therefore was probably a collateral— perhaps an ancestor of the Stesagoras line.

Our question now is whether any Philaid material, either as dated by Hellanikos or by the archon-list, bears any relation to the Herodotean dating of the Kypselids. It may be, for example, a coincidence that Periandros' accession in 612/1 (fixed by the chronography of the Milesian war with Lydia) is $63 = 36 \times 1\frac{3}{4}$ years before the settlement of his great-nephew Miltiades in the Chersonese in 549/8. If we had an early (or any) authority's date for the arbitration of Sigeion we could say if this coincidence was exploited, but in its absence the coincidence is not evidence. The date of the archonship of Kypselos is possibly more helpful. This is 48 years, a very long time, before his son's settlement in the Chersonese, and so is most probably chronographic; it is also $45 = 27 \times 1\frac{2}{3}$ years after his grandfather's accession in Corinth in 642/1.[22] It may be therefore that both Hellanikos and the authors of the archon-list agreed with Herodotus on the Corinthian tyranny dates.

If so, it is possible that a fuller acquaintance with the archon-list would reveal confirmatory evidence. Probably however in the present

---

[22] Other possibilities are that (a) Kypselos as a known pre-Solonian archon was carried back a long time before 549/8 when Solon's date was fixed to 594/3; or (b) that 48 years was $36 \times 1\frac{1}{3}$ even for the authors of the archon list. But it seems probable that the 36-year generation divided into thirds was invented for the Olympic victor list, to which it is particularly suited.

state of our knowledge the most that can be said is that such indications as we possess are compatible with the Herodotean dates. Among these indications is the entry of the basileus Epainetos for 636/5, for this name is explicable as the entry necessitated by the *damnatio memoriae* of Megakles the Accursed, archon in the year of Kylon's revolt. This date for Kylon also dates the tyranny of his father-in-law, Theagenes of Megara, as about contemporary with the beginning of the tyranny of Kypselos in 642/1. These dates give a reasonable correlation with the Kypselid dates of 642–568; but this is not proof, either for Hellanikos or the archon-list, that they shared the Kypselid dates of Herodotus.

c. Hippias' Olympic Register and Kypselid relations with Olympia. The method of composition used by Hippias of Elis in compiling his Register of Olympic victors is unknown, especially the degree to which he made use of previously published material. Some instances however may be provisionally identified: Kylon's insurrection was dated by the Athenian archon-list to 636/5, and Hippias placed his Olympic victory at the preceding Olympiad, 640/39. The victory of Parmenides of Kamarina in 528/7 is a chronographic interval after Antiochos' date for the foundation in 601/0: $63 = 36 \times 1\frac{3}{4} = 27 \times 2\frac{1}{3}$ years.

There is a pair of Corinthian entries at 728/7 and 724/3: the second of these victors, Dasmon or Desmon, is otherwise unknown. The first is Diokles, eromenos of the Bacchiad Philolaos, who went to Thebes and there made the Adoption Laws of the Thebans. This Corinthian Diokles is also homonym to the Syracuse law-giver of 413/2, and his victory is dated by Hippias $315 = 27 \times 11\frac{2}{3} = 36 \times 8\frac{3}{4}$ years before the Syracusan legislation.

Another entry of interest is that of Lygdamis of Syracuse, the first pancratiast, in 648/7. This is the year also used (by Philistos) for the Myletid commotion in Syracuse and the foundation of Himera; and the Syracusans are said to have believed that Lygdamis was as large a man as the Theban Herakles. Both the year and the victor therefore seem to have been well-known in the traditions of Syracuse, but we have too little information to explain them or to set them in context.

An entry of which we do not know the date was the chariot victory of Periandros mentioned by Ephoros.[24] If this was placed at any

---

[24] 70 F 178.

213

Olympiad from 612 to 588 it would tell us nothing of Hippias' dates for the tyranny; and if it had been placed higher or lower we might have heard of it from one of the sources on the tyranny.

Most of the useful evidence from Olympia on the Corinthian tyrants comes from outside the entries on the victors in the games. Kypselid devotion to Olympia was famous for the dedications there; Nikolaos of Damascus[25] in an elaborated version of Kypselos' hazardous youth, says that his childhood was spent at the sanctuary: this is romance, but useful in showing how emphatic was the tradition of Kypselid devotion; and it implies that the Bacchiads had no influence at Olympia.

The stories of the dedications name either the Kypselidai or Kypselos as the dedicator: the surviving example (the Boston Phiale) names the Kypselidai. The 'Kypselos' of some at least of the stories must be Kypselos II (Psammetichos) and in the literary tradition the name may have begun as an error for Kypselidai, and so become attached to Psammetichos.

One of the stories is that on the fall of the tyranny the Corinthians wished the gifts to be rededicated as from the city instead of the dynasty: but the Eleans refused. Presumably this belongs to the same political context as the Elean ban on Elean entries to the Isthmia, which is undated but must reflect a period of hostility, similar to that which caused the refusal of the permission to rededicate the Kypselid offerings.

The hostility seems to be illuminated by the accounts of the Elean wars with Pisa in 588/7–585/4 and 572/1–569/8. Pausanias[26] reports that Damophon of Pisa provoked the Eleans into invading his territories, but he persuaded them to retreat and[27] on Damophon's death, the Sixteen Women arranged the peace terms, and became the body responsible for holding the quadrennial Heraia. In 572/1–569/8 however[28] Pyrrhos, Damophon's brother, led an alliance of Pisa, Dyspontion, and Triphylian Makistos and Skillous against Elis and was defeated: all these cities were destroyed, and we learn from Strabo[29] that the expelled Dyspontines went to Epidamnos and Apollonia. These two Corcyrean colonies connect this Elean war with the

---

[25] 90 F 57.
[26] VI 22.3.
[27] VI 16.5.
[28] VI 22.4.
[29] VIII 3.32.

Corcyrean revolt and Periandros' reign in Corcyra, within the years 572–568 on Herodotus' dating; while the ritual importance of the Sixteen Women makes it likely that the account of these wars goes back to Hippias, who would certainly be concerned with such matters relevant to Olympia, and would also wish (it can be supposed) to explain why entries before 572–568 named Pisatai of Dyspontion, and those later Eleans of the same city.[30]

The hypothesis is therefore that, for Hippias, the Elean war of 572–569 was contemporary with Periandros in Corcyra—that is, that for him the Herodotean dates, at least for the final events of the tyranny, were the acceptable tradition. The western events of these years are therefore something wider than the Corcyrean revolt alone: Corcyra, Epidamnos, and Apollonia are to be closely connected with Pisa, Dyspontion, and Triphylia, while Periandros is the great ally of Elis. The hostility of the Eleans to the new Corinthian government in 568/7 accordingly finds a context. How long this hostility persisted is uncertain: the ban on the Isthmia produced a number of stories to explain it, one of which mentions incidentally an Elean theoria to the Isthmian games.[31] Probably therefore at some date the hostility waned, and a new diplomacy, unable to break the oaths of the ban, nevertheless provided for official Elean participation through a theoria at the Isthmia.

We may perhaps suppose that the dates of the Elean wars in 588/7–585/4 and 572/1–569/8 remained orthodox because they were part of Hippias' work, and that when the dates of the Corinthian tyranny were revised the Elean dates remained unaffected. But if the dates of the Elean wars mean that Hippias used the Herodotean dates for the Kypselid tyranny, we should suppose that he obtained these dates not from Herodotus, but from Hellanikos' *Priestesses*. The same dates would be available from Herodotus to Antiochos, and from Herodotus, Hellanikos, and Hippias, to Philistos.

It is therefore quite probably the explanation of Antiochos' high dates for Akrai and Kasmenai that he wished to place these foundations before the year 642/1, taken as the date of the usurpation of Kypselos. The absence of oecists for these foundations then probably means that Syracuse was in some way at odds with Corinth towards the end of the Bacchiad oligarchy: and this period also includes the

---

[30] Extracts from the Register vary in accuracy: e.g. Africanus calls the Dyspontine victor of 772 a Pisatan, Phlegon F 4 calls him an Elean.
[31] Paus. II 15.1; V 2.

war of Corinth with Corcyra in which the naval battle of about 664 was fought, and Thucydides may have obtained his knowledge of this also from Antiochos.

In that case, the story of the trireme, and Ameinokles the shipwright, dated by Thucydides about 704, probably also came to him from Antiochos, but we do not know whether the triremes and the foundation of Corcyra were connected by Antiochos as they were later by Ephoros. Nor is it clear whether Antiochos, dating Syracuse in 736/5, also placed it in the reign of King Telestes.

It is quite uncertain whether Antiochos preceded Hippias and Philistos in making 648/7 an important year in Syracusan history. Since however Philistos dated the Myletid commotion to this year, it is likely that (at least in general terms) he agreed with Antiochos that the years 666/5 to 646/5 were a period of Syracusan political estrangement from Corinth, and connected with Corinth's war against Corcyra. He may indeed have taken this period of war and difficulty as the necessary and proper context of his series of mid-seventh century foundations, and held that Greek weakness and disunity provided in some way the opportunity for the Carthaginian capture of Ebesos in 654/3, which provoked the Greek foundations of Akragas, Selinous, Himera, and Lipara.

iii. The formation of the orthodox chronography: a. Kallisthenes. One of the obscurer problems of the reign of Periandros is his relation to the Sacred War, in which the city of Krisa was totally destroyed and its land dedicated to Apollo. The specialist history of this war was compiled by Kallisthenes,[32] Aristotle's kinsman; he gave the causes of the war as insults offered to pilgrims to Delphi, including some Argive women; the war lasted ten years and ended with the capture of Krisa, in 591/0; the land forces of the allies were provided especially by Thessaly and Athens; the navy of Kleisthenes of Sikyon operated in the Corinthian Gulf. Periandros who remained active and ferocious in his old age is not mentioned, nor are his two navies. Their absence must have been convincingly and obviously explained.

The Eusebian dating of the end of the Corinthian tyranny to 588/7 provides such an explanation: 591/0 is then the year when Periandros goes to Corcyra, and we may perhaps suppose that his absence in the preceding years was explained by his occupation in the

---

[32] Jac. 124 F 1.

Corcyrean Revolt. Then the dates of the unknown Eusebian source will have been:

660/59   Kypselos reigns for 28 years
632/1   Periandros reigns 41 years in Corinth
591/0   Periandros in Corcyra; Psammetichos in Corinth
588/7   end of the tyranny in Corinth and Corcyra

and this is probably the nearest surviving version to Kallisthenes' dating, though he himself probably shared the 30 years for Kypselos given by our other sources.

It is therefore unlikely that Aristotle shared the absolute dates for the Kypselid tyranny with Herodotus—yet the 44 years of Periandros are due to his synchronization with the Herodotean Alyattes at the beginning of his reign, and should not have been taken as data to be transferred easily to other absolute dates.

The Apollodoran dates were, probably,

657/6   Kypselos reigns for 30 years;
627/6   Periandros reigns for 40 years;
587/6   Psammetichos reigns for 3 years, to 585/4.

In this version, the revolt of Corcyra and the capture of Krisa could still be dated to 591/0, but the subsequent narrative will be that of Nikolaos:[33] Periandros returned from Corcyra to Corinth, where he died; Psammetichos-Kypselos succeeded him until the tyranny was destroyed. The lacuna in Sosikrates' text[34] will have contained a reference to Psammetichos and his death.

Strictly speaking, these revisions of the Kypselid dates are derived from the Athenian archon-list. This placed Solon's archonship in 594/3, and consequently his departure from Athens and visit to Delphi in 591/0: hence the story that he was present at the fall of Krisa. But the early evidence is in favour of a date for Solon in the later 570's, so that his visit to Delphi would come at the end of the decade, just where the earlier version of the Kypselid dates would place the Corcyrean and Elean wars. Thus it seems that through Solon's official date, Kallisthenes arrived at a date for the Sacred War,

---

[33] 90 F 59.
[34] 244 F 332: the lacuna will be due to a haplography: τελευτῆσαι αὐτὸν ἔτεσι τεττάρακοντα καὶ ἑνί, ⟨Ψαμμήτιχον δὲ τρία ἔτη βασιλεύσαντα, ἔτει ἑνὶ⟩ πρὸ τῆς λθ' ὀλυμπιάδος.

and to explain Periandros' failure to appear in that war was forced to one of the high datings of the Kypselid tyranny.

We are therefore brought to the proposition that the Sacred War in fifth-century tradition was part of the general warfare of these years: Corinth against Corcyra, Elis against Pisa and her allies; Thessaly, Athens, and Sikyon against Krisa. The destruction of Krisa, the expulsion of the Dyspontines, the treatment of the Corcyrean boys, show a common savagery by the victors in all these theatres of war, and suggest that the underlying reasons for the alliance of Corcyra, Pisa, and Krisa were substantial and threatening.[35]

It appears therefore that the Herodotean dating of the end of the Kypselid tyranny—the last three years of Periandros and Psammetichos—may well be sound and historically accurate. The great weakness in the rest of his scheme is his reliance on the Milesian date for the end of the war between Miletos and Lydia, which provides a duration for Periandros of $43\frac{1}{2}$ years. Correspondingly, Herodotus fails to report or use the Corinthian tradition of the length of Periandros' reign, though he reports 30 years for Kypselos. His dates for the accessions of Kypselos and Periandros are consequently chronographically derived, and not historical.

They are also probably too early: the archaeological evidence from Akrai and Kasmenai shows that Kypselos' accession should be later than 642/1 by at least some 15 years.

On the historiographic side of this problem however the important question is whether the Corinthian figure for the length of Periandros' reign was ever published by any ancient historian.

b. *The survival of a historical date?*   It is of course always possible that the Corinthian figure for the duration of Periandros' reign was published in the prose Eumelos, or in the introduction to some Περὶ Ἰσθμιῶν or Περὶ Ἀγώνων, and lingered there unnoticed, or in some romance of the Seven Sages, and so remained outside serious history. 'Publication' in the context of our present discussion means use by a historian, criticizing the Herodotean or Apollodoran datings, and being rejected in turn.

We have already seen that some unknown authority gave the

---

[35] The Krisaian adherence to the rebel alliance was presumably marked by a 'discovery' and publication of the last line of the third oracle in Hdt. V 92.

Bacchiad oligarchy 117 years, which were placed by Eusebius from 777/6 to 660/59. But if they were originally reckoned from 747/6, they would place Kypselos' accession in 630/29. Thus Kypselos, reigning 30 years, would give Periandros' accession date as 600/599.

There is supporting evidence, weak, but existing. The Parian Marble dates Alyattes' accession to 605/4, which yields the date of 600/599 for the end of the war with Miletos and the synchronism with Periandros.

It seems then probable that the Corinthian figure for the duration of Periandros' reign was in fact published before 264/3—probably some time before, to allow for knowledge of it by the chronographer of Lydia, and for the knowledge of his calculation to reach the Parian.[36]

Periandros, acceding in Corinth in 600/599 and going to Corcyra in 571/0, has a 29-year reign in Corinth, and this probably was the figure published. It is however a question whether the Corinthian figure did not intend to include the three years in Corcyra, for the derivation from the figure of the date 600/599 for the end of the Milesian war with Lydia is a little too convenient: the 12-years' war then begins in 611/0, and this year is $168 = 36 \times 4\frac{2}{3}$ years before the expulsion of the Neleids from Miletos in 443/2, instead of $180 = 36 \times 5$ years as in Herodotus. It seems wiser to suppose that Periandros died in 568/7, in his 29th year, and therefore acceded in 596/5. Kypselos' thirty years then begin in 626/5, and this is sixteen years after 642/1. The Antiochine datings of Akrai and Kasmenai are perhaps at least fifteen years too early, so that this reduction represents something like the archaeological minimum; it also seems to represent the maximum reduction of the orthodox figures which can be obtained from any direct or indirect historiographic evidence.

iv. The main contacts. We can now survey the main points of contact between Corinthian and western history:

a. The foundation of Syracuse. The foundation of Syracuse seems

---

[36] This points to a fourth-century source; and consequently the candidate is Herakleides Pontikos, who worked on the Corinthian tyrannical genealogy, and apparently preferred low dates for this period—at least, he made Solon only a senior contemporary of Peisistratos: see also 'The Accepted Date for Solon' in *Arethusa* 2.1 (1969) 62 ff.

always to be dated on Syracusan, not Corinthian information; and from this is inferred an approximate date for King Telestes or for the beginning of the oligarchy, for Ephoros certainly, and perhaps Antiochos also, place the foundation within the reign of Telestes; Apollodoros placed it early in the oligarchy. Telestes is, within the meager tradition we receive, a representative of monarchical legitimism, and relatively to him the oligarchs are expansionist if not progressive, extending the privileges of kingship over a very large cousinhood. The tradition about the Syracusan founder Archias as a person is generally hostile, presenting a highly romanticized and dramatic view of the leader of an *agela* (an institution unknown, probably, in historical Corinth) anxious to enroll a boy of non-Corinthian origins.[37] More practically, we may suppose that a Bacchiad who led a colony to Syracuse under Telestes was held to be uncomfortable with, or hostile to, monarchical legitimism; while a colony in the early years of the oligarchy would be an expression of the general expansionism of that period. We infer that whatever the specific narrative given by any historian, the colony was closely associated with early oligarchic expansionist policies; and these were dated from Syracuse. The value of the synchronism is uncertain because so little is available for analysis.

b. Syracusan estrangement from Bacchiad Corinth. The group of seventh-century dates comprises: 666/5 foundation of Akrai; 664/3 war between Corinth and Corcyra (Messenians at Rhegion); 648/7 Lygdamis of Syracuse at Olympia and the Myletid commotion in Syracuse; 646/5 foundation of Kasmenai. The two colonies show Syracuse embarking on a phase of her own expansion, and another aspect of this phase should be seen in Lygdamis' victory. The Corcyrean war is linked with the colonies through the absence of Corinthian (or other) oecists. We infer a historiography of expansionism in Syracuse and Corcyra colliding with a growing exclusiveness in the Bacchiad oligarchy, and account for the too-early dates of the colonies by the necessity to place them before the overthrow of the oligarchy dated by Hellanikos and Herodotus to 642/1, or about fifteen years too early. In this case therefore mainland history establishes the limits of dating for Syracusan events, but it is Corinthian

---

[37] Broadbent *Studies in Greek Genealogy*, pp.39 ff.

history dated by Milesian chronography, not Corinthian history proper.[38]

The *terminus ante* for the resumption of normal relations between Corinth and Syracuse is given by the foundation of Kamarina with her two oecists in the early years of the sixth century. This diplomatic triumph is then probably due to Kypselos.

One effect of the reduction of the date of Kypselos to 626/5 is of course to raise the question whether the upper terminus for the period of Bacchiad estrangement from the colonies should also be brought down: it looks very much as if the period of estrangement should be about twenty years later than the traditional dates. This seems to suit the archaeological evidence for a certain failure of Corinthian exports, slight but noticeable, around the middle of the seventh century. It was at this time also that the Ripe Corinthian narrative style was beginning to be formed which, from another point of view, is or implies a reconciliation of the orientalizing revolution with traditional narratives, no doubt much to their modification. Since the style was formed in Corinth, the main desires for this reconciliation were presumably operative there: and it is easy to see that a growing Bacchiad rigidity might be one side or aspect of the traditionalist forces.

We should probably connect the Myletid commotion in Syracuse with the estrangement, but whether we should reduce the date together with that of Kasmenai seems no less uncertain than whether the Myletids were pro- or anti-Corinthian, or whether a general tension had aggravated some local disagreement past bearing. We are in a similar state of ignorance about Lygdamis the pankratiast: his Olympic victory may be a fiction; it may if true be misdated.

---

[38] We should also note that in dating the colonies before the accession of Kypselos, Antiochos may have over-interpreted his evidence which— deriving from Syracuse—probably required only that the *terminus ante* should be the effective action in the west of Kypselos' new policies. We are told however that for his first ten years, Kypselos (besides confiscating Bacchiad property) tithed the whole Corinthian economy: whatever this meant in fiscal detail, it must imply a highly restrictive general economic effect in some aspects. Thus if Kypselos accedes in 626/5, his restrictive period is not ended until 616/5, and how soon Syracuse responded to the development thereafter is of course questionable. Historically therefore we need not place the foundation of Kasmenai within the period of Syracusan estrangement, earlier than 620–15; and this probably allows the identification of Monte Casale as the site of Kasmenai.

c. The first Corcyrean revolt.   If the campaigns against Corcyra, Krisa, and Pisa were all contemporary and aspects of a single struggle, the primary historiographic question is how this fact was not remembered strongly enough to override the learned arguments in local histories which led to their almost complete separation in the traditions we receive. Partly perhaps this is due to the absence of local histories of Corinth and Corcyra, the two places where the overall designs and policies of the campaigns were likely to have been remembered. Also, there is no evidence that Syracuse was directly concerned, so that is is unlikely that the Syracusan historians made any significant contribution to the treatment of this period in mainland history.

The attention of the Sikeliote historians was fixed instead upon the Akragas controversy, which includes Ebesos, Lipara, and the tyranny of Phalaris and therefore covers, and extends beyond, the period 572–569. The historical question is whether in fact there was an important connection between the whole Akragantine series of events, and the mainland crisis. The Carthaginian advance to Ebesos is represented as a defeat of the Rhodians in the west; the foundation of Lipara is a result of a Carthaginian defeat of Knidians; a fairly close connection between Knidos and Corcyra is shown by their co-operation in founding the Black Corcyra soon after 600, and in the Knidian diplomatic activity over the Corcyrean boys in 568/7. It is probable therefore that Corcyra was vitally interested in, and deeply affected by the defeats of the Rhodian and Knidian enterprises further west: and that this was in some way a contribution to the decision to revolt from Corinth.

For the historiographic tradition therefore we should have to consider the separatist accounts of (1) Corinth and Corcyra; (2) the Sacred War; (3) the Elean subjugation of Pisa and the Dyspontine linkage with Corcyrean colonies; (4) the Sikeliote events and their linkage through Knidos with Corcyra. The main tradition in each case is clearly highly local, and the linkages, though they exist, are seen from the local point of view. The historian who strives after the discovery of a larger context is Philistos, and (whether our present reconstruction is right or not) the archaeological evidence proves him in detail wrong.

v. Conclusions

(1) Syracusan historiography probably confirmed, or even provided,

222

for Corinth the approximate date for King Telestes and the beginning of the Bacchiad oligarchy.

(2) The Hellanikan and Herodotean chronography of the Kypselids probably provided for Antiochos a *terminus ante* for the dates of Akrai and Kasmenai; and for the seventh-century war with Corcyra and other events.

(3) Sikeliote historiography shares with mainland learning the separatist accounts of the events before, during, and after 572–569. The separation could arise because of the absence of Corinthian and Corcyrean historiography, where the unity of the events could have been recorded; Philistos' attempt to reconstruct the unity is a failure.

B. THE 'MESSENIAN' CORRELATIONS.

It is an impressive fact that the Sicilian colonies were founded from distant metropoleis: Euboia, Corinth, and Rhodes. Yet it would seem as likely for the Ionian as for the Aegean sea that long-distance voyages presuppose a varied, small, and dense local traffic between neighbors, and the use of the small ports and havens for shelter by the remoter voyagers. Such a situation is represented in Italy by the foundations of Italiote cities and villages by the cities (and villages) of Achaia and other regions of the Corinthian Gulf; to balance our general notions of activity in the Ionian Sea we should enquire into the situation, in the colonial period, of the western and southern Pelopennesian ports and havens, and their use by Euboians and Rhodians in their long-distance voyages.

The direct connections between the southern Peloponnese and the colonial west are limited, in our surviving sources, to Italy, and to Zankle in Sicily. The Sikeliote historians however, from Antiochos onwards, were concerned also with Italiote affairs, especially through the cities on the straits. The question therefore arises how far they integrated the Italiote with the Sikeliote material, and whether they looked at the Ionian sea as a whole; and whether their work made any contribution to the ancient historiography of the southern Peloponnese.

This historiography was entirely dominated by Spartan tradition and propaganda before 369/8; thereafter Messenian propaganda took its place. It is unclear and disputatious how far we can penetrate through the propaganda. It did not for the ancients, so far as we can see, and does not immediately for us, emerge with any certainty what

223

was the political situation on Sparta's western and northern borders at any particular time in the eighth and seventh centuries. We have a number of names of districts and peoples, but how far *polis* organization, even in the loosest sense, was advanced in the western Peloponnese in these centuries is quite obscure; and even darker is the problem of what may have preceded it. How many wars of conquest, or how many substantial 'Messenian Revolts' there were, divided the ancients: all agreed that the first war of conquest was conducted by the Spartan Theopompos (in the eighth century), and that the last great revolt before the restoration was that which took advantage of the earthquake in the 460's; all agreed also that the poet Tyrtaios was contemporary with a Messenian war or revolt in which Sparta was hard-pressed. But some, including Plato, (Apollodoros) and Strabo, recognized a revolt about 490 which others (Herodotus[40] and Ephoros) ignored; and there was wide divergence of opinion on which war it was that Aristomenes conducted for the Messenians: Myron of Priene put him in the Theopompos war; Ephoros in the Tyrtaios war; and the Cretan Rhianos in the war of 490, which was conducted on the Spartan side by Leotychides II. The mainland tradition was therefore highly controversial; we look now at the colonial traditions to see whether they are derivative or independent.

i. The foundation traditions. Sparta's one colony, at Taras, was agreed to have been founded at the end of the Theopompos war: if this is true, the war is given a *terminus ante* by the archaeological date of the foundation in the neighborhood of 720 B.C. This agrees, as we have seen, with a cousinly generation-value for the royal genealogies at Sparta. The surviving chronographic dates are however ⟨708/7⟩ from Timaios and 706/5 from Eusebius: the latter synchronizes Taras with Corinthian Corcyra, and probably is based on a combination of reckonings: $216 = 27 \times 8 = 36 \times 6$ years before the destruction of Eretria in 490/89 (a reckoning referring principally to the Eretrian settlement in Corcyra recorded by Plutarch); and $195 = 39 \times 5$ years before the expedition of Dorieus and the destruction of Sybaris of 511/0.

Some historian therefore saw, in the foundation of Taras, Spartan cooperation with Corinth against the Eretrians of the west; contrarily Antiochos held that Metapontion was organized by the Achaian

---

[40] But Herodotus knew of something about 500: V 49.

cities as an outpost against Taras. The archaeological date is not long after 700; Strabo[41] reports that the site was originally occupied by Pylians who sailed from Troy with Nestor, and that the historical city continued a hero-sacrifice to the Neleidai. It looks therefore as though the Achaian organization of the city consisted in supporting a Pylian or partly Pylian population. Eusebius synchronizes the foundation of Metapontion with that of 'Pandosia', which as we have already seen probably means a Rhodian settlement later absorbed into Siris. Siris itself was founded from Kolophon before the death of Gyges (say 655 ±5), and the Neleid tradition of Kolophon was strong in Mimnermos' time.[42] These assertions suggest an alignment of Sparta, Taras, Corinth against the Eretrian and Achaian colonies, Metapontion with its Pylian and Neleid traditions, and Siris with its Rhodian background and Ionian-Neleid tradition.

The cities of the straits have more complex histories. Their Euboian founders are Chalkidians, not Eretrians, and their partners are called 'Messenians' not Pylians. Strabo[43] says that the Messenians of Rhegion had been the peace party after the sacrilege at the shrine of Artemis Limnaia, and had meantime been living in Makistos: they provided the governing group at Rhegion down to the time of Anaxilas (494/3–476/5 according to Diodorus). Pausanias names Alkidamidas, the great-grandfather of Anaxilas, as the leader of a Messenian settlement at the end of the Theopompos war; and Gorgos and Mantiklos at the end of the Aristomenes war in the time of Anaxilas. This last settlement however, according to Pausanias,[44] consisted largely of the populations of Pylos and Mothone, together with a remnant of the inlanders; Pylos and Mothone had been holding the coastlands during the fighting,[45] and Strabo[46] similarly says that the 'descendants of Nestor' had fought on the Messenian side. Moreover, according to Pausanias again, Gorgos and Mantiklos moved from Rhegion to Zankle, whence they ousted the recent Samian settlement and gave the city the name of Messene: the priests of Herakles Mantiklos still existed at the time of the restoration of Messenia in 369/8.

---

[41] VI 1.15.
[42] Strabo XIV 1.4.
[43] VI 1.6.
[44] IV 23.1.
[45] Paus. IV 18.1.
[46] VIII 3.30.

It is clear that these Rhegine traditions are much more closely connected with developments in the mainland historiography of 'the Messenian Wars' than those of Metapontion, and that different historians had different narratives. Pausanias' tale seems to combine different elements: Gorgos the son of Aristomenes is especially the contemporary of Anaxilas, and so is fixed to the period around 490; Mantiklos is the son of Theokles, the seer of the kings Androkles and Phintas of Hyameia, whose context seems to be quite different.

ii. The kingdom of Hyameia. Ephoros[47] says that, under its first Dorian ruler Kresphontes, Messenia comprised five kingdoms: Dorian Stenyklaros, and non-Dorian Pylos, Rhion, Mesola, and Hyameitis. Hyameia appears in Pausanias' narrative as a political unit under the kings Androkles and Phintas who, with Theokles the Iamid of Elis as their seer, fought Anaxandros of Sparta at the Battle of the Boar's Grave, where Herakles had exchanged oaths with the sons of Neleus. This kingdom, according to Pausanias, had survived the Theopompos war, and its kings were descended from the peace party in Messenia before that war.

Phintas of Hyameia bears a name given also to a king of Stenyklaros, for whom Eumelos the Bacchiad, the Corinthian epic poet, wrote a processional hymn to be sung by a Messenian choir at the Delian festival. Eumelos is otherwise said to have been an older contemporary of Archias of Syracuse (in 758/7 or 736/5), and Eusebius accordingly enters his name in the *Canons* at 760/59 and 744/3. Eumelos mentioned the names of Sinope and Borysthenes, taken from a city and river of the Euxine, and no doubt the early date for the colonization of Sinope is derived from this fact. But so far as we know, these places cannot have been visited by Greeks before about 675, and this should give a terminus post for the poetical career of Eumelos.

The ascription of the processional hymn to the time of Phintas is presumably due to the mention of his name in the poem: and if Eumelos wrote for Phintas about or after 675, the king cannot be the Phintas of Stenyklaros who ruled before the Theopompos war. The king in question must be Phintas of Hyameia who was killed in battle with Anaxandros of Sparta. Indeed, it seems probable that Phintas of Stenyklaros is a fictional double of the Hyameian, invented to provide

---

[47] 70 F 116.

a patron for the eighth-century Eumelos; and that his supposed Stenyklarian ancestors are in origin the ancestors of the Hyameian. His father Sybotas founded the cult of the river Pamisos, perhaps in his time the eastern frontier of Hyameia; Sybotas' father Dotadas 'made a port at Mothone, though Messenia already had others', no doubt pre-eminently at Pylos. Dotadas' father Isthmios established the cult of the sons of Asklepios, which in Pausanias' time was centred in the Rhodos at Gereneia, where Nestor buried the ashes of Machaon. Isthmios and his father Glaukos (and Glaukos' grandmother Merope) bear names especially reminiscent of Corinth and are certainly more appropriate to coastal than to Stenyklarian persons; while Glaukos' father is Aipytos, who has a Neleid homonym in the founder of Ionian Priene; Kresphontes the founder of the Dorian dynasty, also has a Neleid name.[48]

There is of course no need to emphasize the artificiality of this king-list: what is important is that the artifice seems certainly to have been originally exercised on Hyameian, not on Stenyklarian, material.

Now we cannot suppose that the Messenian serfs under Spartan rule either exercised this artifice, or remembered the courtly religious verse of Eumelos. The place where these traditions were remembered and elaborated will certainly have been Rhegion, where the Messenian governing group provided the necessary aristocratic and courtly society. It will be the intermixture of the Rhegine with the mainland historiography which provided the basic muddle in the historiography of the Messenian Wars.

One inference is however quite clear: Theopompos of Sparta conquered Stenyklaros, Anaxandros conquered Hyameia. We can probably add also that Anaxandros conquered Mesola, for (apart from the obvious geographical inferences) Pausanias[49] reports that Anaxandros captured the 'Messenian' Kleo, priestess of Thetis, together with the wooden image of the goddess, and that the Spartan cult was established by Anaxandros' queen, Leandris. The new 'cosmological' fragment of Alkman[50] may plausibly be taken as a hymn for the institution of the new cult, publishing the appropriate mythology. If this cult of Thetis is to be connected with the cult of

---

[48] Known historically at Miletos: J. P. Barron 'Milesian Politics and Athenian Propaganda' in *JHS* 82 (1962) p.3.
[49] III 14.6.
[50] F 5 Page.

227

the Nereides at Kardamyle[51] Anaxandros' conquests included the coastal strip of Mesola.

We possess therefore the fairly artificial traditions of the kingdom of Hyameia as some material for considering the history of the Ionian sea in the early colonizing period. In Pausanias' account, the royal lineage is related to another in Arcadia, and, if for convenience sake we put them side by side, and calculate in 27-year generations back from the first fully Spartan generation in Messenia, we obtain:

Crude dividend (*terminus ante quem non*)	Hyameian Neleids	Arcadia (*Phigaleia*)	
815	Kresphontes m. Merope sister of	Laias	
788	Aipytos	Boukolion	
761	Glaukos	Phialos	
734	Isthmios founded the Rhodos at Gereneia	Simos	Theopompos' conquest of Stenyklaros; foundations of Taras and Asine. (Asklepiad cults of Kos Knidos etc. spread to Gereneia?)
707	Dotadas built the port at Mothone	Pompos received Aiginetan traders	Neleid and Rhodian settlements at Metapontion and 'Pandosia'. Rhodian Gela 684±7.
680	Sybotas: cult of the river Pamisos	Aiginetes	
653	Phintas: patron of Eumelos of Corinth and member of the Delian League; killed in the Spartan conquest	Polymestor captured a Spartan army; died childless	Anaxandros of Sparta (661±4–627±3) conquers Mesola, Hyameia (Pylos, Rhion). Kolophonian settlement in Siris 655±5. Corinthian war with Corcyra and estrangement from Syracuse.

(According to Pausanias, Phintas was allied to Argos, Arcadia, Elis. Elis is represented by Theokles the Iamid, father of Mantiklos; Arcadia apparently by Polymestor; Argos should perhaps be represented by her victory at Hysiai 662±7 (669/8 is 252 = 36 × 7 years before the destruction of the fortress at Hysiai by the Spartans in 417/6.)

626 onwards   All the Messenian kingdoms under Spartan rule.

The most interesting statements in these fairly artificial traditions are those of the generation of 707: the port of Mothone and the arrival of Aiginetan traders in the Arcadian uplands. These state exactly

---

[51] Paus. III 26.7.

what we should expect at this time: the foundations of Cumae, the straits settlements, Taras and the Achaian cities, the primary colonies in Sicily, all before about 710, are establishing a network of sea-routes and trade; and this activity is beginning to affect the whole surrounding area of coast and hinterlands. In the Arcadian case, it is a matter of being drawn into the trading network; in the Hyameian case, it is a matter of investment in order to compete, no doubt, with Pylos, Asine and, perhaps, Rhion.

At the same time, these traditions throw some light on the political situation north and west of Sparta at this time. Hyameia is clearly an independent kingdom, unconcerned as yet with the fate of Steny-klaros, and competing for the fruits of the new economic development with the equally independent Pylos (and Rhion) and—no doubt—with the new client-state of Sparta at Asine. The chief trading connections of the south-west Peloponnese at this time are apparently with Corinth, Aigina, and Rhodes: we should probably at this period add Crete, or those Cretans who co-operated with the Rhodians in the reinforcement and regular constitution of Gela.

The remaining two Hyameian generations occupy approximately the middle of the seventh century, and with the Pylian foundation of Metapontion as an ally of the Achaians against Taras, and the strengthening of Rhodian representation in the west, we seem to see an increasing competition between the various parties in the exploitation of the west. Hyameia is not said to have played at first any direct part in this, but with the second generation she develops full connections overseas, employing a Corinthian poet and participating in the Delian festival, boasting (according to Pausanias) an Olympic victor and an official Elean seer. With this tradition of expansiveness, it is quite possible that the war with Sparta was initiated by Hyameia,[52] perhaps after the Spartan defeats at Hysiai by Argos, and in Arcadia.

The question now arises when the men of Hyameia, settled in Rhegion, began to call themselves, or to be generally recognized, as Messenians and Dorians. The stories of Isthmios' cult-foundation at Gereneia (where Nestor 'buried the ashes of Machaon'), and of the Battle of the Boars' Grave (where the Neleids met Herakles) together with the names of Aipytos and Kresphontes, suggest that originally they thought of themselves as Neleids and closely related to the

---

[52] The Messenian sacrilege at the sanctuary of Artemis Limnaia is placed before the conquest of Stenyklaros by Pausanias, but was probably before that of Hyameia for Antiochos.

229

Pylians. Strabo[53] says that after the death of Menelaos, the Neleid kingdom was enlarged, so that by the time of the Return, Melanthos ruled Messenia: this implies that the non-Dorian kingdoms of Pylos, Rhion, Hyameia, and Mesola were all Neleid. Eumelos of Corinth, writing in Phintas' time, took the trouble to claim that Neleus had been secretly buried on the Isthmus of Corinth: we seem to see the Corinthian poet contemplating Miletos and her associated Neleid cities in the east, and the Neleid kingdoms of the south-west Peloponnese, in their meeting at the Delian Festival, and recommending their participation in the Isthmia. We should probably add to these considerations that some Mycenaean tombs in Pylos were discovered in the eighth century and a hero-cult of their occupants begun:[54] presumably these were 'the Neleidai', and it is a question whether these heroes were so named by unaided local tradition, or under the influence of Ionian epic as known, for example, to the painter, the exporter, and the purchaser, of the Ischia cup. In view of all these indications it seems unlikely that the Hyameians, in the generation of their arrival in Rhegion, thought of themselves as Messenians. On the other hand, the Messenian name and concept of Messenian unity were entirely acceptable to Anaxilas about 490. We are thus faced with a double question: when was 'Messenian' unity forged on the mainland, and when was it accepted in Rhegion, so that the transformation of Hyameian into 'Messenian' traditions was begun?

iii. The unity of Messenia. Pausanias reports that Alkidamidas the Messenian was the great-grandfather of Anaxilas of Rhegion; Strabo[55] says that the Messenian ancestors of Anaxilas withdrew to Makistos and sailed thence to Rhegion. The statements, both by date and place, suggest that this emigration was a consequence of the Elean war against Pisa, Skillous, Makistos, and Dyspontion in the years 588–5 and 575–69, when the Dyspontines went to the Corcyrean colonies of Epidamnos and Apollonia.

One result of this conclusion is that Rhegion in these years was as ready as Corcyra to admit the enemies of Periandros. Another is that Alkidamidas and his followers form one of the two possible occasions

[53] VIII 4.1.
[54] T. B. L. Webster *Homer and Mycenae* p.137; Per Alin: *Das Ende der Mykenischen Fundstatten auf dem Griechischen Festland* in *Studies in Mediterranean Archaeology* Vol.I (Lund 1962) p.81.
[55] VI 1.6.

for the bringing of the Messenian name to Rhegion. The other occasion is the reception of Gorgos 'son of Aristomenes' by Anaxilas about 490: this however appears to be in the nature of a reinforcement, for Anaxilas uses the Messenian name on his coinage as though it were already famous, and Gorgos is called 'son of Aristomenes' as though that hero were already established as the representative of Messenian resistance. Aristomenes' name is also used in the courteous little story which explains and excuses the peasant origins of Gorgos' wife.[56] Rhianos was perhaps moved to make the war of about 490 the Aristomenian war because of the stories of Gorgos, and of his sister who married Theopompos of Heraia, Olympic victor in 504 and 500; but the evidence taken as a whole (such as it is) suggests that Aristomenes was already a name to conjure with, and that Messenian identity was already established. Alkidamidas is thus the main candidate for the office of bringing the Messenian name to Rhegion.

There is no *a priori* reason to doubt that Messenian unity was forged in the long resistance struggle against Sparta led by Aristomenes, 'the chief glory of the Messenian name'. Ancient historiography however identified this struggle variously with the Theopompos war, the Phintas war, the Tyrtaios war, and the Gorgos war; and in Pausanias' narrative it is combined with all the last three of these. For the modern, Gorgos is firmly fixed to about 490 by Anaxilas; the Phintas war can be disentangled and placed within the years about 640. The Theopompos war is much too early for the Messenian name if the Pylians of Metapontion were not yet Messenian soon after 700, and the Hyameians of Rhegion not yet Messenian about 640.

The remaining possibility is then the Tyrtaios war, when the Spartans were admittedly hard-pressed. Verses attributed to Tyrtaios[57] named Aristokrates of Arcadian Orchomenos and Pantaleon of Pisa as supporters of the Messenians in the Tyrtaios war: Pantaleon was the father of Demophon who quarrelled with the Eleans in 588–5 and of Pyrrhos who was defeated in 572–69. Pantaleon's date should therefore be late in the seventh century. Aristokrates is reported to have had a daughter Eristheneia, who married Prokles of Epidauros and was the mother of Lyside, who married Periandros. Periandros and Lyside had two or three sons who survived childhood but were

[56] Paus. IV 19.5.
[57] Strabo VIII 4.10.

dead by 572, and a daughter mentioned by Herodotus: the marriage must therefore have taken place at least about the time of Periandros' accession in 596; Lyside will then have been born within the decade 620–10, and her mother in the region of 640. This dates her father Aristokrates as an older contemporary of Pantaleon of Pisa. These biographical statements are consistent with Plutarch's report[58] that Messenia was restored in 369/8 after a subjection of 230 years (which would bring the great revolt to an end in 599/8). This historiography clearly gives us a date in the last quarter of the seventh century for the Tyrtaios war.

Indications of date for Aristomenes himself are more difficult to find. Gorgos, 'son of Aristomenes', and his sister who married an Olympic victor of 504 and 500 obviously refer to the war about 490. Some other marriages of Aristomenes' womenfolk are undateable:

(1) the marriage of his sister Hagnagora to Tharyx of Phigaleia. Tharyx was presumably ancestor of a Phigaleian Tharykidas who was an Olympic victor about 368/7, and of another Tharykidas who lived about 240. Pausanias probably got the names of Hagnagora and Tharyx from Rhianos' poem, and he reports also[59] what is perhaps a story associated with this marriage: in 659/8 the Spartans captured Phigaleia and expelled the inhabitants, who were returned to their city by the valor of a hundred picked men of Oresthasion. The tone of this story of a desperate venture strongly resembles the guerilla tales of Aristomenes, and perhaps came to Pausanias from the same source, Rhianos.

(2) a daughter of Aristomenes is reported to have married Damathoidas of Triphylian Lepreon. Damathoidas' name does not fit the epic hexameter, and consequently Pausanias cannot have received this from Rhianos. An ally in Lepreon is perhaps most likely to have been asserted of the exiles in Makistos, and Pausanias' handbook probably collected it from some remotely Rhegine source.

On the other hand, the marriage of Aristomenes' youngest daughter to Damagetos, king of Rhodian Ialysos, is connected by Pausanias[60] with the genealogy of the famous Diagoras and his sons, who won a series of Olympic victories from 464/3 onwards. Pausanias gives two names in the lineage between King Damagetos and the victor Diagoras: it has often been noted that these are not enough to

---

[58] *Apoph.* 194B.
[59] VIII 39.3.
[60] IV 24.3.

separate Diagoras in 464/3 from the Tyrtaios war, while they are too many to allow King Damagetos to be contemporary with the war of 490 (if kings can be supposed in Rhodes at so late a date[61]). Pausanias' lineage therefore cannot represent Rhianos, nor his own dating of Aristomenes to the Phintas war, nor Plutarch's date: so far as we can see, his text must be wrong. The year 659/8 for the Spartan capture of Phigaleia is $195=39\times5$ years before the Diagorid victories begin in 464/3; and Plutarch's year of 599/8 is $135=27\times5$ years before the same date. Both datings therefore imply:

698		Aristomenes	Hagnagora $=$ Tharyx	
659	Damathoidas $=$ dau.		dau. $=$ Damagetos of Ialysos	599
620			Dorieus	572
581			⟨Damagetos⟩	545
542			⟨Dorieus⟩	518
503			Damagetos	491
464			Diagoras	464

The restoration of the two names preserves the nomenclature cycle of the lineage, permits the explanation of their omission in the text by a simple haplography, accounts for the two chronographic dates, and shows how events around 600 B.C. could be identified with the Phintas war. Certainly the ithegenically valued date of 599/8 is the better derivative from a lineage of this type.

Tyrtaios' naming of Aristokrates and Pantaleon, and the genealogies and chronographies of Aristomenes' relatives and descendants, therefore both point to the end of the seventh century for the great and stubborn revolt in which the concept of Messenian unity was made. The stories of Aristomenes' discovery of the treachery of Aristokrates of Arcadia, and the wandering of the survivors from Arcadia to the west coast of the Peloponnese presumably mean that

---

[61] Non-political *basileis* would seem to be irrelevant to the story.

Pantaleon of Pisa, and his sons, remained faithful to their alliance until their power was destroyed in 572–569. If it was at this time that Alkidamidas left Makistos for Rhegion, the traditions of Messenian unity had three generations in which to grow, and assimilate the Hyameian, before Anaxilas.

The development of the mainland historiography in the Messenian case clearly draws upon Spartan tradition for the Theopompos war, the Tyrtaios war, and the Thetis incident in Anaxandros' war; but it is unlikely that Spartan tradition mentioned Aristomenes at all. Messenian tradition as preserved at Rhegion had every reason to bring together Phintas and Mantiklos of the Hyameian tradition, and Aristomenes, Alkidamidas, and Gorgos of the Messenian. Corinth, as the main support of Sparta in the Peloponnesian League was naturally seen, retrospectively, as the ally of Sparta also in the Phintas war: and therefore the historical place of Eumelos, the Bacchiad poet became a problem, resolved by the postulation of another, Stenyklarian, Phintas earlier than all wars. We may suppose that this had happened in hymnography and restoration propaganda before any serious historian examined the Messenian problem: and our sources do not include an extended treatment by a serious historian.

iv. Western and mainland historiography. The apparent series of Spartan major wars in Messenian territory can now be listed as follows:

(1) the Theopompos war: Spartan annexation of Dorian Stenkylaros. Nothing survives of the pre-Spartan history of Stenyklaros. We do not, therefore, know the political organization of these Dorians before they were annexed. The foundation of Taras was one of the consequences of the war, and the archaeological evidence dates it about 720. The Theopompos war may thus be placed in the years around 730.

(2) the Anaxandros war: the conquest of Mesola and Hyameia, probably about the same time as Spartan defeats by Argos (at Hysiai) and Arcadia. We have no history of pre-Spartan Mesola,[62] but the Hyameian traditions were, it seems, extensively preserved at Rhegion and we can follow to a slight degree the history of the kingdom in the eighth and seventh centuries. The Spartan conquest seems to belong

---

[62] The Thetis cult and those of Achilles elsewhere in the south Peloponnese may mark havens used by Aiginetan shipping.

to the years around 650–40, and the Thetis cult provides a date for Alkman.

(3) the Aristomenes-Tyrtaios war: a revolt of Dorian Stenyklaros and the coastal areas, supported by Aristokrates of Arcadia and Pantaleon of Elis. The Messenian name and unity, and Dorian identity, were created in this protracted struggle, and carried to Rhegion by Alkidamidas and his followers. The Spartan reconquest of Messenia may have been complete by about 600, but the Messenian remnant may not have been expelled from the western Peloponnese until the period 572–569.

(4) the Gorgos war about 490. The Spartan victor was Leotychides II, and Gorgos led the remnant of his followers to Rhegion and thence (together with a Mantiklid?) to Zankle-Messene.

Of the two remaining non-Dorian kingdoms, we hear nothing about Rhion; the men of Pylos are said by Pausanias to have gone to Rhegion with those of Mothone (the Hyameians), so that it appears that we should credit Anaxandros with the conquest of all the coastlands: Hyameia seems certainly to have been the leading kingdom, and perhaps exercised some sort of overlordship.

The two great sources for the history of the Messenian wars were clearly the poems of Tyrtaios, and the body of traditions brought back from Rhegion at the restoration in 369/8 and worked up, variously, into a history of Messenia. The central difficulty seems to have been the reconciliation of the Rhegine material with Tyrtaios' statement about the Theopompos war, that 'Our fathers' fathers fought' it. This was taken to mean that the Theopompos war was two generations before the Tyrtaios war, and nearly all the difficulties and confusions seem to arise from the attempts to fit the Rhegine traditions into this scheme.

The Syracusan historians Antiochos and, perhaps, Philistos wrote before the Messenian restoration, and presumably represented, each in their own generation, more or less the current state of Rhegine traditions in their treatment of that city—which in neither case may have been, for the foundation period, more than brief. The first historian to attempt the inclusion of Rhegine material in general Peloponnesian history would be Ephoros, and his treatment probably remained orthodox at least for the school histories—even though specialists and particularly non-historians like Pausanias' main sources, might disagree with, modify, or poeticise his scheme.

235

v. The Ionian Sea. In classical times the voyage from Kythera to Corcyra took five days, though this period might of course be lengthened by storms. We must assume that the boats making this coasting voyage normally needed at least four overnight havens besides their termini, and apart from shelters needed especially about Cape Akritas. One of these overnight stops might be made among the islands, for example at Leukas, which was officially Corinthian from about 620 onwards, and may have been less regularly so before.

Kythera, the starting-point of this route, seems to have been Argive down to the time of Chilon of Sparta. This probably means that it was annexed after the defeat of Argos about 547/6; it then remained a royal domain, outside the Spartan state proper. In the archaic period, political Argos is often equivalent to economic Aigina, and if the Aiginetans had been organizing the port facilities before 547/6, they may have continued to do so under Sparta, paying the revenues to the Spartan instead of to the Argive kings.

The last mainland stop before Leukas may often have been at Kyllene, the port of Elis, which in part of our period, say from about 630 onwards, would pay its revenues to Pisa. The alliance between Pisa and the Messenians in these years suggests a common interest in the coastal trade, and also an encouragement of the imports of metal and weapons (for Pisatan, Messenian, and Arcadian use) which were presumably paid for by agricultural and naval supplies, the flax for which Elis was famous in later centuries, and the slave-prisoners of war captured by the Messenians.

Between Kythera and Kyllene two overnight stops would be needed, and Cape Akritas had to be rounded. The coastal village which appears first in the records is Gerenia, which could have served for boats from Kythera or Crete unable to round Cape Akritas and needing shelter. The connections of Gerenia seem to be with Rhodes, Kos, and Knidos, whose boats would use Cretan havens rather than Kythera, and in the early period the next regular stop may have been Pylos. But around 720 there were apparently two developments near Cape Akritas: the survivors of the Argolic Asine established themselves with Spartan help on the eastern side, while the Hyameian Dotadas made a port at Mothone on the western side. We may suppose that before this Asine was known especially to Argives and Aiginetans coming from Kythera; but the traditions of the foundations at about the same date point to a great increase in the density of traffic as well as (perhaps) a desire to compete with Pylos. Sometime

236

after this, the Pylians export some of their population to Metapontion, under Achaean protection against Taras (perhaps the trading partner of Asine).

The rise of the kingdom of Hyameia and its general expansiveness from something like 710 to around 640 would create an important demand for, among other things, metal and weapons. After 640, this market would shift to Pisa and be intensified in Sparta: in the last quarter of the century, during the Aristomenes war, much of the metal and metal goods import was probably paid for by exports of slaves captured in the raids by both sides. How far the work of the ports as servicing the long-distance trade (especially Asine, Mothone, and Pylos) was affected by the war is quite unclear; the connection between Aristomenes and Damagetos of Rhodes should indicate Rhodian dislike of Spartan control.

With the end of the revolt around 600 the demand for metal and the supply of slaves in the south-western Peloponnese would both greatly diminish: Sparta and Pisa would however still need some metal. This may explain Sparta's new export of Lakonian pottery; no similar development in Pisa is known, but the growth of the Olympic festival would increase the income from harbor and market dues.

The rise of the kingdom of Hyameia from about 710 onwards, and of the Pisatan tyranny from about 640 onwards are thus to be taken as natural results of the use of the Ionian Sea by longer-distance traffic, able to supply new goods, or goods in quite new quantities, in return for harbor facilities and the products of the hinterlands. The Hyameian and Pisatan periods of this development moreover seem to correspond fairly closely to the periods of Bacchiad expansion at Corinth, and the period of Corinthian estrangement from her major colonies at Corcyra and Syracuse followed by the tyranny. The periods thus belong to a wider context of political and economic development, of which we should be able to discern the main processes.

PART EIGHT

THE ORGANISATION OF THE INTERNATIONAL MARKET c760-c560

IN THE PRECEDING DISCUSSIONS, the degree of the dependence of ancient historiography on institutional data is very clear; and at the same time most of the details we have examined have been traced back either to the Sikeliote historians or to universal historians of the earlier periods—Herodotus, Hellanikos, Thucydides, Ephoros, and the latest Eratosthenes-Apollodoros. A minute examination of the Eusebian tradition has produced a date for Leontinoi, two new names (Maroneia and Kardia, both in the Aegean) and a chronographic pattern, but only the haziest adumbration of the work of the 'sea-power' historian among the Eusebian sources. One question which arises is clearly whether this 'sea-power historian', by using the device of sea-power, carried the traditional treatment of the colony dates away from the institutional towards the examination and formulation of processes and trends in what we should recognize as a more modern historiographic manner. From the study of the colony dates alone however no useful discussion of this question can be started.[1]

Any modern study of the Sicilian colony dates must nevertheless enquire into processes, trends, causes and effects. Since we start from institutional material, however, we should not seek to escape from it in such an enquiry, but rather to select some—to our eyes—institutional subject which we know (or can certainly suppose) both existed at the time of the colony foundations and was non-institutional in ancient eyes; and which united the colonizing movement both geographically and through time in a way which approaches the modern notions of underlying historical movements. If at the same time this subject is in any way related to 'sea-power' and can use the

---

[1] It is pursued in the second volume of Studies in Chronography: *The Thalassocracies*.

abundant archaeological evidence, these are likely to be great advantages.

A subject which to some degree fulfils all these requirements is that of the organization of the international market in the two centuries with which we have been concerned. We have no direct information on this subject from our ancient sources: what we have to do is look at all the events (and the historiographies) which have already been discussed from this single point of view.

A. c.760–c.695: THE EUBOIANS. The earliest events attributable to this period continue trends already established: the search for metals and the search for agricultural land. The occupation of Ischia and Cumae in Italy by Euboians before 750 shows the same search for metals in particular, and trade in general, as is shown by the Euboian settlement at Al Mina in Syria by about 800; the Spartan annexation of the plain of Stenyklaros about 740–30 and the emigration of Achaians to the valleys and plains of south Italy show the same searches for agricultural land as had already caused many similar movements in and from the Aegean.

Between about 750 and 696 therefore the Euboians are trading, probably especially in metal, from Cumae in the west to Al Mina in the east. Since we have no notion of the density of this trade from any direct evidence, we can guess very little about its organization: we should in general include not only all the influences which caused the orientalizing revolution from about 725 onwards, but also the specific importations of the Phoenician alphabet and the Phoenician unit of weight and value, the mina. And consequently we should emphasize that the Phoenicians in this period also explore and settle in the west; the substantial finds of Greek pottery in their settlements suggest that the Greek and Phoenician movements were not wholly independent, but that more Greeks were to be found with the Phoenicians than Phoenicians with the Greeks.

At either end of the Euboian trading area at this period we have some evidence which may bear on organization. As we have already noted, in the west Ischia and Cumae were mainly concerned with the metal trade, Zankle and Rhegion with its communications, and Mylai, Naxos, Katane, and Leontinoi with agriculture. This Euboian enclave or small circulation-system would be self-sufficient in metal and food, and probably in shipping also; and feed metal into the 'world market' of the Aegean and Levant. So far as we can tell, this enclave was

239

organized in the years, say, 755–25 and in two political sections: Ischia, Cumae, Zankle, Rhegion, and Mylai on the one hand, and Naxos, Katane, and Leontinoi on the other. The Megarians had some connection with this second political unit for a time, and this (like the name of Naxos) suggests that in this case at least the Euboians were organizing the emigrant population of more cities than their own. In the eastern Mediterranean, archaeology tells us of Al Mina, and the historians who translated or used eastern archives tell us of Greeks at Tarsos and Anchiale supported by fleets; and the Assyrian archives themselves have some scraps of information—including the name 'Ionian' by which Greeks were known to the Semitic peoples (which contrasts with that of the Graikoi by which they were known in Central Italy). In the east also therefore there seems to have been a knot of interrelated settlements at the end of a long communications line, and these settlements were perhaps organized, but not wholly populated, by Euboians. Moreover there is one point of detail which is interesting: no non-heroic foundation legend of Al Mina survives, while the Euboians in the west do not seem to have provided any genealogies to the chronographers.

Within this general picture of an early international market dominated by Euboians, there emerges from about 730 onwards the new east-west trading and manufacturing power of Corinth. This was based on much older foundations of a north-south trade through the isthmus on the one hand, and an acquaintance with western waters at least as far as Ithaka on the other: the traditions of the founding of Syracuse and the ending of the Bacchiad monarchy, and the archaeological evidence of the orientalizing revolution centered—for the mainland—in Corinth show an expansiveness which was in some ways obviously a good deal more dramatic than the Euboian, even when we make allowances for the presence of genealogies and associated material in Dorian Corinth and Syracuse.

For the question of Corinth in relation to the organization of the international market we have a number of pieces of evidence. In the first place, Corinth in the years from 730 onwards rapidly became the dominant producer of fine pottery, so that her trading area is traceable in a way in which the Euboian is not. As is the case however of other trace materials, we must not mistake absolute certainty for relative quantity—it is likely that the total value of the fine pottery trade was small compared to that in metal.

Secondly, the archaeology of Thera gives us some direct evidence of physical market organization at this time. The harbour was apparently used as a meeting place for traders, those carrying Corinthian goods on the one hand, and those coming from the east, Cyprus and Crete, on the other. The native Theraian culture continues quite unchanged: so far as can be seen, the Theraians neither produce for the market nor consume its goods. But foreign objects are found in the graves, nevertheless; and we should probably suppose that the Theraians charged harbor and market dues paid for by 'gifts'—that is, although the Theraians did not produce for the market, they enjoyed revenues from it.

It is this evidence from Thera that gives some backing to what might otherwise be dismissed—the slight and mainly inferential evidence for Corinthian influence in Hyameia in the eighth century, and the possibility that the cult of Asklepios at Gereneia (and elsewhere in Messenia) may show Rhodian, Koan, or Knidian influence at this early date. With the Theraian evidence in mind, it is clearly possible that the Neleid kingdom of Hyameia also enjoyed revenues from the markets it provided: with a far greater hinterland, it is obviously much more likely than in the Theraian case that it began to produce foodstuffs and ships' gear for this market, and in turn that its culture was open to Corinthian and western influence. Also, it is traditionally in the last quarter of the eighth century that a population from Argos settles the port of Asine; that the Hyameian king 'built a port at Methone' and that the Aiginetans (specialists in the carrying trade) opened up western Arcadia.

The general picture is therefore that the Euboians by 750–725 had established a firm and characteristic organization of the 'international market', quite closely connected with the Phoenicians in some areas, into which other communities now push or are drawn: Corinth as producer or trader; Aigina as trader; Thera, Hyameia, and Syracuse as in varying degrees providers of harbors and markets and recipients of their revenues. Previously agricultural 'cities' also show some awareness of this situation: Sparta after the annexation of Stenyklaros establishes Asine and Taras.

This Euboian market organization suffered a severe setback in 696, when the Greeks supported the revolt of Kilikia against Assyria, and their settlements at Tarsos, Anchiale, and Al Mina were destroyed. The Greek settlements in Cyprus may also have been discriminated against (for example, by being refused admission to harbors under Assyrian control). Euboian losses were probably severe, not so much in immediate quantities of men and goods (however great these were) as in the disorganization of the market structure they had built. Probably also at this time Rhodes lost the obvious outlet for her surplus man-power and turned instead to the 'reinforcement' of her western post at Gela, calling back her eastern interests to Phaselis, safely within the Phrygian sphere of influence. This will be only one among many examples at the time, of various cities, previously working within the Euboian system, who were now forced, or seized the opportunity, to pursue independence in their foreign trade.

B. c.695–c.645: BACCHIAD CORINTH. Greek knowledge of the Propontis and Euxine seems to have begun about 675, and presupposes advances in shipbuilding of which we hear romances and rumors in the west in earlier years. These seem to be connected with a clash between Eretria and Corinth on Corcyra, and the Corinthians here are sometimes represented as partners with the Spartans of Taras, who were opposed by the Italiote Achaians, the Pylians of Metapontion, and, presumably, their partners, the Rhodians of 'Pandosia'. If the effect in the east of possessing more powerful and larger ships was the exploration of the Propontis and Euxine, in the west the immediate advantages would be larger cargoes and more frequent voyages, both of which demand better organization in the main supply centers, the principal port towns. It may be therefore that in the stories about Corcyra we have reminiscences of a clash between forms of market—and credit—organization which issued in some places in political consequences.

From the stories of Bacchiad wealth, we should suppose that Corinth was a leader in the new market organization, and that her government became expert in deriving revenues from harbors, markets, and sales. Without such a rival, the Euboians might have rebuilt their organization after 696, but the restoration levels at Al Mina show Euboian influence markedly less and disappearing in favor of East Greek and Corinthian imports.

The Kimmerian devastation of Phrygia dated by later Greek sources to 676, probably dislocated the metal trade within Asia Minor and left Lydia isolated. Lydian attempts to meet the new situation included a change of dynasty and alliance with Assyria: almost certainly there developed also a Lydian market for Greek metal and metal goods—the 'Brazen men' from Ionia and Caria in the 660's may have been armed in Greek-supplied metal worked by Greek and

Asiatic smiths. Correspondingly this is the time (in the years about 650) when Eumelos of Corinth looks east and west at the Neleids and when the Delia and Isthmia are important festivals. It is also the time of the akme of the kingdom of Hyameia, and the period when the Rhodians press into the western metal trade with their own colony at Naples; it is the time of the Kolophonian colony at Siris which 'no doubt shared the overland trade to the coast of the Tyrrhenian Sea'.[2] Such a boom in the Greek metal trade from the fall of Phrygia onwards would to some extent at least protect the older fashioned elements in international trade from the competition of the moderns.

The Lydians however must be regarded not only as consumers *tout court:* the kingdom had something to contribute to the market organization as a powerful consumer. A number of forceful attacks on neighboring Greek cities are recorded at this time: Smyrna was captured and destroyed, Kolophon occupied, and other towns invaded and diminished. On the other hand, Greek settlements in the southern Propontis were encouraged. It seems clear that Gyges was certainly not content to let his kingdom lie at the mercy of economic forces; and in fact Lydia was sufficiently large and wealthy to be an economic force in her own right, capable of defending herself against an international market which, after *c*.675, was represented west of Lydia only by small city-states. Consequently Gyges was able to force them to re-deploy their resources and especially their man-power, and no doubt to cut the boom-condition profit margins and transit revenues very considerably.

The situation between Lydia and her Greek suppliers in fact is probably only the best-documented instance of a problem of market organization beginning to emerge fairly generally at this time. In mainland Greece, the great political powers of this period are exemplified by Argos and Sparta, the rulers of large and fertile plains. The growth of an international market cannot have failed to raise the question of the destination of the agricultural surplus—in dues and taxes to the kings, chiefs, and priests, or in prices to the traders. Very soon, within this conflict, the most rustic royalty must have come to prefer regular trade to piracy; and the freest trader must have come to prefer some regular authority to dealing with bandits. The conflict itself therefore contained the seeds of its own solution, and the importance of Gyges' wars with the Greek city-states seems to lie in

---

[2] Boardman *op. cit.* p.195.

the fact that he appreciated this and forced the Ionian cities to the same acknowledgment. Probably Argos (in relation to Aigina) and Sparta (in relation to Hyameia) were coming to a similar appreciation; certainly the rise of narrative art in Corinth from about 650 onwards speaks in the same sense, and the seventh-century war of Corinth and Corcyra may have originated, at least in part, in a conflict between a new attempt at regularity and the older traditions of a more rapacious boom-situation.

C. c.645–c.630: RESULTS OF THE KIMMERIANS. The Kimmerian advance into Lydia and Ionia in 648 or later must have suddenly and greatly depressed the international market, and we should suppose also a dramatic fall in political revenues from harbors and markets. It is in these years, for example, that Thera unwillingly and slowly exports part of her man-power to Kyrene; and it is probably to these years that we should assign the traditions of Bacchiad avarice at Corinth. In the west, where Corinthian exports had almost entirely dominated in the first half of the century, there is now some increase in imports from Rhodes and East Greece, and even more significantly, the rise of local manufactures at Syracuse, Megara, and Gela. The foundation of Selinous from Megara about this time shows a transference of manpower primarily into agriculture; and generally over the whole area of the 'international market', as the metal and associated traders met their crisis, we should expect the relative values of agriculture to rise. This change, for Argos and Corinth, comes to fruition (so far as our records are concerned) in the next period, but it may have been very early in the years around *c*.645 that Sparta conquered and destroyed Hyameia. Undoubtedly this ended the participation of the south-western Peloponnese in the international market, except presumably for the port-dues of Asine, Pylos, and Mothone—and these will now have gone to Sparta instead of local revenues.

With both Corinth, under Bacchiad 'avarice', and Hyameia, under Spartan rule, hostile in lesser or greater degree to the depressed international market, even Cumae may have felt political effects and decided that the cities of the straits should have their freedom, Zankle was already fully populated (and, if Himera is as early as this, overpopulated for the conditions obtaining), but Rhegion summoned, or at least accepted, reinforcements from Chalkis and Hyameia.

In this great depression of the metal and associated trades, and of political revenues from international trade, we are not to assume (except in Hyameia) that all other trade was equally disastrously affected. Some local trade channels opened up or expanded by international trade would to a considerable extent continue, and as the exchange-value of metal fell, that of agricultural products would relatively rise. As, moreover, Ionian resistance to the Kimmerians stiffened under the inspiration of Kallinos, the demand for raw metal in Ionia would never wholly die away; and (north and south of Ionia) in the secure islands of Lesbos and Rhodes especially, agriculture provided an economic base on which something of participation in international trade could be expanded.

D. c.630–c.600: THE RECOVERY. The skeleton organization of international trade would thus survive, though the shifts in the channels of its flow were important. Lesbos, commanding the approaches to the settlements first in the Propontis then in the Euxine; Naukratis in Egypt founded by about 620; the opening up of the Tartessian metal supplies, show the new pattern. In fact, we should suppose that Ionia and Lydia had fairly recovered by about 620; what had gone for ever was the Phrygian organization of the metal trade in Anatolia, and its links with the dying Assyrian empire.

The metal trade itself in this new period must have taken a new shape determined by the economic rise of new powers which needed weapons and fleets, and especially by (1) the Lydian advance into Phrygia and command of metal supplies: we do not know how long this took, but may suppose it was roughly complete by 600; (2) the arrival on the international market of (no doubt relatively cheap) abundant supplies of Tartessian metal; and (3) the invention of coinage, which transformed the noble metals from luxury into useful and finally much demanded goods.

It seems most likely that the first 'coins' were an emergency measure—small lumps of silver, electrum, and perhaps gold paid out in small transactions whose scale was determined by the impoverishment due to the Kimmerians. The usefulness of the rapid completion of such transactions was first seized upon by the Lydian and Ionian states—the 'small transactions' were probably from the first at state level. But the value of coinage in serving as a common medium for both local and international trade was apparently first seen by the Aiginetans. So, although coinage was probably invented as an emergency device, it survived and developed because there were organized

245

markets, local and international, which could use it as they revived and opened up new channels.

In the terms of trade obtaining in the period *c*.645–*c*.630, Argos must have become one of the wealthiest states. We are told that Pheidon began as hereditary monarch (no doubt on the basis of the wealth of that period) and became a 'tyrant', and in the plain of Elis, Pantaleon of Pisa similarly founded a tyranny: in both cases, and in the foundations of tyrannies in Sikyon, Corinth, Megara, and Epidauros), we are probably to see the recognition that the balance of the economies needed deliberate and centralized organization, especially of the relationship between agriculture and its surpluses, and international trade. It is probably within this recognition that we are to see the Aiginetan realization at the end of the century that coinage could be a common medium between local and international trade, replacing both the iron skewers already used as local currencies, and the silver and other bullion, weighed in minae and talents, used in international trade.

Corinth, in the crisis years seems to have felt the faltering of the international market especially deeply. Kypselos' biography, in the late romantic version, asserts that his first important office was that of polemarch, and that on the judicial side of that office he had to deal with cases of debt. The polemarch, as judge, would be concerned with relations with foreigners, so it is a fair inference that Kypselos found these conditions of indebtedness in the foreign trade markets in Corinth. When he took over the government, it is said that he confiscated Bacchiad property and tithed Corinth for ten years; he founded settlements in Leukas and elsewhere which were, no doubt, financed in kind by the tithe and within a few years would be producing an agricultural surplus; he closed the Isthmia festival, a chief place for advertising and displaying imports from the east; he married a daughter to Tisandros of Athens (a food-exporting area at that time), and expressed a devotion to the Olympic festival and cult in the plain of Elis. From this time onwards, archaic and classical Corinth was not to be without a firm agricultural base, and a dispersed population providing a circulation-system in itself, capable of feeding products into the international market but no longer disastrously dependent on that market in the old Bacchiad manner. The stories of Kypselos' mild and benevolent tyranny therefore probably reflect a real unity of support for his policies as uniting the very different sectors of the Corinthian economy; and the cult of Eunomia, Dike, and Eirene, regarded later as typically Corinthian, may well have begun to take shape in his time, as the regular control, balanced development, and united effort required to reorganize the Corinthian economy.

In the west, Kypselos' policies seem in the end to have healed the estrangement from Corcyra and Syracuse. But by 600, Corinth's sphere of influence is no longer the Greek far west: Rhodian Ebesos and Spanish Rhode may both have been established by 600, and about the same date Corcyrean Apollonia is importing from Rhodes. The Achaian Italiotes are still within the Corinthian sphere, and expanding: Sybaris has founded Poseidonia by about 600, so trade will now bear the cost of overland transport; but the Samian and Phokaian trade with Tartessos may have by-passed the Corinthian domain entirely, and by about 600 Phokaia had founded Massalia. The Corinthian sphere of influence is by this date an enclave within a geographically extended international market.

In the southern Peloponnese the years about 630–600 seem to include at least the beginning, and perhaps the main part of, Aristomenes' revolt against Sparta, and the patriotic Spartan poetry of Tyrtaios. We are told that at first the revolt greatly impoverished a number at least of the Spartans; and that the military operations associated especially with Aristomenes' name were raids, sometimes at least with considerable slaughter. It is very difficult to believe that a war of this type did not produce a sizeable slave-trade, especially in non-combatants, from both sides, which would pay for their metal imports and, on the Spartan side, for their Cretan archers. The Aristomenian period as a whole must have been one of considerable depopulation and disinvestment, partly in Sparta at the beginning but mainly in Messenia in the later part of, and after, the war.

It is a question whether the slave-trade now became established to a much greater degree than previously. In the conditions of the eighth- and seventh-century colonies in the north and west of the Ionian sea, we may readily suppose a certain amount of slave-raiding and kidnapping as a by-product of metal prospecting; and as the Italiote and Sikeliote cities grew at the expense of the native populations, a certain small but fairly steady flow of captives into the slave-trade. The recovery of Lydia and Ionia, the rise of Lesbos, Rhodes, Chios, and other islands during this period and the opening up of the Egyptian market through Naukratis would probably provide sufficient points of sale: the mainland Greek demand for slaves at this period was probably not great—a generation later, Solon of Athens was able, apparently fairly easily, to trace and ransom Athenians previously sold as slaves, and this presumably means that the slave-trade on the Greek mainland was a small and fairly tightly-organized concern still. The probable importance of the Aristomenian war and its results was that (in a Greece generally on the brink of over-population) it introduced the idea of deliberate exchange (by emigration and colonies) of certain sectors of the free population for a slave population doing more or less the same work but able to demand a much smaller share in the results of its production. In this sense, rather than in any immediate change in the rest of Greece, we probably should see the Aristomenian war as the critical point of time at which the slave-trade began to become established.

E. c.600–c.575: CORINTH AND AIGINA. With the end of the Aristomenian revolt, the Spartan supply of slaves to exchange for the metal her armies needed would also practically cease. It is however at this time that Lakonian pottery begins to capture part of the international market for fine wares. The major purchasers were Samos, Naukratis, and Kyrene in the east and south; and Taras and elsewhere in the west. Since Samos had once 'helped Sparta against the Messenians', and Taras was a Spartan colony, it seems certain that this export was politically organized. It was presumably in this period, or later, that the Spartans took the 'Lykourgan' decision not to mint a coinage, but to retain the old iron skewers for local trade and thus prevent the local movement of goods within Lakonia and Messenia from feeding in to the international market. In these circumstances, it is interesting to speculate on the organization of the production of Lakonian ware as well as of its exportation: the elements both of political initiative and of political control must have been great, and information from the archaeologists on the number of workshops and of painters and potters would be of value.

The development of the metal trade in this period must have been affected by the extension of the Lydian empire under Alyattes and the increase of metal production in the east; the Carthaginian annexation of Ebesos from the Rhodians in the west, and the failure of the Rhodian and Knidian attack on Motye and associated events.

In the first place, the beginning of coinages in Lydia, Ionia, and Argos-Aigina established a new use, and therefore presumably a new demand for the precious metals relatively to the useful metals: this means a new structure within the metal trade. More importantly perhaps, the precious-metal part of the trade is now tied in to the general state of the market in ways (such as the presence or absence of peasant confidence) additional to the older use of bullion.

On the other hand, the minae of precious-metal bullion of the older international trade probably in general circulated far more slowly than the coinages were capable of doing, so that from about 630 to about 575 the increase in velocity of circulation in the East Greek, Aiginetan, and Corinthian trading areas must have been very considerable, while (on the fringes of the coinage-using area at any one time) there must have been much 'stickiness' due to hoarding. The 'fringe of the coinage-using area' may have been geographical (between communities using and not admitting the use of the new coinages) or socio-economic, between classes of the population or economic sectors: and hoarding, taken from another point of view, is one example of the movement of coinage from flows to stocks and the reverse—all the problems of accumulating capital, valuing capital assets, realizing them, or putting capital to work. The forms taken by these problems in the older international trade financed by bullion, or the local trade 'financed' by the iron skewers, would always be greatly extended, and often much modified, as the potential uses of coinage were actualized. By the end of the period 575–525 we should suppose that the range and nature of these problems, in advanced and wealthy states, was such that they could be treated without coinage only by keeping local and international markets separated by political controls as at Sparta.

Sparta transformed not money, but self-reproducing labor, into the capital stock (with politically regulated flows) of serf helots. The costs of this transformation were military and political in the main— man-power of a certain kind; but required also a minimal supply of certain goods, especially metal imports, and leather probably from her own hill pastures. After the Aristomenian war (we are told) the Spartans captured and lost Phigaleia in western Arcadia: this incident may have begun the long Arcadian war mentioned by Herodotus, in which the Arcadians were in general successful in driving off the Spartan attacks. The 'finding of Orestes' bones' at Tegea, probably in the 550's, is generally regarded as the beginning of the formation of the Peloponnesian League, a change in Spartan policy from force to diplomacy, admitting that the costs of further enserfment were too high. But if Sparta had not the military man-power, and could not afford the metal, to extend the capitalization (so to speak) of the agricultural labor of the Peloponnese, the acceptance of her diplomatic overtures by other states also implies that they were prepared to accept the exclusion of the southern Peloponnese from the international market. The dying away of the Lakonian pottery exports in the second half of the sixth century shows that this situation was stabilized, even for Samos and Taras.

In Corinth, the years c.600–c.575 cover the greater part of the tyranny of Periandros, about whom we have many anecdotes if a little history. One of these is the famous story of how Periandros was advised by Thrasyboulos of Miletos to 'cut off the heads' of those of his subjects who grew taller than the average. This suggests—since it is growth, not innate nobility that is in question—both that there was considerable amassing of capital by individuals in Periandros' Corinth and that above a certain level the state took all (or at least too much). In such a situation, capital is usually kept or transferred abroad: in this case, we may suspect, to Corcyra and elsewhere. Within Corinth therefore it may be that the central problem was that of the destination of accumulated capitals—to the international market, or to Periandros' treasury.

We are informed of two major expenditures from this treasury: the foundation of the colony of Potidaia (thus extending to the Aegean Kypselos' policy of settlements in the west), and the building of two fleets for 'continuous war'. We are not told where these wars were (except for a possible poetic allusion to a capture or sack of the port of Kerinthos in Euboia), nor of any Corinthian conquests in Periandros' time (before his last years): if there had been defeats amounting to a destruction of a fleet, we should certainly have heard of them against the general background of the tradition about Periandros' wealth and power. The Arion story tells us that Periandros was stern against piracy, but this can hardly have kept two fleets busy for nearly thirty years.

We are however also told that Periandros did not restore the festival and trade-fair at the Isthmia, and that his father's fiscal policy (at least at first) had been to tax at the point of production, not of exchange: the same is implied, perhaps, by the decapitation story for Periandros himself. These statements about a trading community in the same generation as the initiation of the phenomenon of exported Lakonian ware, suggest that Periandros' fleets were used mainly for a certain kind of 'continuous war'; for convoys for traders, and the presence of Corinthian power at the point of sale. It seems likely

250

therefore that both Sparta and Corinth at this time attempted a political direction and management of certain sectors or areas of the international market. No doubt Alyattes was making the same attempt in Lydia, where the old Asiatic form of the check-and-bullion trade (with state or temple backing) may have been well-remembered and in some modified form combined with the new coinage situation.

If this is the case, then Periandros' failure to start a Corinthian coinage (at least early in his reign), his failure to restore the Isthmia, and the origin of the great crisis of 572–69, may all ultimately arise, from the same roots: a long-continued policy by Periandros of taxing production to pay the costs of guaranteeing markets.

The Aiginetans seem to have started buying Athenian pottery and selling it in Egypt at Naukratis, about 620—or at the time according to the dates suggested above, when Kypselos is tithing Corinth at the points of production, and so, presumably, raising export prices. About 575, Athenian pottery begins to be a notable export to Central Italy, and about the same date Athenian exports to the Euxine cities become regular and substantial.

In the archaeological evidence for Athenian exports we are probably to see at work the Aiginetan trading area: we collect therefore that about 575 Athens was feeding slaves, pottery, and oil, and agricultural produce into the international market represented by Aigina; and if Aigina, instead of Corinth, could bring into the market, even marginally, so large and relatively wealthy a community as Athens at this time, then we should suppose that she was at least as capable of opening up other places. In other words, the hypothesis is that in Periandros' time there came into being a certain confrontation between guaranteed Corinthian and free Aiginetan markets. It is likely that the confrontation took time to emerge: for in the beginning the prosperity of the free market may have been depended to some considerable degree on the general security furnished by the guaranteed market, and notions of regularity and balance developed there. We may suspect also that in general the Aiginetan authorities and Periandros knew their relationship reasonably well, and were able to avoid major conflicts: yet it is Periandros' war on Epidauros, the mother-city of Aigina, that begins (according to Herodotus) the great crisis of 572–69. It would seem therefore that in the end Periandros took the initiative against a free market grown to threaten his own organization of markets functioning under political control and naval guarantee. If we are to give weight to the tale that one of Periandros'

251

sons was killed in a revolt in the Corinthian countryside against his father, then the threat had bitten deep into the Corinthian economy itself before Periandros took his precipitating action.

F. c.575–c.560: THE RISE OF ATHENS. If the hypothesis of a confrontation between protected Corinthian and free Aiginetan market organization is correct, the situation of Athens, and the Solonian solution, should illuminate and be illuminated by, these circum stances. The 'Corinthian party' in Athens should be represented politically by the Philaid kinsmen of the Kypselids (one of whom was archon three years before Solon), and economically by the maintenance and establishment of institutions working regularly and politically like the colony at Sigeion. The 'Aiginetan party' should be represented by a thrusting export policy taking advantage of such backwardnesses as debt-slavery. In the early years, the capture and securing of legal title to Sigeion is probably a clear example of how the two trends had not yet diverged.

The Solonian reforms seem in fact to favor neither party: they establish Athens on an independent basis, with backward institutions abolished and replaced, exports confined to industrial goods but these given every encouragement. Both the 'protectionism' of Corinth and the 'freedom' of Aigina are avoided, and no ideological target is set for Athens. This absence of an ideological target is the most important historiographic fact about Solon's Athens, and any reconstruction of his historical context must explain at least this. The hypothesis of the confrontation of Corinth and Aigina as leaders of different forms of market organization offers the beginnings of an explanation.

In foreign affairs proper the picture seems very different. Solon's archonship and reforms are probably to be dated to 573/2, and the great event ascribed to Athenian foreign policy while Solon is in Athens is the Sacred War and the destruction of Krisa: Solon is credited with mobilizing the Delphic Amphiktiony, while the sea-blockade was entrusted to Kleisthenes of Sikyon with (probably) some unspecified help from Argos (since outrages to Argive pilgrims are given as one of the causes of the war). It is probable however, that, as part of the general crisis of 572–69, the Sacred War was primarily caused by Delphic participation in a more general hostility to Periandros, marked by the 'discovery' and addition of the line 'yourself and your son, but not your grandsons' to the older oracle supporting Kypselos' usurpation. Such an addition would certainly demonstrate 'to Periandros that Delphi and its controller Krisa was aligned with his enemies in the Corinthian countryside and Corcyra, where his sons were killed.

The fighting against Krisa continued until its destruction: and during this period, in foreign affairs, Solonian Athens must be seen as committed to the Corinthians under Periandros.

Indeed, at the beginning of the crisis, Corinth is the political victor: Corcyra is reduced, Krisa destroyed, the Eleans (having expelled the Pisatans and Messenians) are firmly attached to the Kypselid dynasty. But at the end victory lies on the other side: the first known initiative of the republican government in Corinth is the re-establishment of the Isthmia festival and trade-fair. This implies the search for non-guaranteed markets in general economic policy, and in fiscal policy a movement from the taxation of production to that of taxation of exchange (import and export dues and sales taxes). It is true that the new Corinth wishes to retain the political and no doubt also the economic allegiance of Corcyra—that is to retain a guaranteed market base for her new development; but Corcyra won her independence when the Knidians persuaded the Samians to return the prisoners. Corinth then quarrelled with Samos, which had (apparently) been a guaranteed market for Lakonian ware, if not also for Corinthian goods. The political disintegration of the guaranteed-market system can thus be traced through 568/7, when Periandros died in Corcyra and Psammetichos in Corinth was killed and a new government established; when the Corcyrean boys are freed, Corcyra becomes independent, and Corinth quarrels with Samos; and 567/6 if this is the true year of the establishment of the Isthmia and the Elean ban upon it. At the end of these events, the Kypselids still rule in Ambrakia and retain the allegiance of Elis, but elsewhere (including Corinth) the guaranteed-market system has broken down.

A question of considerable interest is whether the Corinthian coinage began in the last years of Periandros or the early years of the republican government, for the policy and economic implications are in either case considerable. The coinage is abundant from the first issues, which—if dated before 569/8—can only mean that it was issued as a wartime measure to pay Periandros' allies in Elis, Thessaly, Athens, and Sikyon; and finally, such an issue can only be regarded as a self-defeating attempt to turn a principal device of the free market organization against the members of that market.

On the other hand, if the coinage began under the new government, it would be part of the same policy as that shown in the re-establishment of the Isthmia festival, and the abundance of the early issues would demonstrate a determined attempt to break into the international 'free' market, at the same time as Athens was rapidly advancing in all areas where pottery is the archaeological trace material. On this evidence, as well as the archaeological, we should probably think of a date in the 560's for the beginning of the Corinthian coinage.

Athenian consciousness of the new vigor of Corinthian rivalry is shown through the later years of the decade: if the Isthmia was established in 567/6 (with the Athenian *prohedria*), Athens elected a Kypselid archon and established her own festival of the Panathenaia in 566/5 (or, perhaps more probably in 562/1); about the same time there was Peisistratos' victory over Megara, in which the Corinthians cannot have had no concern; and perhaps on his usurpation of power in 560/59, Peisistratos married the Argive widow of a Kypselid. These Athenian hints to anti-Kypselid Corinth undoubtedly betray an awareness of danger; and the Corinthian coinage has its place among these dangers.

G. THE MARKET c.760–c.560. One side of the Greek market development in this period has scarcely been mentioned but certainly needs to be explored: its use of Asiatic experience. From the foundation of Al Mina to the Kimmerian devastations, any experienced trader from one of the older civilizations could have seen in the Greek international market only a petty provincial pioneering area feeding some metal, textiles, and slaves into the great Levantine system: and providing at times some political nuisance by a marginal increase of resources for potentially rebellious city-states on the fringes – Phoenicia, Cyprus, Kilikia, and (least of all), the Aegean coast, and at other times the reverse political nuisance of pirates and raiders, as in Egypt in the 660's. The total value of the trade, measured in Phoenician minae, would certainly be relatively small, even though, within the area, it was great enough to cause the orientalizing revolution, and to require political changes and new thinking in at least the most advanced communities—and in these fields the dominant tradition (in the sense that it established the limits of the possible) was still that native to the province.

The Kimmerian devastations however seem deeply to have affected the market as a whole, just at the time when Corinthian poetry and narrative art were beginning to place the results of the orientalizing revolution in a net and framework of tradition. The effect on some advanced areas was so great that for them (as they were then constituted) the market was destroyed: Hyameia is the extreme example; the dependence of the Bacchiad oligarchy on market revenues in Corinth, and of the population of Thera in revenues from a market in which they did not noticeably participate, was also very great; but the agricultural states or sectors probably enjoyed a relative benefit. The reconstructed market in the following years consequently shows new features: Corinth under the Kypselids and Lydia under Gyges' successors probably both sought to establish state or state-guaranteed trade on the old Asiatic model; Sparta joined in this movement to a slight extent, but in the main insisted on complete separation between the local movements of goods within her territory, and the reviving international market. Aigina on the other hand turned to the integration of local and international trade and full exploitation of the new device of coinage: and this sector of the market no doubt emphasized its freedom as the Corinthian sector grew more protectionist.

The opening up of the far west in Spain and Gaul provided new resources, new entrepreneurs, and an area where protectionism was, for Greeks, impossible: Kypselid Corinth finally fell in conflict with the eastern fringe of this area, in Corcyra. In this sense, the fall of Kypselid Corinth is also the end of the Greek international market as a petty province of the Levantine: for the next two centuries the history of the first fully independent European international market will be the history of the rise, rule, and decline of Athens. It was, apparently, Kallistratos of Athens who taught Philip of Macedon so to organize the economy of his kingdom that Macedonian armies, in the end, brought the Levant into the international market that the Athenians had organized.

TABLE XIII

THE IONIAN SEA AND THE INTERNATIONAL MARKET

The Ionian Sea western shores	eastern shores		*The International Market*
			Al Mina.
Cumae and its shipping routes. Sicilian colonies begin. Achaian Italiotes. Taras.	Hero-cult in Pylos. Mothone in Hyameia. Aiginetans in Arcadia. Spartans annex Stenyklaros. Asine.	*c.*760–*c.*695	Formation of Euboian-organized market with two enclaves at the end of long communication routes. Within this: Bacchiad oligarchy and expansion at Corinth; and market in Thera; the orientalizing revolution. Phoenicians in the west. Assyrian destruction of the eastern enclave.
Gela reinforced from Rhodes and Crete.		*c.*695–*c.*645	
Pylian Metapontion, Rhodian 'Pandosia', Kolophonian Siris, Selinous.	Bacchiad wealth, Hyameian expansion, Isthmia, Delia.		Improved shipping affects port and market organization. Kimmerian devastation of Phrygia. Greek exploration of Propontis and Euxine. Reorganization of Lydia; the 'coasts and plains' problem of the destinations of the agricultural surplus.
Local manufactures. Hyameians in Rhegion.	Bacchiad avarice. Fall of Hyameia.	*c.*645–*c.*630	Kimmerians devastate Lydia and Ionia; depression of market; Theraians at Kyrene.
		*c.*630–*c.*600	
Syracuse and Corcyra resume relations with Corinth. Sybarite Poseidonia. (The far west opened.)	Pheidonian Argos. Kypselid and other tyrannies. Aiginetan coinage.		Recovery of Lydia and Ionia; rise of Lesbos; colonies in Propontis and Euxine; Naukratis; Tartessos. Emergency 'coinage'. The The tyrannies and balanced and controlled economies. Aristomenian war: the slave-trade.
(Massalia.)	Lakonian pottery	*c.*600–*c.*575	'Balanced control' of economies developed into quasi-Asiatic protectionism in Corinth: confronted with Aiginetan freedom and development of the far west.
Akragas, Lipara.			
Messenians at Rhegion.	Solon of Athens: Sacred War; revolt of Corcyra; Pisa destroyed.	*c.*575–*c.*560	Fall of Kypselids: end of protectionism. Isthmia; Corinthian coinage.

INDEXES

ABBREVIATIONS

AJA	*American Journal of Archeology*
Ath Pol	Aristotle's *Constitution of Athens*
Barbarian:	*Excepta Barbari:* a translation into Merovingian Latin of a lost Alexandrian original, printed as an appendix to Schoene's Eusebius, and in the Teubner series with a reconstituted Greek text
Diod.	Diodorus Siculus
Eus.	Eusebius
Gelzer	H. Gelzer: *Sextus Julius Africanus und die byzantinische Chronographie* Leipzig *1880-98*
Hdt.	Herodotus' *Histories*

All references of the forms Jac. 554 F 1, or 554 F 1, are of course to:

F. Jacoby: *Fragmente der griechischen Historiker* (1921–).

References to the commentaries are given as Komm(entar) with volume and page numbers.

JHS	*Journal of Hellenic Studies*
JNES	*Journal of Near Eastern Studies*
Steph. Byz:	Stephanus of Byzantium
Thk.	Thucydides' *History*

ANCIENT SOURCES

These are listed alphabetically under the names of authors or reputed authors. When the text is discussed textually, the entry is asterisked. For historiographic and chronographic discussions of the work of an author in general, see the Index of People and Places.

Spelling: the general rule is transliteration of the Greek; where there is an accepted English form, this is preferred (e.g. Jerome is preferred to Hieronymos). In some cases, consistency is unattainable, and I agree with the critics that Dionysius of Halikarnassos looks odd. I would add that Dionysius of Tell Mahre looks odder, while Dionysius Telmaharensis is, to my taste, both a disguise and a barbarism, excusable and necessary in the heading of a Latin rendering of the work, but not required in a discussion in English.

Africanus: source for Eusebius
           source for *Excerpta Barbari*
Alexander Polyhistor 273 F 81
Alkman F 5 Page
Anakreon F 101 B
Antiochos 555 F 2
             F 2, 4, 5, 6, 9
             F 9
             F 10
             F 9, 10, 12, 13
             T 3
Apollodoros 244 F 69
            F 331
            F 332*
Archilochos F 146 B
Aristainetos 771 F 1
Aristarchos ap. Σ Pind. *Pyth.* 6.5a
Aristophanes of Byzantium
   ap. Σ Pind. *Ol.* 3.68a
   ap. Σ Pind. *Isth.* 2 inscr.

Hieronymos: see Jerome
Hippias of Elis: *Olympic Victors*
Hippostratos 568 F 2a
        F 3
        F 5
      Sicilian Genealogies
Hippys of Rhegion 554 F 1
        F 3

Ion of Chios F 17

Jerome (Hieronymos) *Chronici Canones*
    Latin representative of Eusebius
    on Gelon and Hieron

Kallimachos F 43 Pfeiffer
Kallisthenes: see Aristotle
Kephalion: *The Nine Muses:* 93 F 1
Konon 26 F 1.3

Lindian *Anagraphe* Jac. 532, entry 17
                        28

Marcellinus *Life of Thucydides*
Marmor Parium: see Parian Marble
Memnon 434 F 1.12
Michael the Great: *Chronicon*

Nikolaos of Damascus 90 F 57
              F 59

Oracles
Oxyrhynchus Papyri 222 (Jac. 415 F 1)
             2465

Parian Marble Jac. 239: epoch 31
                  32
                  53

Pausanias   II 4.3
          III ad init.
          III 3.1
          III 14.3
          III 14.6
          III 26.7
          IV 18.1
          IV 19.5
          IV 23.6 ff.

Synkellos, *Chronographia*
  Greek representative of Eusebius

Theophanes, *Chronographia*
Thucydides VI ad init.
                    F 19
Timaios Jac. 566   F 21
                    F 60 and 164
                    F 71
                    F 80*
                    F 92
                    F 93
                    F 96
                    F 97
                    F 125
                    F 126
                    F 127
                    F 164

Xenagoras 240 F 15
Xenophon *Memorabilia Soc.* 2.7.2
Zenobius 1.54

BIBLIOGRAPHY

W. Albright: review of Sidney Smith, *Alalakh and Chronology*, *AJA* 47 (1943) 491 f.

Per Alin: *Das Ende der Mykenischen Fundstatten auf dem Griechischen Festland* (Studies in Mediterranean Archaeology Vol.I) Lund 1962

J. L. Angel 'The Length of Life in Ancient Greece' *Journal of Gerontology* 2 (1947) 18 ff.

J. P. Barron 'Milesian Politics and Athenian Propaganda' *JHS* 82 (1962) 1 ff.

J. Boardman *The Greeks Overseas* London 1964

L. Bohanan 'A Genealogical Charter' *Africa* XXII (1952) 301 ff.

D. W. Bradeen 'The Fifth-century Archon List' *Hesperia* XXXII (1963) 187 ff.

M. Broadbent *Studies in Greek Genealogy* Leiden 1968

Rhys Carpenter 'Note on the Foundation Date of Carthage' *AJA* 68 (1964) 178

P. Courbin *La Céramique Géométrique de l'Argolide* Paris 1966

I. G. Cunnison *The Luapula Peoples of Northern Rhodesia* Manchester 1959

J. A. Davison *From Archilochus to Pindar* London 1968

T. J. Dunbabin *The Western Greeks* Oxford 1948

S. Lane-Poole *The Mohammedan Dynasties* London 1894

I. M. Lewis 'Historical Aspects of Genealogies in Northern Somali Social Structure' *Journal of African History* III 1 (1962) 35 ff.

M. Miller 'The earlier Persian date in Herodotus' *Klio* 37 (1959) 29 ff.

M. Miller 'The Herodotean Croesus' *Klio* 41 (1963) 58 ff.

M. Miller 'Herodotus as Chronographer' *Klio* 46 (1965) 109 ff.

M. Miller 'The accepted date for Solon' *Arethusa* 2.1 (1969) 62 ff.

L. Moretti *Olympionikai* Rome 1957

H. W. Parke and D. E. W. Wormell *The Delphic Oracle* Oxford 1956

A. Poebel 'The Assyrian King-list from Khorsabad' *JNES* 1 (1942) 247 ff., 460 ff., and 2 (1943) 56 ff.

C. M. Robertson 'Attic Red-figure Vase Painters' *JHS* 85 (1965) 90 ff.

E. L. Smithson 'Dorians on the Akropolis' *AJA* 69 (1965) 176

E. R. Thiele 'Chronology of the kings of Judah and Israel' *JNES* 3 (1944) 137 ff.

T. B. L. Webster *From Mycenae to Homer* London 1958

Dr. Calvin Wells *Bones, Bodies and Disease* London 1964

E. Will *Korinthiaka* Paris 1955

PEOPLE AND PLACES

YEARS

*All years are expressed
in the nearest Olympic-archon equivalents
translated into years B.C.*

⟨1308/7⟩   Timaios' date for the beginning of Herakles' 36-year generation . . . . 98 f.

1215/4   Philistos' date for the foundation of Carthage, 810 = 27×30 years down to and including the year 406/5: Jac. 556 T 11a, F 47 89

1204/3   murder of Minos in Sikania (Jerome); attributed to Antiochos as $468 = 39 \times 12 = 36 \times 13$ years before 736/5 Syracuse, and $780 = 39 \times 20$ years before the Pan-Sikeliote conference of 424/3 . . . . . 79, 82

1193/2   Timaios' date for the fall of Troy (Jac. 566 F 125): $115 = 23 \times 5$ years after Herakles in ⟨1308/7⟩ . . 97, 99

1155/4   Timaios' date for the Return (566 F 126): $153 = 36 \times 4\frac{1}{4}$ years after Herakles in ⟨1308/7⟩ 98

c. 1150/49   Ephoros' date for the Fall of Troy quoted (without Ephoros' name) by Strabo 13.1.3   . . . 87

c. 1090/89   Ephoros' date for the Return ⟨of Temenos and Kissos to Argos⟩: 70 T 10   . . . . 86, 88

1077/6   Parian Marble's date for the Ionian Migration (Jac. 239) . 171

1074/3   Didymos' date for the arrival of Aletes in Corinth: attributed to Apollodoros 202

1070/69   Ephoros' date for the Return ⟨i.e. arrival of Aletes in Corinth⟩: 70 F 223 . . . . 86, 88, 201

1044/3   Eratosthenes' date for the Ionian Migration . . 171

277

279